Multimedia

DeMYSTiFieD®

DeMYSTiFieD® Series

The Demystified Series publishes more than 125 titles in all areas of academic study. For a complete list of titles, please visit www.mhprofessional.com.

Multimedia
DeMYSTiFieD®

Jennifer Coleman Dowling

New York   Chicago   San Francisco   Lisbon   London   Madrid   Mexico City
Milan   New Delhi   San Juan   Seoul   Singapore   Sydney   Toronto

The McGraw·Hill Companies

Cataloging-in-Publication Data is on file with the Library of Congress

McGraw-Hill books are available at special quantity discounts to use as premiums and sales promotions, or for use in corporate training programs. To contact a representative, please e-mail us at bulksales@mcgraw-hill.com.

Multimedia DeMYSTiFieD®

1 2 3 4 5 6 7 8 9 0   DOC DOC   1 0 9 8 7 6 5 4 3 2 1

ISBN   978-0-07-177064-4
MHID   0-07-177064-X

Sponsoring Editor Roger Stewart	**Copy Editor** Marilyn Smith	**Illustration** Cenveo Publisher Services
Editorial Supervisor Janet Walden	**Proofreader** Julie Searls	**Art Director, Cover** Jeff Weeks
Project Manager Anupriya Tyagi, Cenveo Publisher Services	**Indexer** Jack Lewis	**Cover Illustration** Lance Lekander
Acquisitions Coordinator Joya Anthony	**Production Supervisor** Jean Bodeaux	
Technical Editor Brad Borch	**Composition** Cenveo Publisher Services	

I dedicate this book to my family, especially my husband Bill, my sons Tim and Ryan, and my mother Marianne Coleman. If not for them, it is unlikely I would have been able to focus my time and energy to accomplish my goal of completing this book. My family has inspired me tremendously with their support, patience, and encouragement, and for this I am grateful.

About the Author

Jennifer Coleman Dowling (Wayland, Massachusetts) has an MFA in Visual Design and is an experienced new media specialist, educator, and artist. She is a tenured professor in the Communication Arts Department at Framingham State University, where she teaches courses in digital media and design.

Jennifer has been dedicated to her teaching and professional work for more than 20 years. She has worked in the areas of web design, interactive multimedia, animation, print design, illustration, logos and corporate identity, educational software, advertising, product promotion, and presentation graphics. In addition, Jennifer's artistic accomplishments include the creation and exhibition of hybrid mixed-media pieces that combine traditional art making with digital technology methods.

About the Technical Editor

Brad Borch is an award-winning multimedia producer. He has a BA in Film (Penn State, 1986) and an MS in Instructional Technologies (Bloomsburg University, 1989). He started his interactive media career so long ago that the digital bits he used to craft his first project have long since retired. Brad has worked for various creative agencies and media companies, and currently has his own interactive design consultancy, Activa Digital Media Design. He works primarily in Adobe Flash, producing games and interactive presentations.

Brad resides in coastal Maine with his wife Elizabeth, his children Christopher and Rachel, and a big, fuzzy dog. When he is not sculpting bits into presentations of one kind or another, he is hiking, canoeing, or playing guitar.

Contents at a Glance

Contents

Acknowledgments

Multimedia DeMYSTiFieD® came along at the right time, and I have many people to thank for their interest and assistance. The book has a precision and technical rigor as a result of Brad Borch's editing ability. Throughout the process, I have respected his insight and expertise, which has undoubtedly made for a stronger manuscript.

I am also appreciative of the grant I was awarded by Framingham State University (FSU), which was used to fund the hiring of my research assistant, Luis Rodriguez, whose effort and attention to detail helped bring this book to fruition.

There are others who contributed in various ways to this book that I would like to thank: the students at FSU who were willing to participate in my focus groups and offered their input on the subject, my colleagues in the Communication Arts department, and the professional contacts who generously provided me with their technical input and knowledge.

Introduction

You picked up this book because you are interested in the subject of multimedia, or perhaps you are just unsure of what it means and have looked here to find out. I hope you come to value what this book has to offer.

While working professionally in the field and teaching at the university level for more than 20 years, I have invested countless hours trying to find the best way to communicate with digital media, in addition to explaining the process and demonstrating how it all works. I see this book as a companion for those who want to gain a better understanding of multimedia, as well as a means for sharing with others what I know and enjoy about my chosen discipline.

When people have asked what *Multimedia DeMYSTiFieD®* is about, I try to sum it up as succinctly as possible. This is not an easy task when describing such a vast subject. I have come to refer to it as a *primer* of sorts. The book is an introduction to interactive multimedia, also known as *digital media* and *new media*. The 12 chapters encompass a myriad of relevant and up-to-date topics pertaining to multimedia.

Who Should Use This Book

Multimedia DeMYSTiFieD® is intended to be a self-paced study guide for students who are learning about the subject in class, but it is also a good, solid reference for the independent learner who wants to become knowledgeable about multimedia. It is a consolidated handbook that spans everything from digital photography, sound editing, and web authoring with HTML, to vector graphics, file formats, and computer animation.

Take it along with you to class, or have it on your desk at home or work. Wherever you are working with digital media and interactivity, this book will provide you with tips and information on current technologies, as well as design and production guidelines.

How to Use This Book

This book is organized in such a way that it follows a logical sequence from cover to cover. However, similar to using interactive multimedia, you can flip through at random, look up topics in the table of contents or index, or find individual chapters that pique your curiosity.

My first responsibility with *Multimedia DeMYSTiFieD*® was to come up with a detailed outline that would be used as a guide while writing the manuscript. I found the best way to arrange such extensive content, for myself as well as for the reader, was to break it into four sections. The first section explains what multimedia is, the second delves into the media elements that make up a multimedia project, the third covers the software and hardware tools needed to create multimedia, and the fourth helps you to understand how to pull it all together for the end user.

Throughout the book, you will find terms, steps, web links, tips and notes, tables, and many visual examples and illustrations to demonstrate technical concepts. You will learn how to create multimedia projects with state-of-the-art tools and techniques.

Each chapter begins with a list of objectives and concludes with a summary and quiz to reinforce learning. There is also a final exam. In addition, a list of web resources relating to topics in the book is available online at mhprofessional .com/computingdownload.

This book provides a comprehensive approach to the history of multimedia, the creative and development process, and the production and delivery considerations as a way to offer assistance when working on a college assignment, a business product, or your own independent projects.

Part I

Multimedia Overview: What It's All About

chapter **1**

Introduction to Multimedia

In this chapter, you will become acquainted with the notion of multimedia and the technology behind it. Understanding the basic terms and concepts that relate to combining different types of media together is an important first step on our journey of exploring multimedia. So let's get the proverbial ball rolling!

CHAPTER OBJECTIVES

In this chapter, you will:

- Learn the definition of multimedia and what it means to use it
- Discover the kinds of media used in multimedia and understand how to combine them
- Distinguish between linear presentations and user-controlled interactive environments
- Find out about basic technical concepts and early desktop computers
- Learn a bit of multimedia history and understand the difference between older uses of media compared with current digital media uses

What Is Multimedia?

Multimedia is many things rolled into one. What do you think of when you hear the word *multimedia*? Is it merely a mashup of media elements? Or is it everything we see, hear, read, and touch in web sites, video games, phone apps, retail kiosks, and bank ATMs? These are all forms of multimedia, and the list of uses grows daily. We are drawn into multimedia at every turn, whether we like it or not. The goal of this book is to demystify the meaning and process of creating digital multimedia.

The simplest explanation of multimedia is "the combination of two or more media." However, multimedia is vastly more complex than the term implies. It intertwines a myriad of media elements and, as a result, makes for a more comprehensive end product than when media components are experienced independently.

The *media* in multimedia comes in different forms: graphics, photography, text, audio (sound effects, music, voice-over, and so on), video, and animation. Individually, each one serves as a powerful communication vehicle for both expressive and practical purposes. Melded together, they allow for a more dynamic and engaging experience. The final result is improved on even further when there is cooperation and coordination between the disparate media components.

Marshall McLuhan was a leading and influential media communication theorist who coined the familiar phrase "The medium is the message" (*Understanding Media: The Extensions of Man*, NY, 1964). He believed that it is the "medium that shapes and controls the scale and form of human association and action." To him, the focus should not be on the content or what is being said, but the medium by which it is delivered. The subject matter is by no means irrelevant, but the delivery format is a crucial factor in how the message comes across. This is where the immense power and influence of multimedia lie.

Media, by definition, is the plural of *medium*. It has evolved to mean "facilitating or linking communication"—be it via a phone, the Web, TV, or some other instrument. Speaking directly with a person one on one is immediate and does not require mediation. This is communication in its purest form.

The purpose of a medium is to assist in the conveying of a message. When using more than one type of medium, we refer to it as *multimedia*, whether or not it is computer-based. At one time, media mainly applied to newspapers as a way to disseminate news and information to the masses. Now, media encompasses many forms of communication.

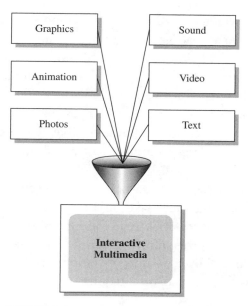

FIGURE 1-1 • Disparate multimedia elements funneling into one unit

The kinds of media elements and how they are used play a significant role in multimedia environments. Consider a web site without any graphics, color, or images. How about a music video without sound? There is clearly something lacking. A combination of media adds richness and provides a complete sensory experience.

As shown in Figure 1-1, multimedia is a synergistic process whereby various media elements work together to make a stronger, more cohesive whole. Take it one step further—get a person involved by providing interactivity with a multimedia program, and there will be even greater potential to increase the educational and entertainment value. Adding user choices with the help of computer code leads to the *interactive* in *interactive multimedia* and generates an engaging, multifaceted experience.

A Concise History of Multimedia

Before we delve into the components and types of multimedia, let's take a look at where the term *multimedia* originates.

Multimedia once meant a slide projector and a tape recorder being played simultaneously. For instance, 50 years ago, photographic images in slide form were projected on a screen or wall while audio attempted to synchronize with the sequence or played as "background" music.

In 1967, pop artist Andy Warhol organized "multimedia" events called the *Exploding Plastic Inevitable*, where he showed films combined with live performances that were illuminated with flashing, colored lights to create a multisensory atmosphere. The technology necessary for joining individual media did not exist at that time. Computers were not accessible to the general public and those that did exist were large, complex, costly, and primarily geared toward scientists and researchers.

Today, the term *multimedia* is associated almost exclusively with the computer, and the components that make up a multimedia program are digital. Various media are brought together to perform in unison on the computer as a single entity, and they are programmed or scripted using authoring software or programming languages. Diverse forms of communication are combined with multimedia to allow for a myriad of outcomes.

Early Multimedia Computing

Up to the 1980s, mainframe computers were the norm as opposed to desktop varieties. These housed vast amounts of data and were primarily used by the military and scientific communities.

In 1975, IBM released the first portable computer with a fixed monitor, keyboard, and data storage. However, it had drawbacks: It required text input, weighed 55 pounds, and cost $20,000, so it was hardly accessible to the masses. In the early 1980s, IBM introduced desktop computers, or personal computers (PCs). The base model had no built-in storage and a text-based screen where input was limited to typing on a keyboard.

As the PC developed, so did its multimedia capabilities. This allowed for regular and widespread use of multimedia and the creation of media elements. At this time, people began using computers for many home and office purposes.

In 1983, Apple Computer, Inc., announced its first desktop computer, which demonstrated an innovative graphical user interface (GUI). It was called the Lisa, and was considered user-friendly because it included a mouse to point and click on interface/screen desktop elements. Other PCs, such as the IBM, did not have these capabilities at the time.

The Lisa was ultimately not successful, so in 1984, Apple released the Macintosh. This was the first commercially successful computer with a GUI that was capable of designing for desktop publishing. This early Mac paved the way for the creation of graphics and page layout design with What You See Is What You

Get (WYSIWYG) technology. This allowed the users to view on their screen an approximate representation of what they would have in their printout, so it was possible to make edits and not need to guess what the final output would look like.

Table 1-1 shows the timeline from the early days of PCs to the current multimedia computers.

TIP *For more information about the history of computers, go to http:// oldcomputers.net/ and www.computerhope.com/history/index.htm.*

You might be wondering where the original concept of multimedia derived from. In the early 1900s, Vannevar Bush, an American computer scientist who

TABLE 1-1 Timeline of Early Days of PCs That Led to Multimedia Computers	
Year	**Technology and Functionality**
1975–1979	First portable computers and game systems; text input only
1980–1987	First personal computers for word processing, spreadsheets, games, simple slide shows; basic interactivity; CD-ROM specification for releasing multimedia titles; better monitors with higher quality color graphics; increased storage
1988–1992	Faster processors and more memory; sophisticated GUIs; interactive environments grow; beginning of the World Wide Web (the Web) with HTML
1993–2000	CD-quality audio and wide use of CDs and DVDs for data storage; 3D computer animation and virtual reality; enhanced presentation software; sophisticated authoring environments; cross-platform developments; the Web becomes interactive with GUIs; widespread Internet and web access
2001–2011	Extensive Internet use with broadband Ethernet capabilities; all-in-one handheld devices for email, Internet, phone, music, video, and photos; game systems and smart phones with Wi-Fi and 3G access; vast search capabilities (such as Google); real-time videoconferencing and live news broadcasts; video on demand (Netflix, Hulu); TV recording devices; social networking; rich multimedia presentations; high-definition TV with Blu-ray technology; downloadable music (iTunes, Pandora)

developed patented devices, came up with inventive ideas about ways to link information. He saw the potential of storing information with built-in connections to other data. Bush called his notion *associative indexing*, which would link information in a way that is more meaningful to the user, rather than the more traditional numerical and alphabetical classifications. He developed the Memex System in 1945, and although it was never implemented, it would have allowed the operator to input notes and drawings using an early method of photocopying. Data was interconnected and could be stored for later recall. His theory led to the development of interlinked hypertext methods, similar to those that are used today.

Douglas Engelbart was another computing pioneer who was way ahead of his time. He is credited with inventing office automation devices such as the mouse, multiple window screens, electronic mail, and videoconferencing during the 1960s. Engelbart was trying to find ways to create a synergy between the user and the computer with an emphasis on human–computer interaction. He worked on collaborative hypermedia systems, which paved the way for current interactive multimedia approaches.

TIP *Learn more by going to The History of Computing Project, at www.thocp.net, which has a vast amount of information about computers. For an interactive timeline of the Internet, go to http://historyoftheinternet.org/.*

Hypermedia and Hypertext

Ted Nelson is a key figure in the evolution of multimedia. As an information technology pioneer who developed the *hypertext* system in the 1960s, Nelson researched the capability of browsing and searching information using a multidirectional, linked approach. He coined the term *hypermedia*, which is nonsequential reading and writing. This coincided with a method he created called Project Xanadu, which was intended to deal with a nonhierarchical approach to storing, presenting, and manipulating data. It demonstrated a form of text that branched and allowed choices to the reader, so users could explore subjects from many different perspectives.

Nelson's explorations opened doors to the multimedia revolution, which ultimately led to the widespread use of the Hypertext Markup Language. HTML is the fundamental web site programming language, or *markup language*, necessary for web pages to be viewed on the Internet.

TIP   *More information on Nelson's hypertext Xanadu project can be found at http://xanadu.com/xuTheModel/index.html.*

The first practical use of hypermedia using hypertext was with a software program called HyperCard, which was introduced by Apple Computer in 1987, as shown in Figure 1-2. It was touted as an easy-to-use "software construction kit," and anyone could be both the creator and user of multimedia. It included buttons, text fields, and menus, and used a metaphor of *cards* (like individual web pages) that made up *stacks* (like entire web sites). The programming language that was used with HyperCard was called HyperTalk, and it was appealing to the masses due to its ease of use. HyperCard was used as a presentation program, like PowerPoint, as well as for designing games and learning tools. This paved the way for more sophisticated software programs that allowed the amateur to create and develop multimedia projects.

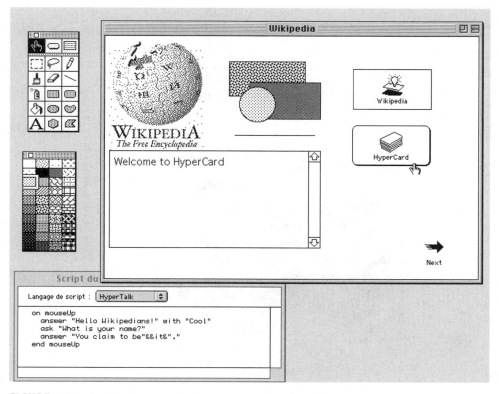

FIGURE 1-2 · Early hypermedia application with HyperCard software

In the early 1990s, there was a surge of multimedia programming, referred to as *edutainment*, that focused on interactive educational projects and books designed for children. CD titles were being produced at a rapid pace, but they were not tested well enough either for significance of the content or technological feasibility. This trend never turned into the revolution that was promised, as it was riddled with hardware and software compatibility problems. It also faced consumer resistance due to cost and unfamiliarity with the use and benefits of such products.

Combining Content from Various Media

The components that make up a multimedia production can be used in various combinations, as in the example in Figure 1-3.

As previously explained, there needs to be at least two kinds of media used in a single program or web site to qualify under the definition of multimedia. Here are some media options:

- Images, including graphics (lines, boxes, circles, rectangles, arrows, borders, and so on), photographs, illustrations, diagrams, cartoons, and color
- Text and typography
- Audio, including sound effects, music, and voice-overs

FIGURE 1-3 · Individual multimedia elements

- Animation, 2D and 3D
- Video
- Interface elements such as backgrounds, scenes, and metaphors
- Navigational devices such as buttons and menus

Linear vs. Interactive Multimedia

As illustrated in Figure 1-4, two important distinctions can be made with re-spect to how multimedia programs are used. One form of multimedia is called *linear* because it plays out in one continuous narrative sequence. Another type of multimedia is called *nonlinear* because information is not laid out in a chron-ological manner, but with many potential directions.

Nonlinear programs are inherently interactive and require active audience participation. The Web is a primary example of this type of multimedia, con-sidering the endless pathways the embedded links provide. Let's explore this a bit further.

Linear Multimedia

Despite the apparent oxymoron, some multimedia programs are linear and designed for sequential viewing and reading of information. They begin at a

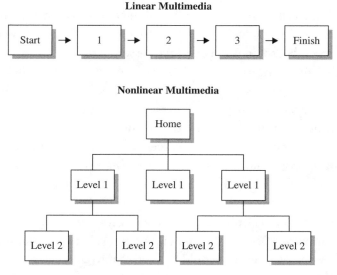

FIGURE 1-4 · Linear vs. nonlinear multimedia

predefined starting point and conclude at a logical ending location. Linear presentations may be automated so that each screen advances at a timed interval.

The linear approach is intended strictly for display purposes and is typically a passive "receiving" experience by the viewer, with no expectation of participating. It eliminates the need to take action (by pressing buttons or keys or touching a screen), and the developer, as opposed to the program user, is in control.

An example of linear multimedia is a PowerPoint presentation given by a town official during a meeting. The presentation is prepared, organized, and controlled by the presenter in a logical sequence. It is intended to present information in a straightforward manner for the purposes of education and discussion. Productions such as these can be as simple as text with bullet points, or multimedia elements—such as photographs, videos, and animation—may be embedded in the presentation. The presenter will press a button or key to begin, as you would do with a video, and play it for an audience to watch and learn without active involvement.

Another example of a simple linear presentation with one primary type of media is a slide show of vacation photographs that are displayed in one direction, with a distinct beginning and end. Additional media elements could be included that would bring it to the level of multimedia, such as active web links to the areas where the person traveled, videos shot on location, and music from the native culture playing in the background.

A linear presentation may also be designed with some minimal control options for either the presenter or another user, by employing computer-programming techniques. If the program is set up to be interactive, it would need to have navigational devices on the screen to click or touch, such as arrows, or a key press option on the keyboard, in order to move forward to the next screen.

Linear presentations are used in place of nonlinear ones when there is no requirement for interactivity. For instance, movies are presented in a linear format, which allows for greater submersion in the experience. You can absorb the information without the distraction of needing to make decisions about what to learn or where to go next. Someone is delivering the content to the audience in the order that it was intended with a predictable conclusion. This method provides a rich experience, yet it eliminates choices and relinquishes control to the presenter.

When the goal is to simply be entertained, gain knowledge about a subject, or become familiar with others' viewpoints, a linear multimedia presentation is preferential. A person or group would be more apt to concentrate on the content of the topic being presented without the possibility of diversions. Interactivity, on the other hand, forces users to make decisions and move through the content at their own pace. Both linear and nonlinear multimedia have their benefits and drawbacks.

Nonlinear Interactive Multimedia

Nonlinear, nonsequential multimedia implies that a person will in some way interact with a computer program. By doing so, they control the experience and dictate their unique journey to their final destination.

Interactivity results when there is some kind of *interface*, or connection between a user and a medium. A range of options or pathways is available to the user by way of menu selections or buttons that will lead to different categories and ultimately provide new information. This results in variable outcomes, which depend on the choices made by the user. The program has predetermined informational hierarchies established by the developer, but the user is free to explore, due to the elimination of path restrictions and time constraints. In this vein, acquiring knowledge by pursuing a random order of routes is encouraged.

An example of interactive multimedia is an educational museum kiosk with a touchscreen that allows visitors to learn more about an exhibit, as shown in Figure 1-5. They can explore historical information by reading text on the subject, viewing images and diagrams, watching videos, and listening to sound recordings.

FIGURE 1-5 • Peabody Essex Museum's multimedia program

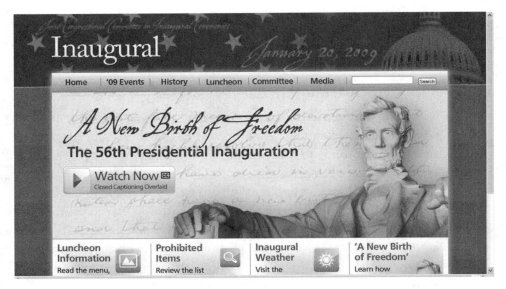

FIGURE 1-6 · A multimedia program for the 56th Presidential Inauguration

Such a program supplements other physical displays to allow for further educational opportunities.

Another example of linear vs. nonlinear multimedia is viewing a video. By its very nature, video is a type of single, independent medium that is typically played and viewed from point A to point B. If presented to an audience, such as in a theater, it is linear, sequential, and noninteractive. There is no viewer participation other than sitting back and watching. The content is presented in a straightforward manner, and it is completely in the hands of the video producer and the person who is controlling the display device.

However, if a video is viewed on a DVD player or streamed via the Internet on a computer or TV, as shown in the example in Figure 1-6, there are many ways to interact with it and control the experience. The video can be paused, rewound, or advanced; different scenes can be selected at random; closed-captioning can be displayed; audio can be adjusted; and the list goes on. This is undeniably a much more lively way to view a movie, even though the video medium itself is inherently designed for passive observation.

Kinds of Multimedia

The following are some examples of different kinds of multimedia programs:

- Educational children's spelling program for use in schools in conjunction with handwriting on the board or on paper

- Retail clothing store with a computer-based interactive customer guide for choosing products and services
- Online hospital training program for a nursing staff that can be completed at work or home
- Informational kiosk at a historical museum with a multimedia program on the social and political issues of the 1970s
- In-store sales and marketing demonstration to persuade customers to purchase office supplies
- Video game based on medieval knights with interactive role-playing options
- Military combat simulations using 3D virtual reality software to prepare soldiers for live warfare conflict (as seen in Figure 1-7)
- Smart phone mini-application to determine the tax and shipping costs for online purchases
- Language learning programs to help prepare for travel

FIGURE 1-7 • Uses of simulation programs in the army

- Live TV broadcast of a singing and dancing competition where the audience can participate by selecting who they prefer with a handheld voting device, and where viewers at home can cast votes via the Web in real time
- Handheld global positioning system (GPS) device for mapping routes while driving, biking, or hiking

As you can see, there are a variety of options when designing for multimedia, ranging from entertainment to business, children to adult, and home use to public kiosks.

Let's Get Technical

Fundamentally, multimedia is a mixture of digital or computer-based images, text, audio, video, and animation that can take many forms. Here, we will cover the basic technical concepts that are essential to understanding multimedia and how it works.

The media elements used in multimedia projects need to be digital (computer-ready) or *digitized* (converted into a digital format) to be used on a computer. The word *digital* stems from the term *binary digits* or *bits*, which is a combination of the two words. These binary or double digits pertain to the value of zeros (0s) and ones (1s) that make up all computer data.

Inside every computer are electronic components that are triggered either by preset commands (what your operating system tells your computer to do) or by input commands (what you are telling your computer to do when you click something or type on the keyboard). The presence of a 0 indicates when the electrical switch is off, and 1 means it is on.

Bits are also related to units of memory, whereby information is stored in a computer. Computing memory has many bits, which are organized into groups of eight, called *bytes* (a byte is 8 consecutive bits). Units include kilobytes (1KB = 1,024 bytes), megabytes (1MB = 1,024 kilobytes), and so on. For instance, a single text character is 1 byte, so the letter *A* is represented in computer storage (or memory) as the following eight binary digits: 01000001. Table 1-2 shows the approximate file size required for various multimedia elements.

TIP *For more about data information, see www2.sims.berkeley.edu/research/ projects/how-much-info/datapowers.html. For a conversion calculator, go to http://users.nlamerica.com/kevin/Bitsbytes.htm.*

TABLE 1-2 Bits and Bytes for Some Multimedia Elements	
Media Element	**File Size Approximation**
Typed word	10 bytes or 80 bits
Typed page	2KB or 2,000 bytes
Low–quality image	100KB or 100,000 bytes
Thirty seconds of broadcast–quality video	5MB or 5,000KB

So, the pictures, text, and sounds used in multimedia are essentially just a bunch of numerical digits. Depending on the combination of electronic switches and quantity of 0s and 1s, the results are unlimited as long as there is enough memory to handle all the multimedia components.

When referring to *memory* in relation to computers, two types are available: active memory, called *random-access memory* (RAM), and memory needed for the software that starts up the computer, called *read-only memory* (ROM). Computers also have internal storage, which is required to save programs and files on the hard drive. Computers are manufactured with memory chips installed, and more can be added to accommodate an increase in software and data requirements.

Still Struggling

RAM is called *random access* because it is readily available and becomes activated as the computer needs it. RAM is the main memory of the computer, and it is needed to run software programs efficiently.

As demand for more memory increases, the greater the need for more RAM, which can be expanded by installing computer chips in the computer. You can do this yourself, but it is recommended that a professional install memory to avoid damage to your motherboard (the primary electronic panel or circuit board inside the computer).

The amount of RAM needed depends on what you use the computer for. If it is mostly for word processing and Internet access, then a minimal amount is needed, and the native RAM is more than adequate. If it is for graphics and video, where multiple programs are open at the same time, then you might need to increase your RAM. If you do not have a sufficient amount of RAM, the programs

(continued)

may not function or could freeze, or files could become corrupted or not open correctly.

The major difference between the data storage on a computer hard drive and RAM storage is that the former is considered more permanent and the latter is only temporary. Anything in RAM will get lost when the computer shuts down. Hard drive memory remains stored in the computer until it is deleted by placing it in the trash (or the recycle bin) and then emptying it. It is easier to understand this concept if you equate it with the desktop metaphor of the filing cabinet (for memory stored in the hard drive) and the desktop workspace (for the active memory).

Analog-to-Digital Evolution

As previously mentioned, media elements must either be converted to a digital format or derive from a digital source in order to be used on the computer. Visual images—such as photos, drawings, and paintings—must be digitized, either by scanning with a flatbed scanner or photographing with a digital camera. Photographic images can also be acquired digitally in their original form by using a digital camera from the start. Either way, they will end up in a computer-friendly format that can be included in a multimedia presentation. Video and audio are similar in that they need to be converted using analog-to-digital technology or captured using a digital video camera in its native format.

The term *analog* generally refers to traditional, physical media, such as video and cassette tapes. This technology was used before the advent of computers that transmitted continuous TV and radio signals resulting in a linear representation. Videotapes were originally developed as a means of recording and playing back analog signals transmitted wirelessly or by cable. Later, they were designed for the home market to record live action for family movies. These days, most video is shot using a portable digital video camera so that the need to use an analog-to-digital converter is eliminated. This process saves steps and is also preferred when producing multimedia, as the screen dimensions and file size requirements are typically small and do not require high-end equipment.

A photograph that derives from a film negative and is printed on light-sensitive paper in a darkroom (or commercially printed) is also an analog source. Music recorded onto vinyl records and movies produced on celluloid filmstrips are other examples.

The analog-to-digital evolution is still occurring as we speak, but much of what is used for multimedia today is digital to begin with. This makes the development of a project easier and quicker, and ultimately cheaper to produce. The arrival of digital cameras in the early 1990s, for instance, allowed photographers to generate average-quality digital images. Over time, lower costs and improvements in technology have spawned numerous brands and models of digital still cameras, and now higher-quality results are commonplace and expected.

In the early days, relatively affordable cameras were very limited. They had a maximum resolution of 72 pixels per inch. The dimensions were limited to 640-by-480 (equal to 6-by-8 inches, or the average dimensions of a 13-inch computer monitor, which was standard at the time), with a 256-color palette, and the image yielded a 900KB file. Average photos taken with a digital camera today are at least 9MB, sporting millions of colors, which is ten times as large with a much higher-quality result.

When scanning or digitizing photographic images for multimedia, the end product and file size are very important. In other words, your goal is to have the highest quality image or sound file possible, but one that is also small enough to play seamlessly on a multimedia CD or the Web.

Another factor in the quality of digital media is that it is dependent on the equipment and technique used to acquire or convert it. A multimedia developer *must* establish in advance what the delivery format will be, as this will determine how the media files will be treated and prepared. More in-depth information on this topic will be discussed later in the book.

Still Struggling

The quality of a photographic image depends on the number of pixels it contains. Simply put, the more pixels that are present in an image, the finer the level of detail and color gradations. Inversely, if the image results in a low quality, the photo will have fewer pixels and the file size will be smaller. Graphics and images will be covered in detail in Chapter 3.

Summary

This chapter covered what multimedia is within a historical context, as well as how and why we use it. You now have a basic understanding of some of the technical concepts centered on multimedia, so you can begin learning about the process of developing it.

By distinguishing between linear presentations and user-controlled interactive environments, you should have an easier time planning your project goals. We also compared older uses of analog media with current digital media to give you a framework for how far we have come and where we are heading with respect to computing and multimedia.

QUIZ

1. **How many bits are in a byte of computer data?**
   A. 2
   B. 8
   C. 100
   D. 1000

2. **What is the term for presentations that are sequential and typically do not have interactivity?**
   A. Linear
   B. Nonlinear
   C. Hyperlinked
   D. Nonhierarchical

3. **Who came up with the original concept of multimedia?**
   A. Ted Nelson
   B. Douglas Engelbart
   C. Marshall McLuhan
   D. Vannevar Bush

4. **In what year was the first Apple computer sporting the innovative GUI released?**
   A. 1980
   B. 1975
   C. 1983
   D. 1990

5. **What is hypertext?**
   A. Douglas Engelbart's invention of office automation devices
   B. An information system that allows for browsing and searching using a multidirectional, linked approach
   C. A programming language that was used with HyperCard
   D. The name of Vannevar Bush's associative indexing system

6. **How many bytes make up an average typed page?**
   A. 100,000 bytes or 10KB
   B. 8 bits or 1 byte
   C. 10 bytes or 10,000 bits
   D. 2KB or 2,000 bytes

7. **Which type of media element is *not* considered digital?**
   A. Audiocassette tapes
   B. Web interface buttons
   C. Computer animation
   D. Scanned images

8. **What does Marshall McLuhan's statement "The medium is the message" mean?**
   A. The way something is delivered is more important than what is being said.
   B. When media elements are combined, they result in a more powerful end product.
   C. Linear presentations eliminate the distraction of needing to make decisions.
   D. Text branched out and users could explore subjects from many different perspectives.

9. **What determines the file size of a scanned photograph?**
   A. The number of colors
   B. The dimensions of the image
   C. The file size or number of bits
   D. All of the above

10. **What term refers to traditional, physical media, such as video and cassette tapes?**
    A. Analog
    B. Digital
    C. Interactive
    D. User interface

The Purposes and Application of Multimedia

This chapter provides an overview of multimedia from four perspectives. First, we'll examine the purpose, or uses, of multimedia in the home, at work, and in school. Then we'll consider the stages involved in developing a multimedia project, which will be followed by a look at the functional roles needed to produce it. Finally, we will introduce the tools and techniques used in working with multimedia, which will be elaborated on in later chapters.

CHAPTER OBJECTIVES

In this chapter, you will:

- Discover why multimedia is used and in what formats it can be presented
- Learn about the advantages of working with multimedia
- Get an overview of the process of developing a multimedia project
- Find out which tools and techniques you can use to work with multimedia

Why and How Multimedia Is Used

What is the purpose of multimedia? Why do we use it? If you want to learn about the French Revolution, why not simply read a long article or book on the topic? Surely everything can be said in text alone, so why bother with photos or documentaries?

If you want to deposit money in the bank using an ATM, why doesn't the bank simply provide you with text describing the sequence of buttons to push? The procedure can be described accurately without the need for graphics and touchscreens.

If you need on-the-job training at the office, why doesn't the company just provide you with a white paper explaining the processes, rather than a slide show or interactive video session?

The answers are obvious. Multimedia helps us understand faster and enables us to do more.

Multimedia is ubiquitous in our society today because, in the context of twenty-first century technology, it is actually essential for maintaining day-to-day functionality. Multimedia plays a key role in commerce, education, finance, and scientific communities.

The three primary purposes of multimedia include the following:

- Storing and transferring information and media elements, such as photo and video archives, blogs, slide shows, and documentaries, to name a few

- Interactivity for self-paced user control, such as museum displays, bank ATMs, and other types of multimedia kiosks

- Presenting information in the workplace or educational settings, such as online lectures, teleconferencing, and digital whiteboards

Multimedia is ideal for learning and training purposes, since the pace can be adjusted, making the experience more individualized. This lets the users analyze and interpret what they are reading, seeing, hearing, and touching at a speed that is comfortable for them. Instructional multimedia is generally accompanied by rich media elements to assist in the absorption, reiteration, and retention of new material.

Defining the end goal and how a multimedia program is ultimately used depends on many factors. For instance, when you use a web site for online banking, you want to be assured that your financial information is secure. Banks have safeguards in place for security protection on their web sites so customers will be comfortable using their services. This is programmed into the web site, so it must be considered during design and development. ATMs also have security measures, but customers interact with them in a different manner. The design and implementation must be adjusted to accommodate the use of a touch-screen and keypad, as well as to allow for check deposits and cash withdrawals. The approach for developing a banking web site will differ significantly from that of an ATM kiosk. For an interactive multimedia program to be effective and successful, it must serve the needs of the intended audience and be placed in the appropriate environment.

We rely heavily on multimedia as a communication vehicle in our personal lives. Social networking sites provide an array of options for maintaining ongoing interactive conversations by means of instant messaging; discussion boards; texting; and posting comments, pictures, and video. In the workplace and educational institutions, videoconferencing allows for virtual face-to-face communication if a live meeting or lecture is not possible.

Multimedia has the potential to offer vast amounts of information for those with an appetite for learning new things. Layers of beneficial resources can be offered, providing ongoing opportunities for acquiring knowledge. However, with the valuable information comes the usual superfluous material, which can lead to frustration and overload. There are typically many directions to go in, with numerous hyperlinks to new locations, but too much of anything, especially multisensory media experiences, gets crowded out by the need to figure out what's important and what isn't.

NOTE *The previous material is based on the Adobe Design Center article "The Value of Multimedia" by Patti Shank (www.adobe.com/designcenter/thinktank/ valuemedia/The_Value_of_Multimedia.pdf).*

Benefits of Interactive Presentations

To state the primary purpose of multimedia is not an easy task. There are many valid reasons to use multimedia at home, work, and school. Hyperlinked information is at the heart of multimedia, where active links lead to other content on multimedia screens and web pages. The Web itself is a form of multimedia due to its interconnected and interactive nature. This method of accessing linked information reflects human thought processes and is analogous to intertwined electronic circuitry.

The use of multimedia encourages us to perform a variety of tasks simultaneously. This notion of *multitasking* began long before computers came along. Today, we just do more of it at a faster rate, and technology is at the heart of it.

It has been argued that multimedia helps us to be more efficient, so that we are not wasting time on laborious tasks that were once completed by hand. For instance, bill paying and online tax filing are quicker and easier than ever before. Increasing amounts of information become available every minute by way of the Internet, and this makes researching, learning, and communicating that much more effective and readily available. There is no doubt that multimedia has a function and purpose, and with the progression of technological capabilities, we are witnessing ever-increasing advancements in its features and attributes.

Studies have shown that multimedia use in educational settings promotes learning, since the student is involved in the process. The learning-by-doing model has been adopted for many decades because it works. Interactive multimedia gives students choices, and it can be modified for individual styles and levels of ability. For instance, in a science curriculum, teachers can use multimedia programs to enhance traditional instruction and to develop students' scientific inquiry skills. Students can visualize molecular structures with rotating 3D models, or study lab processes by viewing videos and conducting virtual experiments while inputting their own data.

Educational multimedia can serve as an enhancement to lectures and presentations with the goal of improving comprehension. Animated simulations help students visualize complex ideas and allow for interaction within virtual environments. If designed properly, instructional multimedia provides continuous adjustments to coincide with a person's learning style, maximizing its effectiveness. The possibilities are endless for educational multimedia uses because the inclusion of relevant concepts and practical information significantly assists the learning of complicated facts.

Interactive multimedia has distinct advantages over individual media, as summarized in Table 2-1.

Avoiding Potential Pitfalls

As discussed in Chapter 1, there are times when interactive multimedia has its drawbacks. There are the inevitable technical problems and limitations that go hand-in-hand with any computer-based production. This is in accord with Murphy's law: "If anything can go wrong, it will." But that's not to say it always will, and with careful planning and anticipation of some trouble occurring, you will most likely have smooth sailing. Later in this chapter, we will discuss the planning stages and development process, which are critical to a successful multimedia production.

TABLE 2-1 Advantages of Interactive Multimedia

Benefit	Capabilities
Many options	Freedom of choice throughout gives the user complete control with many possible directions.
Numerous media elements	Visual images, sounds, animation, video, and text assist in making information more applicable and easier to understand.
Personalized approach	Multimedia is more individual, so learning can be geared toward the particular needs of the person using it.
Self–paced	The pace can be slow or fast to accommodate a person's style and complement that person's rate of absorption and retention.
Level selections	Information can be read in depth or skimmed over.
Audio adjustments	The sound level of music clips, videos, and animation can be customized (increased, decreased, or muted).
Variety of experiences	There is endless variety, so that interest is maintained. Multimedia is a unique experience for each person using it, and it will also differ each time it is used by the same person, based on which path that person takes.
Linked connections	Connections to other information can easily be made by linking words and/or images.
Exploration	Users can investigate and learn by trial and error, without negative consequences.
Immediacy and vastness	Limitless information is right at users' fingertips, easily found with search engines and databases.
Visualization of concepts	Abstract and complex ideas can be visualized and made easier to grasp.
Virtual environments	Virtual worlds can be explored, allowing for full submersion into an altered reality.

Other factors that come into play with interactive multimedia have more to do with the specific media elements that make up the product. When transferring to a digital format, for example, there is an inevitable loss of data information as compared to the original medium. You use an analog-to-digital converter (ADC), but there may be limitations to the conversion capabilities of the technology at hand. Cassette tapes, for instance, can have deformations due to improper storage and handling, which translate over when converted digitally. Although an infrequent occurrence, you might need to obtain an old music clip that is available only on a vinyl LP. The original may have scratches and flaws that will cause skipping or distortion in the audio file when transferring from an analog signal to a digital one. Technical knowledge and skill are required to restore and improve the converted version using digital audio software.

In addition, the compression of files is often necessary to reduce the file size to a smaller amount of disk space so that there is more efficiency. This can affect the quality of the output, as it may not be an accurate representation of the original. Generally speaking, the quality will be sufficient for the purposes of multimedia if using even the most basic digital-conversion technology, since it is for screen viewing, which is inherently small in terms of screen dimensions, with a low pixel resolution.

Table 2-2 lists some of the disadvantages of interactive multimedia. More will be discussed on this topic in future chapters.

TABLE 2-2   Disadvantages of Interactive Multimedia
Limitations with available technology
Problems due to incompatible software, operating systems, and hardware
Limited memory to run programs
Proliferation of new devices with conflicting uses, such as touchscreens, pressure-sensitive tablets, smart phones, mobile devices, game consoles, Blu-ray players, and interactive TV
Confusion due to poorly planned multimedia content and use of elements
Limitations with Internet access due to web browsers and connection speeds
Inadequate audio capabilities and quality (speakers and headphones)
Compromised speed and quality when accessing and viewing images, animation, and videos
Lack of accessibility for users with disabilities
Outdated plug-in software to run programs or files, such as Flash or QuickTime
Costly and time-consuming to produce
Complicated configuration of the authoring environment

Uses of Multimedia

Multimedia has applications in many areas, including entertainment, education, research, business, medicine, banking, military, and commerce. Some of these categories are at times combined with overlapping goals. For instance, educational programs can also be entertaining, and this is referred to as *edutainment*. Multimedia can be used at home, in schools, at work, and in public locations. Table 2-3 outlines the vast number of options available today, and Figure 2-1 illustrates them.

Designing and programming for different types of multimedia varies depending on the fundamental purpose and eventual usage. For example, looking at the underlying source for a web site reveals HTML coding. This is what allows pages to be viewed on the Internet. Hyperlinks are added to web pages to allow users to connect to other web sites, and they may also include Adobe Flash elements (such as animated movies or interactive controls). These are developed using ActionScript programming to further enhance the interactive capabilities (this will be discussed in Chapter 8).

TABLE 2-3 Multimedia Usability Options

Type of Device	Usage
Small handheld devices	Handheld devices (iPod touch, iPad, e-readers, and so on); smart phones; and video game units designed with Internet and email capabilities, apps (mini-applications), and movie and film viewing options
Home desktop computers	PCs for use with software programs, disks (CD or DVD) or web sites on the Internet to create, write, and play
Gaming systems	Xbox, PlayStation, and Wii for video game entertainment
TVs	Cable and wireless Internet with interactive features, as well as systems for viewing and recording programs and movies (DVR or DVD players)
Educational computers	Labs or classroom stations for testing, reading, finding information, and preparing school projects
Workplace computers	Shared or individual workstations, networked for distributing data and exchanging files
Laptops	Portable computers with wireless or hard-wired (Ethernet) Internet access, software, and disk drives (CD or DVD) for multimedia programs

Laptop

Computer station

Music and
video player

Handheld gaming device

Interactive TV

FIGURE 2-1 · Different kinds of multimedia: handheld device, large computer
setup, interactive TV, and laptop

Interactive *kiosks* are another type of multimedia intended for general use in
a pubic setting. These are self-contained, stand-alone computing terminals that
provide access to on-demand information and transactions, as shown in the
example in Figure 2-2.

Kiosks typically have a touchscreen for data entry, along with an on-screen
keyboard and other peripherals, such as card readers and barcode scanners. A
thermal printer is the most common output device if printing is needed. Some
interactive kiosks are equipped to burn custom CDs or DVDs, or download
multimedia files to handheld media players. Some have barcode scanners and
credit card readers, for checking prices, using store coupons and frequent buyer
cards, and making purchases. Interactive kiosks may have a customized, hard-
ened enclosure, or may simply be a standard PC that has been repurposed for
interactive kiosk duties. Outdoor kiosks provide self-service for transportation
companies, theaters, amusement parks, stadiums, and resorts.

FIGURE 2-2 · Home Depot kiosk

Multimedia kiosks (independent computer stations) can be found in the following locations:

- Museums—such as science, children's, historical, and art museums—for finding out more information while visiting an exhibit
- Transportation hubs—such as airports and bus, subway, and train stations—for printing boarding passes and baggage tags, scanning driver licenses and passports, making schedule and seat assignment changes, procuring tickets, and arranging car rentals
- Retail centers—such as stores, malls, and restaurants—for researching and purchasing products
- Performance centers and movie theaters for purchasing tickets

- Banks and loan locations for obtaining account balances, cash withdrawals, deposits, and fund transfers
- Self-checkouts—such as for hardware stores, grocery stores, and libraries—as shown in the example in Figure 2-3.
- Fast-food chains for ordering and paying for food
- Pharmacies for card making, printing coupons, and creating DVDs and prints of digital photos
- Health-care kiosks for check-in, ID scanning, and prescription refills
- Gas stations for filling up and paying for other services, such as a car wash or oil change

FIGURE 2-3 • Self-checkout

Planning Stages and Development Process

When designing a multimedia project, planning as much as possible in advance is crucial for successful results. There are two major considerations: what is involved in the project and who will bring the project from concept to completion.

Web site design requires an initial site architecture plan that focuses on the navigation or information flow of a web site. This helps to determine what will go where and what kind of hierarchical arrangement the content will follow. Setting up the program's infrastructure is essential to navigation design, which is an integral part of multimedia development. As when constructing a building, the underlying structure is the foundation upon which everything else is assembled.

The preparation stage needs to first address the content of the project and how best to organize it. A diagram or flowchart like the one shown in Figure 2-4 is an important early step to show a map or bird's-eye view of the paths or options available. This illustrates the entire scope of the program with navigational routes the user can take, as well as how content interrelates and how it

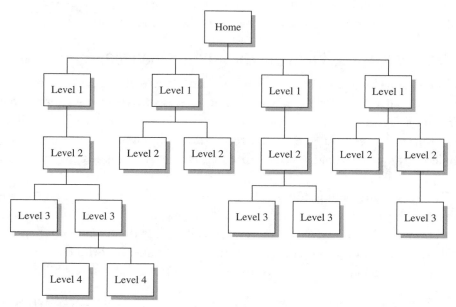

FIGURE 2-4 · A sample flowchart for a multimedia project

is accessed. The flow diagram becomes a useful reference tool, and it may change and evolve as the project progresses.

When developing a multimedia program, key components must be fleshed out by the director of the project. It is important to address some of the primary concerns up front by asking clients if they have considered the following:

- Concept (theme or underlying idea)
- Content (subject matter and media that will be incorporated)
- Aesthetics or *look and feel* of visual aspects (color scheme, textures, layout, and screen designs)
- Functionality of the program features (interactive controls, such as buttons and menus)
- Intended audience or target market
- Program structure (linear versus nonlinear; flowchart showing pathways)
- Interrelationship of media elements: images, text, audio, moving images (animation and video), interface design, interactivity, and navigation

The multimedia development process is a step-by-step plan that guides the project director and team members so that they stay on track. Table 2-4 shows the order of events necessary for the formation of a successful multimedia project.

Roles and Responsibilities of the Multimedia Team

Before establishing the team and each member's role, it is necessary to stress the importance of the client's needs and interests as well as the client's goals for the project. If you are both the producer and client, then your job will be much easier, since you don't need to consider anyone else's preferences. A single person can manage a smaller project. However, designing multimedia is typically a team effort.

Even if you are willing to wear all the different project hats and go it alone, there will be necessary roles that only skilled specialists can fill. Someone *does* need to be in charge, and this person is typically called the *project manager*. The goals and scope of the project will determine the makeup of the team. A multimedia team is likely to consist of the following titles and responsibilities:

- **Project managers** plan, organize, develop, and oversee the project, work with the client, and manage personnel.
- **Multimedia project designers** oversee technical aspects, content, information architecture, media elements, and interaction.

TABLE 2-4 Multimedia Development Process

Stage	Objectives
1. Project goal	Define the project, inquiring and brainstorming for content ideas Research topic Determine budget
2. Concept and planning	Determine target audience (gender, age, education, etc.) Determine product usage or venue (environment in which it will be used, such as computer station, web site, kiosk, or TV) Decide on platform (Mac, PC executable, browser–based) Define hardware and software requirements Outline treatment (a written description or outline of the components and intended experience) Design a flowchart for information design (navigational routes; diagram showing the entire scope with different levels or subcategories) Develop sketches and storyboards (show elements and functionality; visualizing scenes to represent what the user will see and interact with) Set up schedule for goals and monitor budget
3. Design and prototype	Consider overall project design: • Constraints (limitations, expected difficulties) • Conventions (method or mode) • Interactivity (buttons, menus) • Visual metaphor or theme for interface design Consider media elements (backgrounds, illustrations, photos, graphics, text, animation, video, sound, and music) Obtain rights for use of existing materials where necessary Secure resources and talent for media production (photography, video, and music) Develop a prototype to show structure, content, and functionality (a test run that represents the final result)
4. Production	Write and script (refine the plan and prepare the copy or text) Prepare and produce media elements Program/author (integrate content and link the system) Produce the program (upload to a FTP site or master and duplicate CDs/DVDs) Design packaging and written material for print (if applicable)
5. Quality assurance and user testing	Evaluation completed in–house as a tryout of the product prior to distribution: • Alpha testing (early in the development to address problems) • Beta testing (just before final release) Identify and repair bugs or technical glitches
6. Distribution and deployment	Write documentation (user tutorial and installation guide) Produce CDs and DVDs, which includes manufacturing, packaging, marketing, selling, and shipping Install software and configure hardware for stand–alone computers Upload to server, track traffic, and gauge effectiveness based on response to ads and registration logins

- **Interface designers** supervise screen design and user navigation.
- **Photographers, illustrators,** and **graphic designers** create visual elements.
- **Audio, video, and animation professionals** produce sound and moving images.
- **Subject matter experts** provide accurate content on the primary topic.
- **Writers and editors** provide scripts and review text content.
- **Computer programmers** author code and provide functionality and interactivity.
- **Producers** test, implement, and deliver multimedia.

During the initial meetings with the client, you must carefully define the project and have a brainstorming session to generate ideas for program content. In this part of the process, *everything* is possible, but the project goals still must remain within the confines of what the budget will allow.

The content is the subject matter, which includes all the media elements that will be collected and integrated into the project. It is a good idea to make a content list or asset breakdown to categorize what will be created by content specialists, such as photographers and illustrators, and what needs to be gathered from existing materials. Sometimes material is provided by the client; other times, it must be researched and located, which takes time. Obtaining permission to use content will also add to the time frame, so planning ahead and doing the preliminary work are essential. (We'll talk more about copyright issues a little later in the chapter.)

The target audience is an important piece of the puzzle, particularly with web site designs and educational multimedia. You must take into account that not everyone has the same interests, reading levels, and speed at which they access information. Such factors in determining how to design for the intended users include but are not limited to age, gender, educational background, technological skill level, and occupation. The content and features that are included will have an effect on the final decisions for design, concept, functionality, copywriting, video and audio selections, and so on.

This stage is followed by the writer's job to write a description or outline of the multimedia project, and then create a flowchart with the main topics and subcategories to show the full extent of the program. Both the client and team members need to put their heads together at this point to set goals and deadlines, as well as make arrangements for constituent resources, so that the budget and payment schedule can be closely monitored.

Clearly, there is a need for a team, be it small or large, to keep the process of developing multimedia on track. Filling such roles, as well as maintaining ongoing communication among team members, is essential to the success of the project. There must be regular check-ins via email, phone, videoconferencing, or face-to-face meetings. Regular contact with the client for consultation and review is important to ensure that the team is following the schedule and budget. These checks and balances throughout the progress of the project help to make for an effective and efficient workflow.

Information Architecture

Determining the breadth and depth of the program is another key factor that must be tweaked by the team. This relates to the information architecture, where hierarchies are established based on the organization of the information. Levels of a program can be designed as *wide and shallow* (more choices for the user up front, and fewer as they go along) or *narrow and deep* (fewer choices up front, but many categories later on). These structures can work, but they have their drawbacks. Shallow program structures make for unnecessarily lengthy menus, and deep structures require users to burrow through numerous screens for information.

Multimedia can also be a complex network of links, as on the Web, where choices for the user can link within the site itself and also to outside web pages. The selections are limitless in this case, but at times overwhelmingly so. You must consider options for how users can look for and access information, such as the table of contents, site map, search engine, index, and pull-down menus.

Another related factor is where these elements may appear on the screen and how they will work. For instance, will there be a menu at the top with drop-down options, or will all the options be on the left, where each item brings the user to a new page or screen? Is the structure set up as a hub-and-spoke, like a web search engine, which allows for many directions all stemming from one central hub, with a myriad of links from any of the search results? Figure 2-5 illustrates the hub-and-spoke organization, as well as the shallow and deep structures. There are bound to be discrepancies between browsers, platforms, and hardware, so the testing phase (stage 5) is vital before launching the product.

TIP   *An excellent resource for information architecture and organizing content for multimedia in different ways is the Yale Style Manual (http://webstyleguide.com/ wsg3/index.html). The manual includes a number of very good visual examples of flowchart diagrams. It is intended for web-specific applications, but it is an appropriate guide for all multimedia models.*

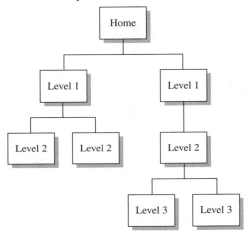

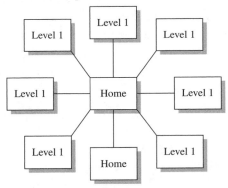

FIGURE 2-5 · Multimedia organizational structures: shallow vs. deep, and hub-and-spoke

Copyright Issues: Securing Permission for Media Usage

A large part of building a multimedia project is the creation or acquisition of media elements. When acquiring existing media, such as a photograph found on the Internet, a developer *must* seek and secure permission for all media elements that are not already owned by another source. You must get permission from the copyright owner before using an element in a multimedia project, or legal action may be filed against you or your company. Owners have exclusive rights to their work, so by infringing, you are depriving them of their constitutional right to maintain possession of their creative efforts. Even if you own a work of art or a music recording, such as audio files burned to a CD, you cannot use them in any form without first seeking authorization.

TIP *Good information about copyrights and fair use can be found at the web site for the United States Copyright Office, www.copyright.gov.*

Original creative works have inherent ownership rights, so that no one can copy or reuse them for financial gain, personal recognition, or professional advancement without repercussions. Obtaining rights to usage of material can range from being complicated and costly to simply getting written permission from the owner. The owner may not want to relinquish the rights, but they may be licensed to you for a fee, allowing you to use the element in your project. If you are creating your own media elements, make sure you provide a copyright notice in some form, either on the main screen or front matter, in order to protect your creative work from infringement by others.

To protect proprietary works against illegal use and to safeguard ownership rights, the Copyright Act of 1976 was enacted. This came about long before PCs and the Internet were in use by the general public. The copyright law does allow *fair use*, which means limited use for educational purposes and in instructional settings. More specifically, fair use includes material that is used for teaching, analysis and criticism, research, and school projects. However, there are still restrictions in place for anything that may be profited from. Also, the owner of the copyrighted materials must be acknowledged, even under fair-use circumstances. Therefore, you have a legal and ethical obligation to adhere to fair-use guidelines, especially with multimedia, since so many aspects deal with media elements.

An option worth considering that will minimize the risk of infringement or unlawful use is to obtain royalty-free or public-domain media. In this case, there are few, if any, restrictions placed on usage. Nonetheless, it is still imperative that you read and comply with usage guidelines. If none are provided, do not assume the item can be used freely.

The following are ways to obtain inexpensive or free media:

- Stock image libraries with a fee attached for single, limited, or unlimited use (photos, clip art, animated GIFs)
- Image databases containing public domain media (those with no copyright restrictions or works from which the original copyright has expired)
- Royalty-free content

NOTE *Beware that some works may contain protections against unwanted reproduction. For example, images may have invisible watermarks or audio files may contain encryption schemes. These mechanisms limit or prevent use of copyrighted material, and they can be used as a tracking device or method of detecting unlawful usage. This is referred to as Digital Rights Management (DRM), and it is constantly evolving to keep pace with the latest technologies and the ever-increasing accessibility to new media.*

Copyright matters are somewhat complex. If the subject is not clear or you have questions, you should consult with an attorney who is familiar with the intricacies of the law or someone who specializes in intellectual property.

Tools for Creating and Preparing Media

A variety of possible media elements were discussed in Chapter 1. Now we need to delve into the tools needed to create multimedia programs. These come in the form of different software programs, and there are many of them on the market.

Table 2-5 lists the tools needed for creating multimedia, along with the associated industry-standard software. However, there are many other inexpensive or free options that can be downloaded from the Web. These freeware and shareware programs are often less robust than the commercial versions but, generally speaking, have the capabilities to get the job done.

Images and video need to be either digitized or converted to a digital format if taken from an analog source (analog versus digital was discussed in Chapter 1), or they need to be taken with a digital camera from the start. If you are acquiring existing media that you did not create—taking media elements from the Web or

TABLE 2-5 Tools for Creating Multimedia

Media	Hardware for Capturing or Converting	Standard Software for Creating or Modifying
Photos	Shoot with a digital camera; scan original printed photos or film negatives with an optical scanner	Photoshop, iPhoto
Illustrations, graphics, and diagrams	Hand-drawn and scanned; clip art from stock image database; create with vector drawing or drafting program	Illustrator, Freehand, Fireworks, CorelDRAW, Xara Xtreme
Pixel-based art	Transfer artwork created using traditional media and either scan or photograph; construct in a raster software program	Photoshop, Painter, Paint Shop Pro
Text	Generate in a word processing or page layout program, and import into a web design program	Word, Illustrator, InDesign, Flash, Dreamweaver
Audio	Transfer from a tape or film to a computerized format using an ADC, or digitize using a digital audio recording device	Garage Band (music creation and editing), SoundBooth (importing and manipulating audio), Audacity
Video	Transfer from a tape or film to a computerized format using an ADC, or digitize using a digital video recording device	Final Cut Pro and Premier (editing nonlinear digital video), Pinnacle and Vegas (PC-based video editors)
Animation	Hand-drawn and recorded on film or taken with a digital camera; imported into 2D or 3D animation programs to further enhance	Flash, LightWave, Maya, After Effects, Toon Boom
Web site development	N/A	Create in an illustration, page layout, or photo editing program and export to web design software (Dreamweaver, Expression Web)
Interface design	N/A	Graphics and web design software for making backgrounds, scenes, and metaphorical scenes
Navigation	N/A	Illustrator or Photoshop for design, and web design software (Dreamweaver) for adding functionality to buttons and menus

CDs—you must either use royalty-free media or obtain permission if it is copyright-protected.

So you have collected all the pieces of the puzzle and are ready to assemble it, but need to know how to prepare everything to ensure it will work correctly in the intended multimedia environment. When saving your media elements, using the correct file format is essential.

Still Struggling

Different file formats allow media to be opened in other programs and platforms. For instance, if an animated web advertisement is designed in Flash, and then saved in formats for both the Web and mobile devices, it becomes versatile and consequently more marketable since it has the potential to reach a wider audience.

Each type of media requires technical knowledge and expertise/skill so that it is produced effectively, is visually appealing, and functions properly. File formats, as well as how to go about gathering and preparing for a multimedia project, will be covered in greater depth in Parts II and III of this book.

Making It Functional and Interactive

Another important consideration with respect to preparation of media for finalizing a multimedia project is the authoring or programming to make the content interactive. This is also necessary to pull everything (all the content and functionality) together to create a unified end product.

Authoring tools are off-the-shelf, end-user software packages, such as Dreamweaver for web design using HTML and Flash for interactive design using ActionScript. Alternatively, you can use a general-purpose programming language, such as Visual Basic or C++. These tools are not geared specifically for creating multimedia projects. They are best used for programs with a lot of data and unconventional display formats—specific control that an authoring tool does not provide or does not manage well.

For web authoring, you need to learn how to work with HTML code. HTML is a markup language as opposed to a programming language, and it uses tags to specify the visual features of web pages, like text styles and image placement. Other types have been added on to HTML to allow customization, such as Dynamic HTML (DHTML), Extensible Markup Language (XML), JavaScript, and Cascading Style Sheets (CSS). HTML editors are software programs, such as Dreamweaver, that allow you to create web pages without needing to know much about HTML.

Authoring, even in its most basic form with simple commands, has a steep learning curve and takes time and patience to master. Tools that provide built-in scripts or behaviors are helpful for those who are not adept with or inclined toward becoming proficient with programming. A good solution is to work with someone who is comfortable with authoring and programming, so you share the burden of making a functional, interactive program.

Still Struggling

If all these acronyms seem a bit much, it is typical computer jargon and takes some getting used to. Using shorthand is commonplace today in all aspects of technology. It makes it easier to remember and convey something rather than long, complicated names. However, when learning such terms, you will not only need to know what they stand for, but also know what they mean. For instance, as noted, XML stands for Extensible Markup Language, which is a set of rules for decoding documents and transferring and storing data.

Finalizing, Testing, and Delivering Multimedia

The last stages in preparing multimedia are the most critical for a successful and properly working product. The user-testing process has two distinct phases:

- **Alpha testing**   This is the first pass early on to check content relationships, address bugs (errors or flaws in the design), and test if the program is functioning. It is generally conducted within a company and typically not with targeted users.
- **Beta testing**   This testing is done just before the final release of the product to make sure it is free of bugs and all aspects of the program are functional.

Comments/feedback and reports on problems are needed to address and correct deficiencies. It is also important to use a representative sampling from the intended audience. This stage of testing is a process that should not be rushed or overlooked simply to meet a deadline, as it can affect the success of the program.

Testing multimedia then results in programming rework to advance the development process to the final stage, which is *delivering*, or distributing and deploying, the product. As indicated in Table 2-4, documentation is written for instructional tutorials and installation guides, and the product is deployed. If it is intended for use on a CD or DVD, it will be manufactured, packaged, marketed, and shipped to retail distribution centers.

Stand-alone computers, such as kiosks in stores and museums, require software installation and hardware configuration. Files are uploaded to the server, and then user traffic is monitored to gauge the effectiveness of the program. This is often based on responses to ads, questionnaires, signing up for access to services or content, and registration logins.

After user testing occurs, it is time to deliver the multimedia project. This has to do with collecting everything and getting it ready so it will work properly in its intended environment. It may need to be installed by the users, which will require a set of written instructions for them to follow. Or it may be preinstalled onto a computer's hard disk or burned to a CD or DVD.

For web-enabled multimedia, files need to be uploaded to an FTP site that is housed on a web server. The Web operates with connections between *servers* (computers that store web site files with software to run them) and *clients* (those who are accessing a web site). This ongoing reciprocal communication between the two is what allows web pages to be viewed and interacted with, regardless of a person's hardware (computer) or software (Internet browser).

Summary

This concludes Part I of this book, which provided a broad multimedia overview. So far, we have addressed what multimedia is, including the historical framework and basic technological concepts, and what interactivity means, while making analog and digital media distinctions. Understanding the purposes and uses of multimedia, as well as what goes into developing and producing multimedia, will help to pave the way to learning about the specific kinds of media that compose a multimedia program.

QUIZ

1. **What is the first step in the multimedia development process?**
   A. Quality assurance
   B. Design and prototype
   C. Production
   D. Project goal

2. **In order to legally use a photograph in a multimedia program, what must you do?**
   A. Determine if it is royalty-free
   B. Find out who owns the photo
   C. Ask permission to use the photo
   D. Change it so it is no longer recognizable

3. **Before distributing a multimedia program, it is important to do what?**
   A. Check on copyright permissions
   B. Test it on the intended audience
   C. Have the software and hardware configurations working correctly
   D. All of the above

4. **Which type of multimedia is a self-contained, stand-alone public computing terminal that provides access to on-demand information and transactions?**
   A. Educational computer
   B. Interactive kiosk
   C. Gaming system
   D. Small handheld device

5. **What does HTML stand for?**
   A. Hypermedia Transfer Markup Language
   B. Hypertext Markup Language
   C. Hypermedia Markup Language
   D. HyperCard Technical Markup Language

6. **What is *not* an advantage of interactive multimedia?**
   A. Virtual environments
   B. Immediate and vast
   C. Limited choices
   D. Self-paced

7. **Who has the primary role on a multimedia team for planning, organizing, and overseeing the project?**
   A. Interactive designer
   B. Project manager
   C. Subject matter expert
   D. Multimedia project designer

8. What is *not* a primary consideration when designing a multimedia project?
    A. Concept or underlying idea of the multimedia program
    B. Content of the program
    C. How many people are on the multimedia team
    D. Functionality of the program features

9. What are the primary tools used to make a multimedia program functional and interactive?
    A. Authoring tools
    B. Designing tools
    C. Video-editing tools
    D. Animation tools

10. Why is planning and testing with a specific target audience in mind important for multimedia that is designed for educational purposes?
    A. To take into account different interests and reading levels
    B. So that it can be assured to provide a learning benefit
    C. The educational content and features will have an effect on design decisions for the concept, functionality, copywriting, and media elements
    D. All of the above

Part II

Kinds of Media: The Essential Components

chapter 3

Graphics and Images

When creating multimedia projects, many factors enter into the equation. A primary component that needs to be addressed is just what kinds of media to include and how to use them. In this chapter, we will cover creating and acquiring graphics and images. We will also look at file formats and color theory in preparation for their use on computer displays.

CHAPTER OBJECTIVES

In this chapter, you will:

- Make sense of all the different ways to create and prepare graphics and images for multimedia

- Find out about digital photography, scanning, and resolution

- Discover the purpose of file formats and how to correctly save image files

- Learn about color theory and the differences between working with color for the screen and using it for printed material

The Role of Graphics and Images in Multimedia

We are a visually oriented society. Human communication has relied on visual messages for conveying ideas since the Stone Age. Images were and still are a vital means of expression and transmission of thoughts, feelings, and information. Digital images on computer screens are no exception; they have simply become more sophisticated with the advancement of software capabilities and high-resolution displays, much like visualizing the real thing.

One of the largest and most prominent aspects of any multimedia program is the *look* of it. This is what people are exposed to right up front—from the overall *interface* (what the user clicks or touches), to the menus and buttons, to the photographs and illustrations.

Graphics and images are integral to the design of a multimedia program. It has been proven that complex ideas such as statistical data and historical timelines are more easily explained and understood when accompanied by visual examples.

Visual images for multimedia are essentially backgrounds, photos, objects, buttons, patterns, graphics, and illustrations. The way that these images are treated and positioned on a screen determines their aesthetic appeal and their overall effectiveness in terms of communication. Users of multimedia will look at and interact with these elements, and the selection and treatment of them should reflect the underlying concept and goals of the project.

Graphics have the ability to attract viewers and lure them in, and maintain their interest. However, there are visuals, and there are visuals—not all are created equal. You want to make sure that images are created and saved properly in order to provide a high-quality and professional end product. Graphics and images can be created from scratch or acquired from other sources.

There are many different kinds of computer graphic images, with a variety of terms and uses associated with them. The two primary categories that digital images fall into are *vector* and *raster*. A distinction needs to be made between the two, as they differ significantly in terms of how they are created, worked with, and prepared. We will first look at the use of vector graphics and then explore raster images.

Designing Vector Graphics

Vector graphics are one of the oldest types of computer images. They were used when computer-generated graphics first came into being in the 1960s.

Vectors are used for line-art graphics, such as illustrations (logos, cartoons, and drawings), type design, and diagrams (charts, graphs, and maps). They are called *vector* because they are objects made up of lines (also called *paths*) that are defined by mathematical equations. Pierre Bezier, a French mathematician and engineer who experimented with techniques for drawing vector curves and lines, invented this type of graphic during the 1960s. He worked for the car manufacturer Renault, and used his knowledge and skills to advance the development of vector graphics for use in numerous applications.

Vector images are also referred to as *object-based* or *object-oriented* because they are fundamentally centered on the creation of forms or shapes. Vector images are resolution-independent in that they are scalable and not dependent on resolution for the quality of the final result. *Scalability* means that vectors can be repeatedly made larger or smaller without sacrificing the integrity of the image. Vector graphics will appear smooth and proportional regardless of their size in dimensions.

Vector graphics, at a very minimum, consist of two end points, also called *control points*, and a path that connects them. Bezier curves allow vector lines to arch and bend smoothly. They can be adjusted repeatedly to obtain the desired shape without losing aspects of the original form. Figure 3-1 shows examples of a vector shape and vector text.

Vector graphics can be angular or curved, as shown in Figure 3-2. Creating curved lines requires a bit more skill and precision, but you can produce a smooth, controllable line and manipulate it by handles on the end points. Angular corners can easily be converted into curved lines, and curves can be converted into corners. Such versatile tools give tremendous flexibility to the design process.

Methods of creating vector graphics vary depending on the software program and tools available. With most vector software programs, you can create a line using one of several tools.

Vector Shape

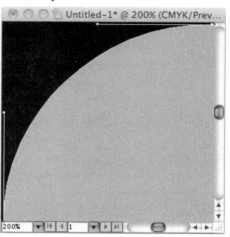

Vector Text

Vector Text Rasterized

FIGURE 3-1 • Vector graphic examples

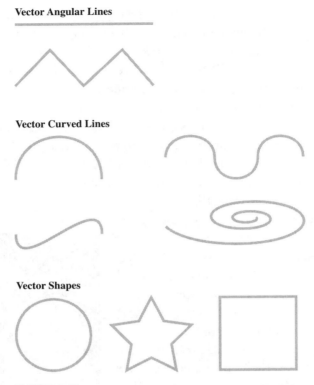

FIGURE 3-2 · Lines and curves created in a vector program

The line tool will make a straight line vertically, horizontally, or at any angle. Percentages can be assigned to accurately alter the direction, or dragging on one of the end points can rotate, stretch, flip, or skew it. The pencil tool provides a free-form approach. The pen tool allows for great precision for creating curved and straight lines and shapes. Shape tools allow for the simple creation of squares, rectangles, circles, ovals, and a myriad of other commonly used forms.

Programs such as Adobe Illustrator and Flash use vector graphics. Flash is designed for the Web, to create interactive web sites and animation. This requires small files to run quickly and efficiently for multimedia and web sites.

Vector programs are used to create logos, clip art, illustrations, icons, and type effects since they are easily manipulated, scaled, copied, and combined. Color is also simple to apply to vector graphics since they are objects made up of lines and curves. Color gradations (called *gradients*) can be applied as well, adding dimensionality to otherwise flat, two-dimensional artwork.

Vector files are typically small since they display line art in the form of mathematical formulas. When vector graphics are saved, anchor points connecting lines and curves, as well as the individual colors associated with each object, are stored in the file's memory. However, vector graphics can also become rather complex. They can be modest designs with few attributes, or layered with many shapes and lines for an intricately detailed visual result. The more graphic elements included in a vector file, the larger the file size in terms of bytes.

Software programs that specialize in 3D illustration and animation, such as *computer-aided design* (CAD) systems, use vector graphics. Such graphics are vector polygons in a wireframe form that use complex gradients and surface-mapping techniques to simulate real-life imagery. One method of creation is for designers to work with 3D models using dedicated software by interpreting (or *rendering*) 2D vector shapes. Shadows and highlights are depicted in a more accurate way using vectors since the mathematical formulas connect one directly with the other; when changes are made to one, it mirrors changes in a corresponding graphic. Another approach is to create 3D models from scratch using 3D modeling and animation software.

TIP   *You can find a good basic tutorial on creating vector shapes in the "Create Vector Graphics in Illustrator and Freehand" article, at http://articles.sitepoint .com/article/graphics-illustrator-freehand.*

Creating Raster Images

Raster graphics are the other major type used to create computer images. This type is commonly associated with digital photography, but it also pertains to other kinds of images that use continuous tone or color.

Most of the visual elements in a multimedia program are made up of raster graphics; even graphics that originate as vectors are converted to raster for screen-viewing purposes. Web graphics are always raster images, with the exception of the Scalable Vector Graphic (SVG) format, unless they are linked image files for the purpose of downloading or sharing. Multimedia programs and web sites use raster images because they are viewed on screen, and digital displays are made up of pixels with specific pixel dimensions (called *screen resolution*).

Raster graphics are also referred to as *bitmapped* images, which means they are literally bits mapped on a grid. Each raster image is made up of data bits that are mapped or fixed to the pixels on a screen, in the same way that text and numbers appear on a screen. These bits are organized in a vertical and horizontal grid, so the resolution of a bitmapped image is determined by the number of pixels in a 1-inch-by-1-inch area.

The *pixels per inch* (PPI) unit differs from the *dots per inch* (DPI) unit, which has to do with the number of dots per inch in a printed version of a computer image. For example, an average laser printer has a resolution of between 300 to 600 DPI, so an image with the same resolution as the printer will print adequately and sharply. Printing images will be discussed later in this chapter in the section on color, as well as in Chapter 9.

Figure 3-3 shows an example of working with a raster image in a software program.

FIGURE 3-3 • Pixels mapped on a grid and colors identified by RGB values

Pixel-Based Displays

Screen graphics are by nature raster images due to the fact that computer displays are rasterized, or pixel-based. The origin of the word *pixel* is two words combined: *picture element*. Hence, pixels are the tiny squares of color that make up raster, or bitmapped, images. A pixel is the smallest unit of data necessary to represent a digital image.

Each of these small squares has a single color property assigned to it, which is defined by the red, green, blue color model. The number associated with it revolves around 8-bit color for a total of 256, the number of colors needed to display a 24-bit color image. This value ranges from 0 to 255, designating how much red, green, and blue the pixel contains. For example, a pure red will have 255, with green and blue both having 0 bits. White contains 255 red, 255 green, and 255 blue. Black contains 0 for all three colors, resulting in the absence of color or light.

The color and brightness of a pixel can be represented in several different ways: hue, saturation, brightness (HSB); red, green, blue (RGB); and cyan, magenta, yellow, black (CMYK). When pixels are added together in varying degrees of colors, they make up the visual data that results in screen-based bitmapped photographs and illustrations.

Computer monitors display images at a fixed pixel size at a low resolution: 72 PPI. On the other hand, software programs can dynamically reduce or enlarge an image to display at virtually any size. When an image is saved at the monitor setting of 72 PPI, there will be plenty of detail, with the added benefit of being a small file size.

Smaller files speed up the processing and loading of images so they appear on the screen more quickly, which ultimately reduces wait time. Images with a resolution higher than 72 PPI will not only load more slowly, but will also display larger on the screen in terms of the dimensions (height and width).

The size of a pixel never changes, but the number of pixels and how an image is represented on the screen will vary. For instance, a larger image with a higher resolution will appear to have larger pixels, since the image is enlarged, but it is merely a great number of pixels representing the image.

Monitor sizes and their corresponding resolution options also factor into the equation. Larger monitors have a higher pixel resolution, which affects how images appear on the screen. For example, a 13-inch monitor (which was standard in the 1990s) is limited to 640-by-480 pixels. Therefore, a multimedia screen at that time needed to be designed at those dimensions, still using 72 PPI for image resolution. Today, a 17-inch monitor has upward of 1680-by-1050 pixels for screen resolution. An image designed for a 13-inch monitor would fill the screen, but on a 17-inch monitor, it would appear much smaller. So multimedia programs and web sites can quickly become outdated in appearance when larger monitors are affordable and more accessible to the average consumer.

Working with Raster Graphics

You can produce raster graphics in a few different ways:

- Use a digital camera, in which case the resulting image originates in a raster format.
- Convert a vector graphic into a raster image to prepare it for screen viewing in a multimedia program.
- Create a raster image directly using a software program that uses pixels, such as Adobe Photoshop or Corel Painter.
- Scan an analog image to convert it to a digital one, which we will delve into later in this chapter.

Raster images are resolution-dependent. (Vector images are resolution-independent; a bitmapped image can be *resampled*, which is reducing or enlarging the number of pixels.) This means that raster images have a set number of pixels, and if the file dimensions are increased, there will be significant distortion of the original, leading to a blurry, low-quality image. Enlarging bitmapped images is a process that is commonly practiced but not recommended, as the integrity of the image is lost.

When increasing the resolution and/or dimensions of a raster image, a computer program will go through an *interpolation* process. Scanners also follow this procedure when increasing an image's resolution. This means *pixels are added* to an image based on existing, neighboring pixels. The final result rarely coincides with the original source, and is typically missing crucial detail and necessary crispness. (Reducing bitmapped images is an acceptable practice, since the reduction process tosses out excess pixels, and the final image is based on the primary pixels necessary to represent the content of the image.) The best option is to rescan an image at a higher resolution, rather than try to stretch it beyond recognition.

NOTE *It is important to maintain a respect for the necessity of high-quality images and not settle for average results, especially when it comes to multimedia. The quality of the images ultimately has an effect on the individual visual attributes, as well as the aesthetic value of a project.*

Figure 3-4 shows an example of a raster image at different resolutions.

Raster images can be produced in two ways: *aliased* or *anti-aliased*. The main difference is that the edges of aliased images are not smooth like anti-aliased ones, as shown in Figure 3-5. The characteristic quality of an aliased image is that the edges appear square or blocky and stair-stepped, due to the lack of blending and shading. With anti-aliased images, pixels close in hue and value are placed next to the hard-edged pixels to give the illusion of colors blending with the background.

Aliasing versus anti-aliasing is mostly important when dealing with text, as it determines the on-screen readability of letters, words, and sentences. Anti-aliased images are preferable to aliased ones, since they smooth out jagged edges and are more visually appealing. They do increase the size of a file, but the difference in size is negligible. In general, it is recommended that anti-aliasing be used unless your intent is to show a harsh, raw image for the purposes of communicating a visual message.

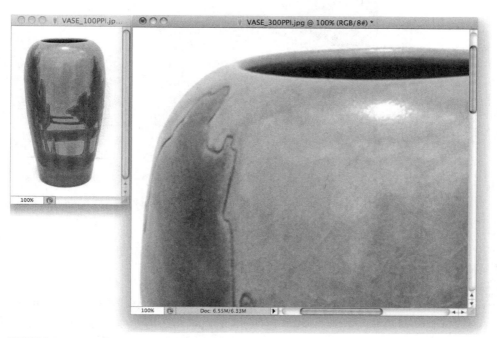

FIGURE 3-4 · Raster image at different resolutions

Raster Shape with Aliased Edges

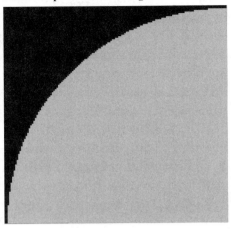

Raster Shape with Anti-aliased Edges

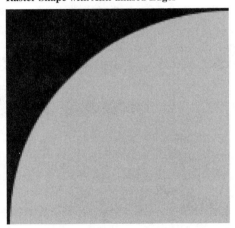

FIGURE 3-5 · Aliased and anti-aliased raster object

Scanning and Resolution

When a visual sample—anything from a printed photograph to a fine-art charcoal sketch—is in its native format (printed on paper, film negative, or slide), it needs to be transformed into a digital file so that it can be viewed and manipulated on the computer. A scanner will capture an image and convert it into a digital raster image.

Image scanners vary in terms of sharpness and resolution as a result of the number of sensors, optical lens, and power of the light source (or lamp) within the scanner. Scanning can be completed using a flatbed, film, sheet-fed, handheld, or drum scanner. Each one has unique properties and purposes. Low-end, inexpensive flatbed scanners are more than adequate for preparing multimedia images, as the files do not require a high resolution for screen presentation.

Scanners are categorized by their *bit depth*, or color depth, capabilities, which pertains to the amount of color that can be reproduced. A 24-bit depth (millions of colors) is required for accurate color. Most scanners today offer this technology and meet these standards.

This is where image resolution comes into play. The greater the number of pixels that an image possesses (higher resolution), the higher the quality of the end product, and consequently, the larger the file size. The image resolution will be higher as a result of the increase in data, which provides a more crisp, clear, and detailed image. If an image is scanned at too low a resolution, it is difficult to improve the quality, even with photo-enhancement software, such as Adobe Photoshop.

Determining scanning resolution depends on several factors, but the primary one is knowing where the image is going to end up. For multimedia, the lowest possible resolution is 72 PPI, since that is the screen resolution. On the other hand, a scanned image that is intended for a newspaper should be scanned roughly between 180 and 200 PPI. This is so that there are enough pixels in the image to be able to print using a halftone screen, which directly correlates with the *lines per inch* (LPI) for the printing device. Magazines typically use an LPI of 133, so the resolution can be safely set to 300 PPI.

Scanning the image at a higher resolution than you need from the start is your best bet. A digitized image can always be reduced in size and resolution, but it cannot be enlarged without losing quality.

In Chapter 9, we will cover scanners from a technical hardware standpoint.

Still Struggling

Printers use a line screen to print halftone dots. The higher the quality of the printout (such as full-color coffee-table books), the higher the line screen, so the greater the number of pixels needed. The general rule is that image resolution intended for print should be twice the line screen. For instance, a newspaper photograph is printed using 85 LPI, so the image resolution needs to be doubled to print properly.

Digital Photography

Digital photography represents a significant portion of the visual imaging category. Taking photos has been a professional pursuit or hobby for many ever since portable film cameras became affordable and accessible to the general consumer market. Today, digital cameras are more widely used, primarily because the technology is cheaper, and the process of taking and seeing instant photographic results makes it more appealing. There is no need to buy costly film and pay to have negatives printed. Also, many settings on cameras are automated, making it much easier to take a decent photo.

A digital photograph can be enhanced with photo-editing tools. For example, Adobe Photoshop includes the Levels tool, which can adjust the tones in an image to balance black and white using a histogram representation, as shown in Figure 3-6. Curves is another Photoshop tool used to adjust color, tone, and value, as shown in Figure 3-7.

You can transfer a photographic image to the computer in several ways:

- Scan a printed photograph into the computer so that it becomes a digital image and is no longer in an analog media format.
- Download images from the Web or an Internet FTP server (networked site).

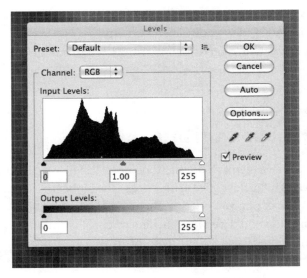

FIGURE 3-6 · Photoshop Levels adjustment dialog box

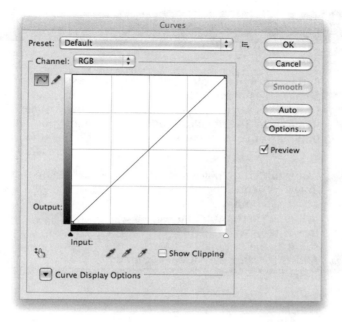

FIGURE 3-7 · Photoshop Curves adjustment dialog box

- Use a digital camera to shoot live images, and then download the photos from the camera to a computer using a USB cable. This is more personal and eliminates copyright concerns.

Once on the computer, digital photos can be handled in the following ways:

- Used as-is in their natural format (not altered at all)
- Have their tones adjusted and colors changed
- Be layered and collaged
- Be manipulated and distorted

After you've completed the process of transferring and enhancing photos, you must save the files in the proper format for the intended multimedia platform or output device. The two primary file formats for raster images are JPEG and GIF. Typically, digital photographs are saved in JPEG format for multimedia and the Web, since the compression scheme is well suited to bitmapped images. Compression reduces file size significantly, making files smaller yet still maintaining enough detail and clarity. Table 3-1 explains the pros and cons of the two main formats.

TABLE 3-1 JPEG vs. GIF File Formats

File Format	Pros	Cons
JPEG	Better for photographs Smaller files than GIF format Downloads faster Remains in 24–bit color mode (millions of colors)	*Lossy compression*, which means some image quality is permanently lost, depending on the amount of file compression
GIF	Better for flat graphics and line drawings (icons, logos, buttons, text) *Lossless compression* (LZW), meaning there is no image quality loss when saved; the file looks the same as the original Allows for transparent backgrounds	Larger files than JPEG format Files must be indexed to an 8–bit palette of no more than 256 colors

We have only scratched the surface of digital photography here. In Chapter 9, we'll discuss the hardware and equipment options for digital cameras.

Clip Art and Stock Images

Due to time constraints or lack of artistic resources on hand during a project, it may be necessary to gather digital images from other sources. Clip art comes installed with many programs, such as Microsoft Word, and can be found online for free use, without copyright strings attached.

Clip art is in a category that ranges from high-quality, detailed, realistic illustrations to low quality, cartoon-style computer drawings. Being selective is a key factor when choosing clip art. It should suit the tenor of the multimedia project in terms of appearance and treatment. There should also be a consistent style throughout the program or web site. There is nothing worse than seeing typical, run-of-the-mill clip art in many different styles within a single multimedia program.

Another option to consider is stock image databases. These are historically stock photo libraries, but now many extend to illustration, clip art, animation, and even web page templates.

The fees for using stock image libraries vary. Some libraries provide royalty-free images for unlimited use at a set price. You may be able to download small thumbnails or use a limited selection of free images, but you still need to register with the site and set up an account to gain access to the library. Some stock image agencies charge fees based on different usages, such as for print or the Web. Others require monthly fees to access the site and download images. These plans vary in cost depending on the number of images you intend to use on a monthly basis. For a single use of an image in a project, there is typically a one-time fee. If the image will appear more than once, or you want unlimited access to usage, then it is another level in the fee structure. Also, often the larger the image is, the higher the cost.

Photographers sell the rights to their images when signing on with a stock photo agency. When an image is purchased to use in a project, the fee provides permission to use someone else's work without infringing on copyright. (Chapter 2 covers copyright issues and suggests ways to obtain inexpensive or free media.)

Using stock image libraries saves time and eliminates the concern over intellectual property issues. You can locate an endless stream of images on Google's image search and Flickr, but these are not necessarily free for the taking. Some of the better-known stock image agencies are Corbis, Getty Images, Shutterstock, iStock Photos, Stock Photo, and PhotoSearch.

A number of stock photo web sites provide royalty-free and public-domain images, which don't require a fee to use. However, there are guidelines as to how to use the images, called *terms of use*, that you should read carefully. If the terms are not obvious on the top menu level, they are usually listed at the bottom of the page. Some sites request that you acknowledge the owner of the image or web site. Others stipulate that images cannot be altered or used for profit, and must be presented in their original, entire state.

TIP   *The ToMuse page at http://tomuse.com/stock-photo-sites-buy-sell-images/ lists ten well-known stock photo sites that offer royalty-free images and explains the services provided by each. The Free Stock Images site at www.freestockimages.net/resource-list/ lists ten free stock image sites.*

File Formats for Screen Display

Files are initially saved in their native format. This means when a media file is saved to a hard disk or stored on another type of drive, it will be associated with the program that was used to create it. If a logo is designed in Adobe Illustrator, for instance, it will try to open first in Illustrator. If it is opened on a computer that does not have that program installed, there will be an error message telling you this is an unknown file type, and you will be allowed to choose the program with which you want to open it. In order for the file to be opened in another program, you must first save it in a format that is compatible with that other program.

Most software programs allow you to save a file in a number of different formats. The final three letters of the file name (also referred to as the *file extension*) indicate which format was used to save the file. The trick is to understand what each one means and when you would need to use it.

Various file formats for media elements are necessary for proper configuration so media files will open and play on different programs, platforms, and browsers. File formatting also provides compression schemes that will consolidate the data to reduce the size of the file. The general rule of thumb when compressing files is that the more you compress, the smaller the file will be, but also the lower the quality of the end result.

Many variables come into play here. Let's say you are working with video files, which are inherently large. If they are intended to be viewed on a screen—either a computer monitor or projected to a large screen—and they are stored on a computer's hard drive, then they simply must be saved in a format that allows for screen resolution. The size of the file is not as important, since it is not going to be delivered via the Web. If a file needs to be on a web site, it will need to be compressed or reduced in size, so that it can be played or downloaded easily. The quality is likely to diminish as a result, but there are relatively few alternatives.

Resolution is what determines the quality of a media file. For image files, the resolution refers to the number of pixels in the image, which will affect the size of the file. The dimensions of the image in inches or the number of pixels making up the image will also affect the file size. For audio files, resolution determines the accuracy of the digitized sound. This is defined by bits (8 bits or 16 bits). The higher the bit rate, the higher the quality of the output, which results in a sound that is similar to the original. For audio files, other factors come into play, such as sampling rates, stereo or mono, and file size requirements.

When it comes to bitmapped images, such as photographs, the resolution is a significant factor that affects the quality, which directly relates to the file size and dimensions (height and width). Another aspect to consider is color. A pixel-based image can be saved in formats such as black and white, web palette, 8-bit, 16-bit, and 32-bit. As noted earlier, this is the bit depth, which has to do with how many colors are available. The more colors requested, the larger the data file in terms of bytes. So, a 4-inch-by-6-inch photo with a resolution of 72 PPI and 8-bit color will be 365KB. If the photo is saved with the same size and resolution but 16-bit color, it will be twice the size, at 730KB.

TABLE 3-2   Common File Formats for Vector Graphics

Format	Where It Originated	What It Stands For
AI	Adobe Illustrator	Adobe Illustrator
SWF	Adobe Flash	Shockwave Format
VML	Microsoft	Vector Markup Language
WMF	Microsoft	Windows Metafile Format
SVG	W3C	Scalable Vector Graphic
CRD	CorelDraw	CorelDraw
PDF	Adobe	Portable Document File
EPS (or EPSF)	Adobe Illustrator, CorelDraw	Encapsulated PostScript

Tables 3-2 and 3-3 list the common file formats for vector and raster images, respectively.

TIP   *For more information about image file formats, check out this web site: www.scantips.com/basics09.html.*

TABLE 3-3   Common File Formats for Raster Images

Format	What It Stands For	What It Means
JPEG	Joint Photographic Expert Group	Lossy compression of digital images to reduce the file size and minimize number of pixels
GIF	Graphic Interchange Format	Lossless compression of digital images with a limited color palette of 256 colors; also used for small web animations
PNG	Portable Network Graphic	Lossless compression but no color palette limit
TIFF	Tag Image File Format	Universal format used for graphic images; compression options, but typically larger than JPEG files; can contain different kinds of data within one file
PICT	Apple Graphic File Format	Compresses both bitmapped and vector images; up to 24–bit color (millions); PDF format is now more commonly used
BMP	Windows Bitmap Image	Saves and stores digital images on Windows PCs; compression options
PDF	Portable Document File	Like TIFF files, self–contained documents

TIP   *For a file format glossary, go to www.crutchfield.com/S-sNOq72obZkH/learn/ learningcenter/home/fileformats_glossary.html. This will help you get more acronyms under your belt. Wikipedia also has an extensive alphabetical listing of file formats, at http://en.wikipedia.org/wiki/List_of_file_formats.*

Color Theory: Pigment vs. Pixels

Color is used to enhance designs, draw attention, create unity, and evoke emotions. Since the subject is so broad, we will mainly focus on the principal differences between printed color and screen color, with respect to the two key color theory models: *additive* and *subtractive*.

Pixels, as previously mentioned, are digital representations of color in the form of light. The full color spectrum is present in natural light or sunlight, which is the *additive* (RGB) color model. Colors on the screen also use this *color space* model, which is based on the fact that on-screen color is made up of light. Pigments, on the other hand, are physical forms of color whose properties are synonymous with dyes or paints. Mixing these together results in different color combinations, which is the *subtractive* (CMYK) color model.

In either case, we need light in order to perceive color. Color is light energy in the form of waves, or *lightwaves*. These waves vary in length (or frequency), which results in different colors. The longest perceptible wavelength is red and the shortest is purple.

On the computer, we make adjustments and work with color in terms of brightness and saturation, as opposed to tone and value as when working with paints and pigments. The HSB color space (alternately referred to as HSV, for Hue, Saturation, Value) is best used for screen processing as it directly correlates with the color and the degree of dark and light. The hue is essentially the name of a color or its description, such as red or blue. Hues are represented in degrees depending on their location on the color wheel. The saturation of a color is its vividness or boldness, and low saturation of a color displays as pale or muted. Saturation is valued between 100% (full color) and 0% (no color), whereas the brightness is just the opposite of saturation and ranges between 100% of the color and 0% (black).

TIP   *The following are a few very good web sites on color theory worth spending some time with: an interactive color guide at http://colorschemedesigner.com/, a color resource for web designers at www.morecrayons.com, and a color theory overview at www.worqx.com/color/.*

CMYK and the Subtractive Color Model

The colors cyan, magenta, yellow, and black make up the *subtractive* color model. These are the primary colors associated with painting and printing (also referred to as the primaries of blue, red, and yellow).

This model is called *subtractive* because of the absorption of wavelengths of light by an object or surface. Mixed together, these primary colors create black (or brown), which is the absence of color. Adding or combining them takes color away, which is why they are subtractive and not additive.

The CMYK color model is also called *process color*. It is necessary for printing large quantity and high-end graphic design pieces.

Many printers designed for computer output use CMYK as color separations, such as desktop inkjet color printers, offset printers for larger output, and large-format printers that use laser technology. The process is to layer these colors, starting with the lightest color (yellow), followed by magenta and cyan, and ending with the darkest (black). White surfaces contain all the colors of the spectrum, whereas black surfaces are the absence of color. White reflects color, so inks are placed on the surface to block all other colors. The opposite is true with black, which absorbs all colors. So printers, in essence, subtract, or take away, color from the white of the paper.

Still Struggling

Each color in the subtractive color model absorbs one-third of the white light spectrum, which translates as its color complement (or opposite color). For instance, when magenta ink is printed on a white paper, it absorbs the green wavelengths or the complementary color of blue light. We are able to see the magenta color since this is the wavelength that is reflected off the paper surface.

Images created on the computer using the RGB model, as described next, can be converted into CMYK in preparation for printing, but there will inevitably be a discrepancy between the colors in the original and the altered image. So, you may wonder why bring up a color model that revolves around print technology if we are focusing on screen-based imagery? When translating computer color to printed color, it is important to understand the distinction so that you can optimize your results, be it for screen, printed output, or both. Figure 3-8 shows an example of working with a CMYK file in Photoshop.

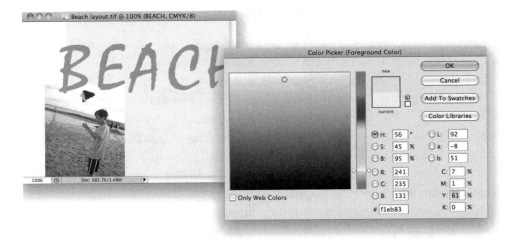

FIGURE 3-8 · Color Picker in Photoshop showing pixel color attributes: CMYK yellow

RGB and the Additive Color Model

Red, green, and blue are the three primary colors in the *additive color model* (also referred to as the *RGB color model*). They are associated with light, primarily colored lights. This model is also used to reproduce color on computer monitor displays and TVs.

Additive color originates as black, the absence of color and light. Beams of light from the three primaries project individual colors of red, green, and blue, and together they add up to white light when combined in equal proportions. Various permutations of these three colors result in a full range of on-screen hues.

Artificial light also uses this model. As in a theater production, lights are projected onto the stage from above. When all three overlap, a bright white spotlight results. When two lights overlap, the resulting colors are cyan, magenta, and yellow. For instance, if blue and yellow cross, a cyan (or turquoise) color results. If red and blue overlap, a magenta color results.

Natural light is equated with sunlight (also called *white light*), which contains the entire color spectrum. As previously mentioned, light is energy (or waves) represented in varying lengths, so colors are perceived as different wavelengths. Red, green, and blue are the three main bands of light energy that make up white light. The different amounts and degrees of combining the three additive primaries result in any possible color—virtually millions of color options.

Different color models will also affect the size of a file. RGB files are smaller than CMYK files, since they have three color channels (or color separations), as opposed to four. Another computer model is Indexed color, which refers to the limited web-safe palette based on hexadecimal code. This type of file is smaller than either an RGB file or a CMYK file, since it is forced to adhere to a palette of 256 colors. Figure 3-9 shows an example of working with an RGB file in Photoshop.

Color for Digital Displays

Visible color results from electron beams in the *cathode ray tube* (CRT), which is contained within a computer monitor. These high-speed beams of light respond to red, green, and blue phosphors, and as a result, most computer displays and projection devices today can display millions of colors (24-bit color). However, some will vary in terms of accuracy in the translation of color. There will always be discrepancies between contrast, brightness, and saturation, which affect how an image appears on screen. One monitor may be bright and more heavily shifted toward a magenta hue; another may be darker and more cyan. The same holds true for TVs, phones, and laptops.

This topic directly relates to the previous one on RGB color, but has more to do with *color space*, which refers to a very specific set of characteristics that enable image data to be mapped correctly to a given device's display capabilities.

FIGURE 3-9 · Color Picker in Photoshop showing pixel color attributes: RGB blue

Computer displays—such as desktop, handheld, LCD projection, and laptop—differ in terms of format (size and pixel dimensions) and manufactured parts. On-screen color is affected by how the monitor is produced, the components used, and the condition of the display itself. Other factors are the ambient lighting in a given room and the settings for brightness and contrast. The software program that is used to create visual images also affects how color displays, and the choice of color model will impact how color is worked with in any given program (such as RGB, CMYK, HSB, Grayscale, or Indexed for the Web). Figure 3-10 shows an example of working with an HSB file in Photoshop.

As explained earlier, computer monitors use the additive color model and the three primary colors of red, green, and blue. These colors can be combined to make up all color combinations, upward of millions of color choices. The white you see on a screen is the combination of equal parts of the three primaries. This process differs from the red, yellow, and blue primaries of the subtractive color model. The opposite happens when mixing paints: They become muddy brown when combined. Furthermore, the intensity of a color on a display will be determined by how much red, green, and blue it contains.

Due to the fact the computer monitors display the additive colors of red, green, and blue, there are fixed percentages of light representing a color. A displayed color constitutes each of the three primaries. Each component ranges from 0 to 1, having to do with the computer's electrodes triggering bits of data.

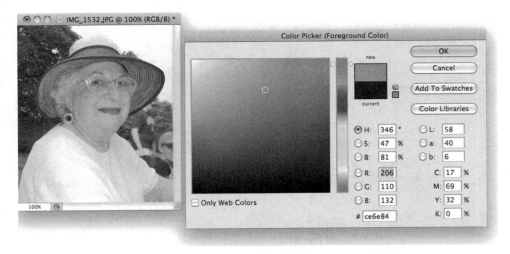

FIGURE 3-10 · Color Picker in Photoshop showing pixel color attributes: HSB Red

So, black is 0 (no intensity or brightness), and white is 1 (pure light as a combination of all three colors). The 24-bit color model can produce more than 16.7 million separate colors. A fully saturated red in 24-bit color will be 8, 0, 0 (8 bits for red, 0 for green, and 0 for blue).

Scanning images affects colors, and the printout differs even further. The original and the displayed and printed versions typically do not look similar.

Color calibration is a method of adjusting displays for accurate color representation. Calibrating computer monitors is important when producing color hardcopy, so that there is consistency among devices, as well as to provide a close approximation between what is on the screen and what prints out.

Since colors on the screen are RGB but printed colors are CMYK, the results of printing will undoubtedly vary, regardless of the calibration settings. There are typically greater discrepancies between screen and print when using desktop inkjet printers as compared with higher-end offset printing because they do not use the capabilities of overlaid transparent inks for large-capacity production of printed material. With such printing techniques, the results will be much truer to the original.

Software programs, such as Adobe Photoshop, can convert RGB colors to CMYK in preparation for printed output. Colors will invariably shift slightly, and depending on the color, the result can range from an imperceptible difference to a significantly darker, duller image. Inversely, CMYK can easily be converted to RGB color mode using software, so they are essentially interchangeable. Figure 3-11 shows a graphic image using the CMYK, RGB, and Indexed color models.

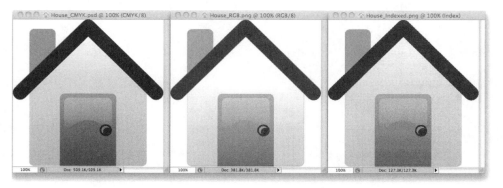

FIGURE 3-11 · Screen vs. print color model (CMYK, RGB, Indexed)

Summary

So now you know some fundamental concepts and strategies when dealing with graphics and images, as well as how to interpret them and work with them for multimedia. Vector and raster images are key concepts when creating, manipulating, and saving computer images. More complex, but just as important, are image-resolution settings and file formats, which are necessary to determine the end quality of digital images.

We also went over color theory, a significant factor when dealing with digital images that will reemerge time and again. Some of these topics are technically complicated and take time to digest and understand, but frequent and repeated exposure to them will help you develop an appreciation for the intricacies of working with digital images.

QUIZ

1. **What kind of images work best when saved in the JPEG file format?**
   A. Vector
   B. Raster
   C. 3D
   D. Text

2. **What is the required pixel resolution of a graphic file for screen viewing?**
   A. 72 PPI
   B. 150 PPI
   C. 300 PPI
   D. 600 PPI

3. **What are vector graphics mostly made up of?**
   A. Pixels
   B. Dots of color
   C. Lines and curves
   D. Bitmaps

4. **Which set of primary colors do computer displays use?**
   A. Red, green, blue
   B. Red, blue, yellow
   C. Cyan, magenta, yellow
   D. Orange, green, purple

5. **Which of the following is a type of file format used for vector graphics?**
   A. GIF
   B. JPEG
   C. EPS
   D. PNG

6. **Which statement is true for image resolution?**
   A. The higher the number of pixels that make up an image, the lower the quality of the end product.
   B. The fewer pixels that make up an image, the higher the quality of the end product and the larger the file size.
   C. The larger an image is in terms of file size, the larger the pixels become.
   D. The more pixels that make up an image, the higher the quality and the larger the file size.

7. **Which color model is associated with paints or pigments?**
   A. Additive
   B. HSB
   C. Subtractive
   D. RGB

8. **Which are the two primary kinds of digital images?**
   A. Vector and object-oriented
   B. Raster and bitmapped
   C. JPEG and GIF
   D. Vector and raster

9. **Which type of graphic is considered resolution-independent?**
   A. Raster
   B. Bitmapped
   C. Vector
   D. Pixel-based

10. **What is light energy in the form of waves, or lightwaves?**
    A. A scanner
    B. Color
    C. Pixels
    D. A computer monitor

chapter 4

Text and Typography

In the previous chapter, we focused on images and color for multimedia. In this chapter, we will concentrate on text and typography for multimedia. Text is a graphic element in a sense, as it has visual attributes along with textual meaning.

Typographic topics covered in this chapter include the design and treatment of type, type fonts and styles, placement and arrangement of type, and preparing text for the screen in terms of readability for users. You will also learn some skills for coming up with the appropriate words and writing effective copy for conveying the content of a multimedia program or web site.

CHAPTER OBJECTIVES

In this chapter, you will:

- Discover how to write effective copy for multimedia
- Learn how to work with text in multimedia programs and web sites
- Find out the differences between viewing type on the screen and in print
- Make distinctions between serif and sans serif typefaces
- Figure out how to best prepare text for reading on the screen

Text Defined

Text is essentially written language represented as a combination of letters and words. It is used to express thoughts, ideas, and emotions. It is the equivalent of the written word.

Type is a form of text. The term originally referred to the design of block and raised letters used for printing. It now means any printed character: a letter, number, symbol, or punctuation mark.

Most of what we read today is typed as opposed to handwritten. On the Web, we can read anything from articles to books to manuals, many of which are hyperlinked to provide additional information about a subject. How well the text is written and how relevant the content is determines, by and large, the success of a multimedia program or web site.

When books and newspapers were the primary media by which information was transmitted, the term *text* was used to refer to the typed words. Generally speaking, text is headlines and subheadings, as well as the main body of written material, treated as a block or mass.

In media, words set as text are called *copy*. Words are combined together to form text. Copy can be both short and long informative passages—be it a book or a newsletter, or a magazine or a poem.

With respect to multimedia, text is words, sentences, and paragraphs. It is used as screen or page titles, captions for pictures, labels for buttons and navigational devices, and instructional information for using the program.

Typing, Texting, and Emailing

Many words that originate as nouns become verbs in computerese, such as *Photoshopping* or *emailing*. With respect to type, we use the word *typing* for the act of creating words on a keyboard.

Texting has become part of our familiar vernacular. The word originated as a combination of two words: *text messaging*. Type sizes are small to accommodate reduced screen sizes, and fonts are typically sans serif, with smooth edges so they are easier to read. *Email* is similar to text messages in terms of screen presentation, with the exception of a limited number of characters. Texting and emailing are growing forms of social interaction by means of text, as opposed to spoken conversation or handwritten letter writing.

When people text, they typically use abbreviated versions of words and acronyms in place of complete words and sentences. Punctuation and grammar are typically ignored with texting, as it is a casual form of communication, intended to be immediate. The shorthand usage is also due to the limited amount of space and restricted number of characters. For instance, a look at a typical smart phone screen or Twitter shows a restricted amount of space and a limited number of characters in which to get your message across.

Still Struggling

Short Message Service (SMS) is the most widely used application today for text messaging. Data messaging has a set limit of 160 characters when texting on mobile devices and cell phones, and Twitter has a character limit of 140 (which can be bypassed by the use of software programs).

Numerical keypads, which were once the standard way to type text messages, present hindrances when texting. This was the norm before BlackBerry introduced its QWERTY keypad, followed by the iPhone's touchscreen keyboard. Keyboards are preferable, as they offer a more natural and faster way of typing.

TIP   *For a* **Los Angeles Times** *article on why there is a 160-character limit to text messages, visit http://latimesblogs.latimes.com/technology/2009/05/invented-text-messaging.html. For a list of text messaging and chat abbreviations, visit www.webopedia.com/quick_ref/textmessageabbreviations.asp.*

Words and Copywriting: How to Write Effective Content

Writing is a crucial part of the multimedia development process. Finding just the right words is not always easy. Writing is a job best saved for a skilled writer, as the value of a multimedia program's content relies on it. However, if you are going it alone and developing your own content, you should aim to produce high-impact copy that will resonate with your intended audience.

At times, you want to communicate a clear message, such as with educational multimedia. In this case, you must also be straightforward and succinct, as well as accurate, or you may quickly lose your audience.

With respect to multimedia, words are typed as readable text, but they are also spoken and sung, and at times become a mixture of visual images and text. With audio, the power of words is enhanced by voice, with all its enthusiasm and inflection. With video, visual images reinforce the words.

Words have powerful effects on people, regardless of whether they are read or spoken. Consider "trigger" words and phrases to jump-start the process of writing for multimedia. Words have emotional triggers in that they invoke and engage the reader's feelings. Some of the primary emotions we all experience are sadness, anger, disgust, fear, interest, surprise, and happiness. When writing copy, we can play off these emotions by using the appropriate words for the intended goal.

Here are some tips to help with writing content for multimedia:

- Plan a multimedia program by writing an outline of the major topics and subcategories to assist in arranging the structure.
- Get to the point and address the main idea early.
- Use action words (verbs that are *active*) to attract attention and move the reader from a passive to an involved state of mind.
- Evoke emotions by using strong words.
- Keep copy brief to facilitate reading on computer display. There should be less text than in print, since people have a shorter attention span when reading text on a screen and will experience eye fatigue more quickly.
- Use hierarchies so headlines are the largest and most dominant elements, subheadings are smaller and appear secondary in terms of importance, and sentences and/or paragraphs are less prominent.
- Sentences and paragraphs should be short. Use a line length of 12 words or less for paragraphs of three or four sentences. Full sentences should be 20 words or less. Use a maximum of five lines or rows of text. (Plan a word count for each screen and do not exceed it.)
- Keep concepts uncomplicated and easy to digest. Address a slightly wider audience range and assume a general comprehension level, so that a variety of readers will be able to understand the content.
- Simplify by limiting the use of unnecessary and excessive words or phrases.

Typography

Type refers to the visual characteristics of text where letterforms are stylized. *Typography* is design composition using type (with an emphasis on *design*), including the arrangement and appearance of type. Typography is a crucial component in multimedia design as a means of merging the content with the visual presentation.

"Typography has one plain duty before it and that is to convey information in writing. No argument or consideration can absolve typography from this duty. A printed work which cannot be read becomes a product without purpose." Emil Ruder (*Typography: A Manual of Design*, Verlag Niggli AG, seventh revised edition, 2001).

The same can be applied to using type in multimedia. For multimedia design, you must consider the best typefaces for the underlying theme, as well as how they will look on the screen. Some typographic considerations are related to readability, such as adequate spacing between lines of text (called *leading*), and word and letter spacing (called *kerning* and *tracking*). These topics are covered in greater depth in the next section. Figure 4-1 shows the anatomy of type and design attributes.

TIP *A good primer on type design with numerous examples can be found at www.thinkingwithtype.com/. For testing fonts on the screen, try this useful tool: www.typetester.org/.*

Fonts and Styles

Letterforms are the unique shapes of individual letters, and typefaces are identified by their letterforms. They are categorized as serif, sans serif, and script. The final form of a letter is a design product, resulting in a series of letters called a *font*.

A *typeface* is a graphic representation of letters, numbers, and symbols in a variety of styles and sizes. It refers to a specific design or *look* of type; a set of characters has a similar structure in terms of proportion, angle, stroke, weight, and detail (for example, Times typeface, all sizes and styles). Styles have to do with the minor enhancements of type (italic, bold, underline, and so on), which are also built into any word processing program.

A font is technically a subset of a typeface; it is one particular typeface in a single size and style (for example, Arial, 12-point, bold). When printing processes were first developed, metal type was used. Each font needed to be

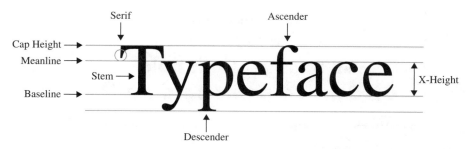

FIGURE 4-1 • Anatomy of type

separated so that it was organized and accessible. Typefaces today are often referred to as *fonts*, so the terms are used interchangeably. The distinction is not as important as it used to be.

A *font family* is a group of related fonts, with similar width and weight attributes, that vary in terms of style, such as bold, italic, condensed, light, and so on. Times represents a font family, for instance, and Times Bold and Times Italic are fonts within the same family. Figure 4-2 shows examples of a typeface, font, and font family.

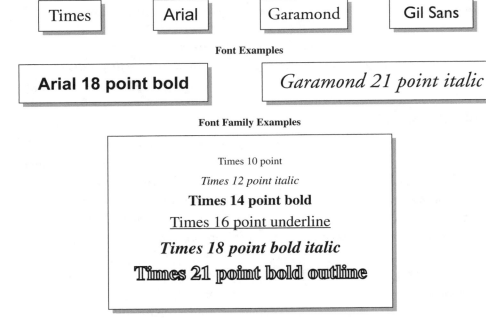

FIGURE 4-2 · Typeface, font, and font families

TABLE 4-1 Text Attributes	
Term	**Description**
Weight	Thickness of the strokes of a typeface
Baseline	Horizontal line underneath letters
Meanline	Line that marks the top edge or height of lowercase letters
Cap height	Line that marks the height of all capital letters in a typeface
Ascender	The upper portion of a lowercase letter that extends above the meanline, such as *b*, *f*, and *t*
Descender	The lower portion of a lowercase letter that extends below the baseline, such as *g*, *q*, and *y*
Kerning	Letter spacing
Tracking	Word spacing
Leading	Line spacing (space between lines of text)
Serif	A typeface with finishing strokes at the top and bottom of letters
Sans serif	A typeface without finishing strokes at the top and bottom of letters

Type is measured in *points*. The sizes of letters are indicated by points and are measured from the top of a capital letter to the bottom of a *descender* (such as with the letter *y*). One inch is equal to 72 points. Print and screen text sizes are measured the same way.

Type has various attributes that affect its appearance and readability. Specific terms are associated with type to identify certain characteristics. Table 4-1 explains these attributes.

Serif vs. Sans Serif

The two varieties of font styles are *serif* and *sans serif*, as illustrated in Figure 4-3. These are mainly distinguished by their visual characteristics. Serif fonts have additional marks or tips at the ends of each letter stroke. They appear to be more classic and old-fashioned looking than sans serif fonts. They are frequently used in print, since the serifs assist in reading longer lines of text from left to right across the page.

Serif fonts originated as Roman letters cut into stone. The extra line was a cut used to add precision to letter strokes and aid readability. All capital letters were used with Roman lettering. However, all capitals, especially for long text

Serif Font Styles   Sans Serif Font Styles

Courier 10 point
Courier 10 point oblique
Courier 10 point bold

Times 12 point
Times 12 point italic
Times 12 point bold

Garamond 14 point
Garamond 14 point italic
Garamond 14 point bold

Verdana 10 point
Verdana 10 point italic
Verdana 10 point bold

Helvetica 12 point
Helvetica 12 point oblique
Helvetica 12 point bold

Arial 14 point
Arial 14 point italic
Arial 14 point bold

FIGURE 4-3 · Serif and sans serif font styles

passages, is much harder to read than a mixture of uppercase and lowercase. These typefaces have thick and thin lines, which don't reproduce well at small sizes on the screen. Using all capitals on the screen is not recommended for anything other than a headline, especially when sending email or text messages, as it is considered shouting or yelling.

Sans serif fonts do not have these added marks and tend to be clean and modern in appearance (*sans* is French for *without*). Sans serif fonts are easier to read at smaller sizes due to the more uniform stroke style.

You will find a wide diversity of font styles that can be used for many purposes. You should carefully choose a type style that is appropriate for the particular subject—one that suits the design and aesthetics of your program. However, for body text, it is more important to select fonts that are readable on the screen.

Typographic Treatment: Designing with Type

Typographic treatment has to do with how type is designed—what is done to the letterforms and words to make it more interesting and visually appealing, and have a greater impact for communication purposes. This process is also referred to as *typographic design* or *typography*. It controls font selection, leading (space between lines of text), kerning (space between letters), and tracking (space between words), as well as bold and italic type styles. Examples of these aspects of type can be seen in Figure 4-4.

Ways we handle or treat type draw attention in the same way that visual images do. Design utilizes type as if the letterforms were images, considering placement, arrangement, and relationship with other elements on the page or screen.

For typography, you must consider and employ design principles as well. These principles are balance, contrast, dominance or emphasis, rhythm and repetition, and variation. The goal is a final design that is visually unified and harmonious. The meaning cannot be ignored, so the synchronous/symbiotic relationship between designing with type and images and the communication of the message must be well thought out.

Designing for multimedia requires an establishment of visual hierarchies with respect to text. Hierarchy is a means of guiding what the viewer looks at. This includes making use of white (or negative) space, using headings and catchphrases that will connect with the reader and garner visual interest, and employing contrasting colors and tones so the text is readable against the background or adjacent graphics.

Text in multimedia programs is used for the following:

- Labeling images and icons
- Providing information about the subject
- Supplying instructions as to how to do something or use the program
- Guiding users through the program (navigation)

Fonts should be kept consistent throughout a multimedia program, so there is a sense of cohesiveness. You should limit the number of fonts in one program or web site to adhere to the design and minimize potential distractions.

When using text in a multimedia program, make sure to consider the content and to use proper grammar and punctuation. Type can be decorative and dressed up, to draw attention and tie in aesthetically to the concept and *look and feel* of

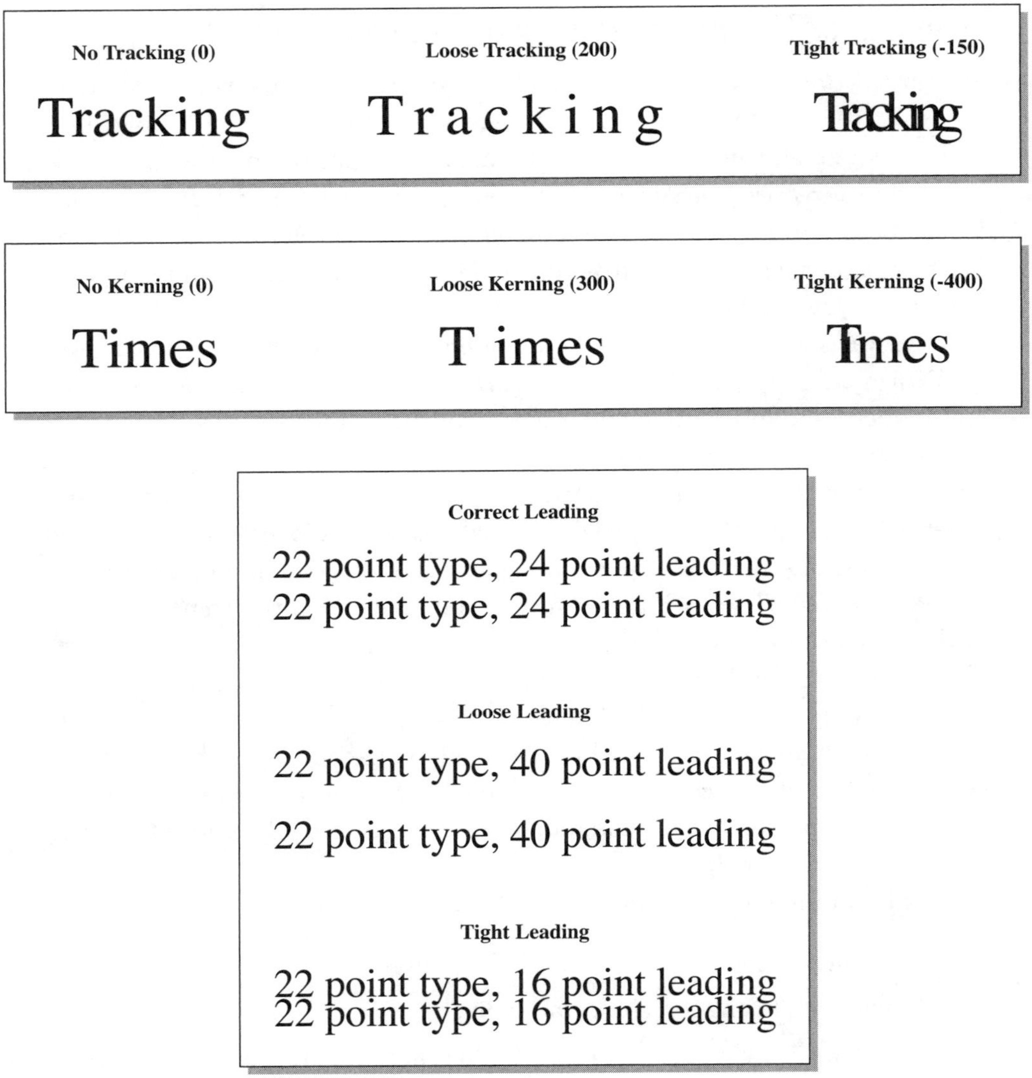

No Tracking (0)	Loose Tracking (200)	Tight Tracking (-150)
Tracking	T r a c k i n g	Tracking

No Kerning (0)	Loose Kerning (300)	Tight Kerning (-400)
Times	T imes	Tmes

Correct Leading

22 point type, 24 point leading
22 point type, 24 point leading

Loose Leading

22 point type, 40 point leading

22 point type, 40 point leading

Tight Leading

22 point type, 16 point leading
22 point type, 16 point leading

FIGURE 4-4 · Tracking, kerning, and leading examples

the interactive program, but the meaning of the words and what it is being said matters most. The text must be meaningful and accurate, easy to read, and fit in visually with the screen designs and interface elements. Typographic design coordinates the meaning of the message with the appearance of type. Type style, treatment, color, spacing, justification, and placement all play a role.

Generally, type used in any kind of presentation can be loosely organized in two categories:

- Blocks of text as information (meant to be read and comprehended, also referred to as *body text*)
- Text that is treated in a more artistic way, which is intended to be part of the design

While both forms of type need to be readable and convey information, the primary objective of body text is to communicate a clear message with the meaning of the words. Body text, or *copy*, should be set in high contrast with small text and organized into blocks consisting of sentences and paragraphs. It is usually left-justified, with the kerning and leading adjusted to well-established (predetermined) standards. Imposing overly creative approaches to body text is not recommended. It is best to keep it simple, using a highly readable sans serif or serif font.

Text included for the purpose of design includes titles, headings, subheadings, slogans, logos, and other elements not intended to be read in large blocks or columns. This kind of text can be treated much more creatively, as it is meant to convey meaning visually as well as by the words that are used. In this case, typeface selection is one of the more important design decisions. Perhaps as much as color, images, and sound, choice of type can convey a distinctive message and elicit strong responses.

Typefaces can have personalities and unique characteristics. They can communicate feelings of enjoyment, silliness, formality, elegance, harshness, seriousness, tranquility, and many other expressive aspects. It is worthwhile to study magazines, books, advertisements, and web sites to get an understanding of how type is used in design to instantly suggest a particular mood.

Placement and Arrangement of Type

The placement and arrangement of type on the screen (also called *screen layout*), as well as visual hierarchies, come into play when considering *how* type is read. It is imperative for the designer to facilitate reading and not hinder comprehension of the material in any way. The treatment of type should be intended for communication and not used purely for expressive, artistic purposes. When designing for multimedia, type needs to be well organized, readable, accessible, and easy on the eyes. Arranging the type is the creative part of using text, and what is referred to as *typographic design*, as noted earlier.

Designing for multimedia requires that you choose type that is eye-catching, as well as make sure that it communicates a clear message. Controlling the visual elements on the screen with hierarchical approaches includes the use of type, as an overall balance needs to be established. Typographic hierarchy places emphasis on what is most important. With text, this means titles and headlines. Subheadings are given secondary importance by their size, color, and placement.

When text is used for multimedia, it is a means of both sending messages and providing information for captions, text blocks, navigational guides for drop-down lists and menu items, and image labels. Text that is easy to read, is informative, and has visual appeal is designed well. Text that is crowded, has minimal contrast, is too long, and is not consistent with other pages or screens could lead to a negative response by the user.

Text *alignment* is another factor when arranging type. Left justification for alignment is the most beneficial, as it is easier and customary to read from left to right. Centered text should be used only for two or three lines, and reserved for a headline or subheading. Copy that is centered challenges the readers, as they are forced to move too much between the beginning and end of sentences. Readers become weary, and frustration sets in when it is too much work to sift through the text. Fully justified text should be used sparingly, as it creates *rivers* of white space between letters, which is distracting to the reader. When text is left-, center-, or right-aligned, the spacing between words remains consistent.

Lastly, a *grid* is a useful tool for aligning text and images. Designers of print publications use grids because they provide structure to a document that is text-laden. The same holds true for screen designs that utilize text. A grid provides proportion to the composition and gives a sense of order. Once the primary grid is established, it can be broken slightly, meaning that text and image elements can be offset, as long as there is a consistent use of such placement from screen to screen.

Preparing Text for the Screen: Amount and Legibility

Text displayed on a screen for multimedia or the Web is a graphic image made up of pixels. Fonts are bitmapped so they can be displayed on the screen.

Text needs to be treated differently for viewing on the screen than it does for reading in print. Making the typeface part of the screen image will help to avoid the problem of users not having the font you used on their system (a substitute will be used, and it typically does not look the way the designer intended).

With this method, text can be manipulated and sized to suit the design, and it will not be dependent on a certain type family to display properly.

Once text becomes a bitmap, it can no longer be edited, as it is part of the screen design, The text becomes an image, and its format is preserved. A downside is that text that is converted to a bitmap takes considerably more bandwidth to store, and cannot be indexed or searched.

Another method is to save (convert) to PDF format, so the type will appear exactly as it is designed and intended, but will remain editable and selectable. You can include information embedded in rasterized text that is used in web pages by using the same wording in the image's alt attribute for image tags (this is text that appears when an image cannot be rendered on the screen). Doing so makes the text accessible to visually impaired users, as it can be converted using speech synthesizer technology, which is a system that converts text into speech.

Screen text is high in contrast and brightness due to the fact that it is being viewed as colored light, as opposed to ink on paper. If a multimedia program uses a CRT-based display and not a backlit Kindle, for instance, the reader's eyes will generally fatigue more easily due to longer exposures to the light emitted from the screen. When viewing web sites, the user can make text in a standard HTML-based web site larger on the screen to assist its readability.

Monitor resolution will also affect how type displays on the screen. A 17-inch or higher resolution monitor will display 12-point type much smaller than a 13-inch monitor. The more pixels you have, the smaller they get on screen, since there will be more pixels fitting into a 1-inch-by-1-inch grid. When pixels are smaller, everything looks smaller—whether images or text.

Text for multimedia should have enough contrast to stand out against the background. There should also be ample white space (or *negative space*) to alleviate crowding and allow for the text to be noticed. Informative text tends to be longer, and in sentence or paragraph form. If a program has more text than can fit on a screen—say, more than three paragraphs—scrolling text fields are a good alternative. The user can scroll through the text, which will be condensed into a small box or container on the screen within the overall interface. However, despite the fact that you can assign a specific typeface, you cannot customize the type formatting, and it typically looks plain and lacks any design attributes.

Sans serif fonts are more readable on lower-resolution displays, but today most fonts are readable as long as they are large enough. Pictures or pictorial icons used for navigational devices, such as buttons, are most effective when text labels accompany them. This helps users identify their meaning and know where the navigational tool will lead them.

Spacing between letters can also affect how we read text. Spacing of letters and lines of text should not be too wide or too narrow. Your goal is to facilitate reading, not make it a challenge for the reader. Too much space can render text illegible. Using varying styles of type (bold, italic, underline, and so on), as well as size differences, draws attention and provides a structure to the information.

Type Sizes and Styles for the Screen

The choice of typeface and the size of the type are crucial for readability on the screen. For instance, 10-point type is adequate for reading text on printed documents, but it is advisable to use at least 12-point type for screen legibility. Fonts appear differently on the screen; for example, Times typeface will be smaller than Verdana set to the same size. Another factor that affects the reading of text on the screen is the amount of text displayed.

The following are some tips when using text and typography on a display screen:

- Limit the use of type with color attributes, as color can become overused quickly and be distracting to the viewer.
- Make sure text stands out against the background so it is readable.
- Tie in the text color with photographs and illustrations for consistency and balance.
- Background textures and patterns should be subtle and take into consideration contrast with type. For example, use light type with dark backgrounds and vice versa.
- When text is used behind photographs or illustrations, make sure it is still readable.
- Text should be anti-aliased so edges are smooth and will blend in with the background image or color.
- Fonts need to have some weight (substance) with uniform strokes. Text should not have lines that are too thin, or they will disappear due to soft edges.
- Choose fonts and sizes that are easy to read on the screen. Use sans serif fonts, like Arial or Tahoma, when the type is going to be small, as these are easier to read (see Figure 4-5).

FIGURE 4-5 · An example of sans serif typefaces used for the Crate&Barrel web site

- Use one or two fonts throughout the program or web site so that the design is clean and consistent, and the readability is not compromised (see Figure 4-6).

- The title of the program or web site should be prominent in terms of color and size.

- Type size for headings and titles can vary depending on the font choice, placement, and color choice. Make sure it is readable and appropriate for the subject matter.

- Lists should be short, with a maximum of five to seven options. Long lists are overwhelming and discourage browsing. If more options are needed, break them into separate categories and pages.

FIGURE 4-6 • An example of a combination of sans serif and serif typefaces used for the *Wall Street Journal* web site

- Type for text blocks should be no larger than 12 to 14 points (depending on the font, the subject matter, and the audience). Less than 10 points is too hard to read; more than 14 points is too large, so the screen appears crowded.

- Paragraphs should be short rather than long scrolls. This is more manageable for the user. Keep descriptive text brief (one short paragraph at most), if used at all.

- When text accompanies pictorial navigational icons, make sure they are simple and clear, so users are not confused by their meaning. Buttons with text labels should be easy to read and clear for quick scanning of content.

- Italicized text should be used infrequently, especially with small font sizes (anything less than 12 points). Italics are difficult to read and will most likely be overlooked.

- If the project will appear on a standard TV, make sure your text does not include any horizontal lines fewer than 2 pixels high to avoid flickering. Also, keep the text away from the edges of the screen, because some TV sets clip the sides of the image.

Screen vs. Print

Table 4-2 distinguishes type designed for screen compared with type used for print. Some attributes remain consistent for both. However, there are a number of considerations when designing for the screen due to factors such as pixel resolution, as well as contrast and brightness discrepancies as a result of how computer displays make use of light. Note that this table is mainly pertinent to body copy, as opposed to text intended for design purposes.

Type on the Web

You need to consider the text attributes in Table 4-1 when working with type in multimedia programs as well as on the Web. HTML was designed for text documents to be displayed on computer screens, so fonts are limited to what the users have on their computer. Typography used for the Web varies depending on whether the site is designed using HTML code or with bitmapped layouts, where the type is part of the interface. When designing web page layouts with programs such as Adobe Photoshop, type will be rasterized. It becomes part of the screen image and is not dependent on HTML text formatting.

With respect to multimedia, font choices are vast due to the fact that type can be rasterized for the screen. If the layout of a web page is designed in a raster program, such as Photoshop, fonts are not a problem. When a web site is designed using strictly HTML code, there is a font limitation due to HTML restrictions. HTML uses text formatting embedded in the code of a web page to designate attributes for text, such as **bold** or *italic*, by using bracketed symbols, or *tags*. These tags are like sandwich bread, as there must be one at the beginning and one at the end. An example of a text tag is `<B>Bold<B/>`.

The settings or preferences of a web browser can also affect how text appears on the screen. With Safari, for instance, the user can change the default text size for all web sites. It is also easy to enlarge or reduce what appears on the screen by zooming in and out while on a web page.

TABLE 4-2   Type for Screen vs. Type for Print

Type Attribute	Screen	Print
Typeface	At small sizes, clean typefaces with minimal ornamentation are best.	Use any typeface as long as it is not too small for the average reader (minimum of 8 points).
Size of text	Larger text is easier to read on the screen. Sans serif typefaces should be at least 10 points. Serif typefaces should be at least 12 points.	Most sizes and styles are readable. Type sized between 8 and 11 points is acceptable.
Legibility	Anti–aliased type (for smooth edges) and typefaces with even strokes allow for greater readability.	Use vector type for clean edges and resizing capabilities.
Kerning and tracking	Letter spacing that is too tight or too wide compromises readability, especially with small anti–aliased type.	Various amounts of spacing are used for both communicating a message and adding visual interest.
Leading	Too much space between lines of text interrupts the flow of reading sentences and paragraphs on the screen.	Increased line space can be used, as there is not a screen–dimension limit. Wider leading is more readable in print.
Amount of text	Use equal amounts of text and images for a balanced design and readability on the screen. Minimize excessive use of text.	Text can be minimal or excessive depending on the purpose of the print piece, and still be readable.
Length of lines	Maintain 10 to 12 words per line when using paragraphs; shorter columns are easier to read.	Using 18 to 20 words per line is adequate. Line length varies depending on the kind of print piece and font size, but generally longer lines are acceptable especially when using serif fonts.
Tone and color	Use contrast so that text is legible, and use spot color in bright hues to draw attention to words.	Colors can be specified since color properties for print are more regulated.

HTML will format the text depending on what is selected by the designer (such as Arial versus Times), but what appears on the web page is ultimately determined by the typefaces that are available on the users' computers. This is less of an issue than it has been in the past, since most operating systems, such as Mac OS X or Windows, have a set of commonly used fonts automatically installed. However, despite advancements in technology, there is still only a handful of fonts that can be used cross-platform reliably. There are standards in place to alleviate this problem, but it is difficult to control exactly how text will appear on the screen with web sites. A font used in a multimedia presentation may not be loaded on the target platform (the computer on which the presentation will be used), the font may not appear, or a substitute may replace it. You should be aware of the limitations of your project when it comes to type.

A method used to control this problem is called *font embedding*. This allows a font used in a multimedia presentation or web site to be tethered to it, so the type will appear as it was intended. Some software programs can embed fonts; others cannot. For instance, Microsoft PowerPoint and Word cannot embed fonts, and HTML (for web design) does not provide any reliable way to embed fonts. You can embed fonts in Adobe Flash presentations and Adobe Acrobat PDFs. This means that you can use whatever font is installed on your system (although there may be legal restrictions, as embedding a font is technically copying it).

Still Struggling

Previously, only seven text sizes were available for web sites when using HTML code, but another technique that is widely used today is Cascading Style Sheets (CSS). CSS consists of technical specifications that allow web designers greater control over the appearance of text. Specific parameters can be assigned to type (style, size, font, color, and spacing), which can be applied to the entire web site. For instance, you can format headlines at 16-point, Helvetica, bold, underlined with a red color using CSS. It allows you to use this style for headlines on all pages in the site.

I have addressed a few different ways of working with text, so let's review them. Selecting fonts from those that are installed on a computer is the most common way to create text. Converting text to a bitmapped format is an assurance that the appearance of the font will not change when viewed on a different computer or platform. The other method of safeguarding the look of type is to embed fonts into the document, as with PDF files. Yet another way to work with text is by using device fonts, which are "hardware fonts" that are built into a computer's operating system and available to all software programs.

Device fonts can be used for designing multimedia and web sites with programs such as Adobe Flash, as they prevent display problems on end users' machines, since these fonts are found on most computers. If the device font is not present when the SWF file is played, a system font that most closely resembles the device font will be used in its place.

A point worth mentioning is the use of Unicode for universal text translation, as it assists in the conversion of letters and words for exchanging information between different written languages. Unicode is a programming code that assigns a number, or *code point*, for each letter or character. Since each character has an individual number associated with it, no two are alike. Unicode encodes, represents, and handles text for global writing and reading capabilities. For instance, HTML documents use a sequence of Unicode characters. If you want to translate a web page into Japanese, you can easily convert it if Unicode was used when the original site was programmed. The most commonly used encodings are Unicode Transformation Format (UTF) character sets, or UTF *charsets*. These sets store strings of Unicode numbers so the amount of memory (or bytes) being used is consolidated.

Summary

In this chapter, we covered text and the attributes of working with type. Designing with type for the screen is an important part of multimedia development, as the type must maintain a clear, consistent message in terms of the subject matter, and it must be readable as well as appear visually coherent and appealing. You learned the distinction between typefaces and fonts, as well as serif and sans serif typefaces, and compared text used for screen and print purposes. More on designing with type will be covered in Chapter 8, when we go over interactive design and HTML tags.

QUIZ

1. **Which of the following is an example of a font?**
   A. Times
   B. Arial, 12-point, bold, italic
   C. Univers narrow
   D. Helvetica underlined

2. **Which style of type has short lines at the beginning and end of letter strokes?**
   A. Sans serif
   B. Serif
   C. Ascender
   D. Italic

3. **Why are sans serif fonts frequently used for the screen?**
   A. Serif fonts have thick and thin lines, which don't reproduce well at small sizes on the screen.
   B. Serif fonts can't be rasterized.
   C. Serif fonts don't look modern enough.
   D. There are fewer sans serif fonts from which to choose.

4. **What is the best arrangement for body text to be read on screen?**
   A. Right-justified
   B. Fully justified
   C. Centered
   D. Left-justified

5. **What is the minimum recommended size for serif type to be displayed on screen?**
   A. 8 points
   B. 10 points
   C. 12 points
   D. As large as possible

6. **Is excessively wide letter spacing recommended for reading text on the screen?**
   A. Yes, when there is enough room on the screen to fit it.
   B. Yes, if you can still read it.
   C. No, because it compromises readability.
   D. No, because it draws unnecessary attention.

7. **Which technique is used to control the appearance of text in a web site?**
   A. Using Cascading Style Sheets (CSS)
   B. Using lists
   C. Formatting with HTML
   D. Using scrolling text boxes

8. **What approach is *not* suggested for writing effective copy?**
   A. Get to the point and address the main idea early.
   B. Use passive words.
   C. Keep concepts uncomplicated and easy to digest.
   D. Simplify by limiting excessive words or phrases.

9. **Which text attribute is described as "The lower portion of a lowercase letter that extends below the baseline"?**
   A. Meanline
   B. Ascender
   C. Descender
   D. Cap height

10. **How does a font differ from a typeface?**
    A. A font is one particular typeface in a single size and style.
    B. A font contains related font families.
    C. A font is a design of type for a set of similar characters.
    D. A font has many sizes and styles.

chapter 5

2D and 3D Animation

In this chapter, we will move away from static images of graphics, illustrations, and photographs and embark on a journey to discover the power of moving images. Animation is used in multimedia presentations and on the Web to draw attention, provide entertainment, and explain concepts. We will discuss both traditional and digital animation, along with the principles of animation and what it means to develop a narrative sequence and storyboard. 2D and 3D computer animation will also be covered, including how to save animation files in the correct format for final output and usage.

CHAPTER OBJECTIVES

In this chapter, you will:

- Learn about the different kinds of animation, including traditional and computer-based approaches
- Discover why and how animation is used in multimedia
- Get a fundamental idea of the differences between 2D and 3D computer animation
- Find out about file formats for saving animated movies

Animation in Multimedia

Animation is another word for animated or moving images, but actually is an optical illusion. Motion is simulated by quickly presenting a series of images. The same holds true for film and video. The illusion of movement is possible due to a physiological phenomenon called *persistence of vision*. This is a human attribute whereby the appearance of movement results when viewing images shown in rapid succession. It is considered a time-based medium, similar to film and video, since it plays out over the course of time.

Animation comes in many forms, including photos that fade in and out; web interface buttons that expand or bounce when rolled over; cartoon characters that walk, jump, and run; company logos that fly in from the distance on a computer screen; and special effects added to a live-action movie. Animation is used for entertainment, games, advertisements, demonstrations, and instructional purposes.

You'll see animation everywhere you look today. It can be found in all forms of multimedia technology: TV, the Web, kiosks, gaming devices, cell phones, ATMs, self-checkouts, billboards, store signage, and so on. Animation attracts attention and captivates interest, but only momentarily if it is not done in an effective, well-thought-out manner.

Animation is a versatile and powerful communication delivery mechanism in its own right. Information presented as moving images is more likely to be noticed and retained by the viewer. An animation can be as simple as an ongoing stream of images or words, or it can be a multifaceted story layered with meaning and rich characters.

In multimedia, animation can be used in a variety of ways: as part of a user interface to highlight key concepts, for navigational devices where buttons jump or spin when rolled over, to draw attention to active areas on the screen, and placed within a window for informational purposes. Figure 5-1 provides some examples.

Animation is frequently incorporated into interactive programs. It is especially useful in educational multimedia. It has the ability to simplify a complex concept by providing information in a visually appealing sequence. For instance, an explanation of outer space is easier to grasp with an animation showing the movement and relationship of planets. It is not feasible to photograph or take video in such cases, so animation is a valuable substitute. Animation can also present an imaginary world of fantasy as an escape from real life.

FIGURE 5-1 · Kinds of animation

Animation has come a long way since its inception, and it continues to evolve with the advent of new technologies and software capabilities. All of these qualities combined provide infinite possibilities with a multifaceted and complex medium.

Functions of Moving Images

Take a walk through Times Square in New York City, and you will witness the epitome of overstimulation and excessive information from a myriad of animated signs and flashing lights. This is an extreme scenario of a public exhibition of multimedia and animation, and in varying degrees has become commonplace in large, cosmopolitan centers. However, when too many senses are being stimulated at once, it is difficult to know where to look and on what to focus. So, the question is when and how to use animation for effectively communicating a message.

Animation that is used more selectively will make its point clearer and draw attention. When animation is used for advertising, it is a form of entertainment and is typically fast-paced and exciting. When it is used for the purposes of demonstrating a concept, it is educational and informative by nature.

Edward Tufte, an expert and author on the subject of information design and visual communication, believes that animation should be purposeful and not used unnecessarily. He states, "Animations are usually going to work better when they describe something that actually moves. For reasoning about cardiology, animation and sound are obviously useful and relevant. For reasoning about typography, probably not" (www.edwardtufte.com/bboard/q-and-a-fetch-msg?msg_id=0000Ri, May 25, 2003).

Advantages and Disadvantages of Animation

The following are some of the advantages of using animation in a multimedia program or web site:

- Adds value and significance to information being presented
- Draws attention to buttons and navigational devices
- Provides feedback to users when accessing "active" areas
- Facilitates the use and making it more functional
- Gives the content more meaning
- Encourages action and involvement
- Demonstrates complex concepts

But there are also disadvantages of using animation, as follows:

- Overwhelms the users with too much movement (can become bother-some and no longer noticeable)
- Adds no value (for instance, when used on the screen as a decorative element)
- Impedes the individual pace
- Forces users to watch, which can be a deterrent
- May take additional bandwidth and require additional plug-ins

Animation is a primary element in multimedia presentations as it has a way of captivating an audience. It uses visual impact and sound to elicit curiosity and pull people in. Animation provides some form of a *story* that unfolds over time. Various elements—such as music, voice, sound effects, background scenes, graphics, and color—typically accompany it in some form.

Animation is not just necessary with multimedia; it is expected. We live in a fast-paced society and choose to have some form of media in front of us, in our hands, at every waking moment. It is commonplace today to witness and engage in a high-speed turnover of bright and colorful images, loud and jarring sounds, strong and bold words, flashy videos, and engaging animated movies. TV encourages this pace, as do movies and advertising in general.

In educational multimedia, animation can engage learners by providing in-depth explanations when text and pictures will not suffice. Animation that is seamlessly integrated into multimedia is better than forcing the use of it so that it sticks out like a sore thumb. In other words, if animation is used appropriately, it is not noticeable as such, and it is most likely done well.

Interactive Animation

Interactive animation is an additional function of movable images that is integral to multimedia, especially for use with entertainment programs and games. This type of animation gives the user control over virtual environments with respect to figurative movement.

Digital game consoles were first introduced with the Odyssey in the early 1970s by Magnavox, but the graphics were crude and the games had limited capabilities. Today, game players can create alternate 3D personas called *avatars*, which can interact and communicate with other characters playing the same game. They can either be teammates or opponents, but the purpose is to encourage interactivity and active participation.

An example of a video game and entertainment system sold today that provides such capabilities is the Xbox 360. Xbox LIVE is an additional Internet service that lets users interact with each other in real time and download games. Another feature that can be purchased for the Xbox system is Kinect, which gives the user the capability of interacting with games, music, and movies without needing a controller or handheld device. Your entire body becomes the means by which you control the game; you move in front of a sensor that picks up gestures and body positions, as well as responds to voice commands and facial expressions.

The following are various types of current interactive game systems (consoles) that use animation features:

- **Apple iPhone and iPod touch**   Portable handheld devices that use applications downloaded from the Internet. They have an animated user interface.

- **Nintendo DS series**   Portable devices that use game cartridges. Some models offer Internet connection and 3D screen effects.

- **Sony PlayStation**   Both console and portable devices with online features. The PlayStation uses game disks.
- **Nintendo Wii**   Consoles with remote controllers. The Wii also uses game disks.
- **Microsoft Xbox 360**   Consoles with live capabilities and online features. The Xbox is controller-free with Kinect.

Kinds of Animation: Categorizing and Evaluating

Animation comes in many forms—from cartoons, to fine-art films, to advertisements, to scientific explanations. Traditional animation, which is created by hand using film techniques, employs methods such as clay animation, stop motion, cut paper, rotoscoping, and drawing on individual cels.

Most animation today is created entirely on the computer or with a combination of traditional approaches and digital techniques. 2D animation is typically flat and combines individual frames to depict motion. The illusion of depth can be created with methods of shading, lighting, layering, and perspective. This type of animation is sometimes called 2½D. It uses the same conceptual space as standard 2D animation, but employs various techniques to simulate the dimension of depth (the z axis). The conceptual space of 2D and 2½D animation differs significantly from true 3D animation. 3D animation uses the dimensionality of software programs capable of rendering vector objects to make animation appear very realistic and lifelike. Animation has the ability to evoke different moods and reactions in the viewer.

The length of an animation is determined by its purpose, including where and how it will be viewed. For instance, animated ads that appear on web pages are naturally short and communicate a direct message quickly, in order to be effective in a limited amount of time and not become an annoyance to the user. Dramatic stories are better suited to lengthier movies, because adequate time is necessary to evolve a narrative story and fully develop the characters.

Some recurring themes appear in animation, such as drama, fantasy, action, literature, mythology, humor, slapstick, animated characters, cartoons, and 3D virtual environments. These thematic approaches can be applied in combination, but a single, clear message is best to avoid diluting the meaning.

With so many kinds of animation techniques to choose from, determining what to use and how to use it is a good initial step. When working with animation, it is helpful to first look at creative professional examples to see how it is done. Examine all different types of animation, as well as old and new animated movies, from Disney's 1930s *Snow White* (the first full-length hand-drawn animated movie) to Pixar's *Toy Story* (the first feature-length computer-animated movie). This process will help you learn how to come up with an inventive concept, build a narrative, create storyboards, and develop characters and their personalities. It will also help you to understand and become more aware of film attributes, such as pacing, tempo, sequential movement design and implementation, and the integration of moving images and sound.

The following are questions that you can use as guidelines for evaluating animation. They are intended to give you a basic idea of what makes for effective, engaging animation when you begin to create your own (or hire someone to do it for you).

Treatment:

- Is the animation 2D or 3D, or a combination of the two?
- Does it use vector images (illustrations and graphics), raster images (photos), or both?

Quality:

- Is it is high- or low-quality in terms of technique?
- What is the creation method and animation approach?
- How much detail is present in the artwork and backgrounds?
- Was artistic and technical effort applied in executing the piece?
- Is it visually appealing?

Story/Narrative:

- Is there a storyline with an introduction and conclusion, or is it all glitz and no substance? If so, is the story convincing and/or emotionally engaging?
- Does the narrative sequence flow and sustain viewer interest?
- Is the process from introduction to conclusion complete or fragmented? Is it logical, or does it jump around with no sense of order or plan?
- Is there uniqueness and authenticity (a fresh approach), or is it formulaic?
- Is the concept evident? Is there an underlying idea that runs throughout?
- Is it playful and fun (entertaining), factual and/or historical (serious), or open to interpretation?

Characters:

- Are the characters lifelike humans or animals, cartoons, or anthropomorphic objects?
- Is there enough character development so viewers can relate or connect with the characters?
- Are there interrelationships between characters, or is there a single, isolated character presented alone?
- Do the characters possess realistic movement?

Purposes:

- Is the animation intended for the Web, multimedia, TV, or a mobile device?
- Does it use characters to promote a product (is it used for advertising and commercialized)?
- Is it designed for entertainment, education, or both?
- Does it present a social commentary?
- Is it part of a portfolio to demonstrate creative skills and animation capabilities?

Audio:

- Is there use of music, sound effects, voice-over, or a combination of all three?
- How are the audio tracks used or applied?
- Is the audio appropriate and/or effective?
- Is the timing of audio synchronized to the voices or action?

Misc:

- Are transitions from scene to scene quick clips, smooth segues, or morphing effects?
- Is the tempo or pace—the underlying beat or rhythm—too fast or too slow?

Traditional Animation Overview

Until the camera was invented in the early nineteenth century, visual forms of entertainment were limited to theatrical and dance performances, fine art (painting, drawing, and sculpture), and hand-drawn cartoons. Cameras paved the way to the development of moving images and eventually led to filmmaking with sound. Animation was also on the rise at this time.

Animation began as hand-drawn pictures that were quickly flipped to create a sense, or *illusion*, of movement. This led to the use of photographs that were shown in rapid succession so that they appeared to be moving. Eadweard Muybridge, a British photographer, was a pioneer in the field of moving pictures. As early as 1872, he experimented with successive images of running horses, and eventually used photographs of humans to demonstrate the capabilities of capturing fluid motion.

Early inventions that made use of animation techniques were mostly Victorian era toys. Here are some of the first animation devices (some are illustrated in Figure 5-2):

- **Thaumatrope**   This was a disk with images on each side that was flipped using string to show a combined image (1824).

FIGURE 5-2 • Examples of early animation devices

- **Phenakistoscope** This used a spinning disk attached to a handle (1831). Its name was derived from the Greek phrase "deceiving viewer."

- **Zoetrope** This used a cylinder with vertical slits to produce an illusion of action (1834). Its name was derived from the Greek phrase "wheel of life."

- **Kineograph** This was a flip book. The word means "moving picture" (1868).

- **Zoopraxiscope** This was a primitive version of later motion-picture devices that projected images, but predated the celluloid film strip (1879).

The term *cel animation* comes from an abbreviation for the clear *celluloid* sheets used for drawing the film frames in traditional animation techniques. This method was employed by Disney in the early days of animated filmmaking and continued for more than 60 years, and it is still in use today. However, the cel animation process requires 24 individual drawings for each second of animated film. Due to its labor-intensive, time-consuming, and costly nature, this approach has fallen out of favor and been largely replaced by digital animation.

Principles of Animation

Many animated effects can be used in an interactive program or web site. Some of these are animated text, color changes, rollover effects for user navigation, images moving across the screen, transitions and fades, looping images, and morphing objects. Using animation in some form and applying these techniques offer an effective way of making the screen come alive.

In order to be effective and demonstrate convincing movement, the creation of animation should follow a set of fundamental principles, such as tempo, pace, timing, mood, anticipation, squashing and stretching (see Figure 5-3), character development, and posing. These are basic yet time-proven techniques that show how characters and objects move and interact in space.

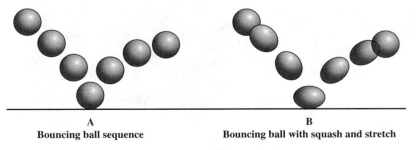

A
Bouncing ball sequence

B
Bouncing ball with squash and stretch

FIGURE 5-3 · Examples of the squash and stretch animation principle

Concept Development and Storyboarding

The development of any animation needs to follow some basic planning steps so that there is a sense of logic behind it. These progressive stages will vary depending on the purpose of the animation; however, most animation projects require some basic procedural guidelines.

The first consideration is the conceptualization of the animation, or coming up with a concept. The *concept* is the underlying idea or theme that drives the entire animated movie. This stage involves establishing the structure or framework of the animation.

For an animation to make sense, there needs to be a fundamental logic, and this reasoning is applied to the *story*. The use of a story is not restricted to longer animated movies with numerous characters. It applies equally to TV commercials as it does for abstract, fine-art animation. Dramatic structure is the glue necessary for holding the animation together. There should be a sequence of events where timing and emotion come into play. Typically, characters are used to convey emotions and conjure empathy with the audience.

Animation is in essence a form of *visual storytelling*, similar to the oral tradition of telling stories where information is recorded and communicated in a variety of ways. The main difference is that animation uses moving images, along with sound, to tell a convincing story. A story is another word for a *narrative*, and sequential (or noninteractive) animation is a visual means of conveying this narrative.

Still Struggling

Narratives, or stories, need a well-thought-out plot with a sequence of events. For an animation to be cohesive and complete, these events should involve an introduction, conflict, climax, and resolution. Using this formula will give your audience the invisible structure they need so they can follow the story and remain interested.

Once the concept and story structure are established, the next step is drawing *storyboards*. They are necessary in the process of developing the story and planning the action in the animation, and they will save the production team a great deal of time in the long run. Storyboards help to develop how the animation will unfold. They need to be done before any animation work begins so that the overall plan is in place prior to the onset of the project.

NOTE *Although we are discussing storyboards in the context of animation, the use of storyboards originated in filmmaking, where it is still widely used. In fact, visualizing the story from various perspectives using techniques commonly undertaken in filmmaking (such as camera positions, actor's points of view, and so on) is a skill that, when transferred to animation, makes for a much more compelling narrative.*

Storyboards are early visual representations of the narrative, in the form of hand-drawn sketches laid out in horizontal rows of boxes that depict the sequence of events in an animation. A typical storyboard represents individual frames in the story, with characters or major elements showing the setting or environment and any changes in action or camera angles. Specific information and directions are usually written under the sketch, including the timing and the length of each scene. An animation storyboard should have enough detail to explain how the entire story plays out. Figure 5-4 shows some examples.

FIGURE 5-4 · Storyboard examples

The last phase in planning the animation concept is writing the *treatment*. This is the typed description of the animated movie combining specific details with significant moments in the story. Each scene is described so that it is clear what is happening and when. *Script* development is also part of this stage, where the dialogue, character placement, and scene arrangements are worked out. It is vital to resolve these components for team members in various roles of the production process, especially those involved with audio and voice recordings.

This leads us to the inclusion of *sound*. Audio for multimedia will be covered in depth in Chapter 6, but it is important to touch on it with respect to animation. Animation can be created with or without sound, but you must consider the fact that the user may not have adequate output (speakers could be broken or the sound feature could be on mute), or a person could have poor hearing. For animated movies intended for sequential viewing, as opposed to those presented in an interactive environment, audio is an integral part, as it adds an entirely new dimension to it.

A *synchronized soundtrack* is used when dialogue is needed. Actors' voices are recorded so they coincide with characters' facial movements. A soundtrack generally sets the tone or mood of the piece by means of music, which might be vocal or instrumental. Music can tell a story in its own right, and, coupled with animation, lends itself to creating powerful narratives. Selecting the music, sound effects, and/or voices that are appropriate for both the animation concept and the theme of the multimedia project is key to its success, and must be well thought out before launching into the development of any animation.

Differences Between 2D and 3D Computer Animation

Computer animation programs make use of similar approaches and terminology as traditional cel animation by utilizing layers, onionskin, keyframes, and tweening effects. Cel animation on the computer mainly uses transparent effects. There is still work to be done when using computer animation, such as drawing characters and scenes, but the software takes care of many aspects with automated features, which eases the burden somewhat and minimizes the time involved.

Animation can fall into the categories of two-dimensional (2D) and three-dimensional (3D). What are the differences between these, and why is it important to make a distinction? One reason has to do with the style of animation, and the other is the execution of it, meaning techniques, equipment, and software.

2D animation is visually flat with minimal depth, using an x axis and y axis to define the space. These axes map coordinates on a grid, so lines and shapes are assigned to specific points. Despite the flat quality of 2D graphics, making use of scale differences and color shifts can imply a sense of perspective.

Some animation software packages, such as Toon Boom Studio, specialize in the 2½D animation technique mentioned earlier in the chapter. They also contain special tools to create animated characters, and include the ability to automatically synchronize speech and sound effects with characters and events. Toon Boom also supplies a library of assets for characters, backgrounds, and props to facilitate the animation-creation process. In addition, such programs may include the capability of producing storyboards, with the added benefit of being able to generate animations directly from the storyboards.

3D animation, on the other hand, applies digital treatments of light, shadow, and texture that are rendered on the surfaces of wireframe objects modeled with vector graphics. 3D graphics and animation tend to be a more accurate representation of the appearance and movement of real objects and scenes, whereas 2D animation typically appears more simplified and cartoon-like. 3D computer animation adds a third dimension to the x and y axes, which is the z axis. A common feature is a *camera* that provides the ability to move in and out of this 3D space. This type of animation is more complicated than 2D animation and requires a setup of appropriate 3D software and technical equipment. Another factor is the steep learning curve, so it is necessary to allow adequate time and patience to get up to speed with the attributes and techniques.

Both 2D and 3D animation use a *timeline*, where individual frames contain imagery that will combine to create movement. The timeline is both time-based and frame-based, so that animators can plan and adjust the tempo, pace, and length of an animation.

2D Computer Animation: Frame-by-Frame and Tweening

2D animation can be created entirely on the computer using software designed for 2D graphics and animation. Alternatively, hand-drawn images, collages, or objects can be scanned and imported into a library of *assets*, or elements that will be placed into individual frames of the animation. A library or repository such as this can contain graphics, photographs, text, audio, and video.

2D space requires an arrangement of shapes and lines within a *composition*. This rectangular frame can be thought of as the lens of a camera to assist in directing the audience's attention. Relationships between objects and the space they occupy on the screen determine the layout and positioning of elements in a 2D environment.

 2D computer animation stems from traditional methods of drawing separate images for each frame. It uses a variety of approaches to make objects, images, and characters move on screen. The frame-by-frame approach is most similar to traditional cel animation, where changes to individual elements are drawn on each frame of an animation. To create natural movement and blend one frame with the next, it is helpful to use an *onionskinning* feature (see Figure 5-5), which most animation software offers. This allows you to simultaneously view the image before and after the one you are working on. This method works well for character animation, which requires walking and running cycles. Creating frame-by-frame animation can be time-consuming and slow, since each frame represents an individual drawing with subtle changes from one to the next.

FIGURE 5-5 • Onionskin feature in Flash software

Still Struggling

The frame rate, which is also *frames per second* (FPS), is 24 FPS for film (movies and traditional cel animation), 30 FPS for broadcast quality video (TV), and 10 to 15 FPS for multimedia and the Web (computer screen).

As a result of the frame rate, different approaches need to be taken to successfully produce a 2D animation, such as shorter length movies, a team approach, or an extended time frame to complete the project. Animation for multimedia and the Web is typically not long in duration.

Computer programs can simplify the animation process by allowing for *tweening*. With tweening, digitally generated frames are inserted in between key frames or end frames, as illustrated in Figure 5-6. This method works well when something needs to move across the screen and change its size, shape, or color over time, such as a logo, text, or simple objects. Tweening saves time and labor, but tends to have more of a technical and computerized feel to it than frame-by-frame animation.

An important aspect of tweening is easing. *Easing* is simply the rate at which an object being tweened changes. For example, if you were tweening a bouncing ball, the speed of the ball from the top to the bottom of the bounce would increase. The ball would move down slowly and accelerate gradually. In this case, you would *ease-in* the tween.

Tweening can also apply to virtually any characteristic of an image that can be changed over time. For example, the transparency of an image (also referred to as the *alpha*) can be tweened, as well as its color and scale. In addition, some programs allow an object to be *shape tweened* (also called *morphing*). This technique automatically calculates and displays the transition that one shape goes through as it changes into another shape.

Inverse kinematics is an animation technique where one object is connected to another object so that when one object moves, the object it is connected to also moves. Software that can calculate where one object will be based on its relationship to another object can make the animation of complex scenes with connected parts much easier. For example, making realistic movement such as walking or jumping is facilitated using this technique, which is used in both 2D and 3D animation programs.

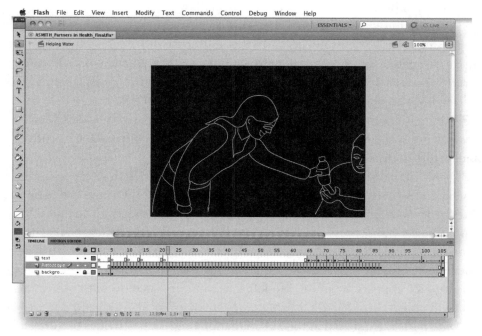

FIGURE 5-6 · Frame-by-frame animation in Adobe Flash (top) and frame-by-frame combined with tweening in Adobe Flash (bottom)

TIP   *Some well-known software programs for 2D animation are Adobe Flash, Toon Boom, Adobe After Effects, Alchemy Mindworks Animation Workshop, and Anime Studio. You can also find free and open source animation programs on the Web. An extensive list of animation software programs with descriptions can be found at www.animationprograms.biz/top-animation-programs/.*

3D Animation: Modeling, Ray Tracing, and Rendering

3D animation computer animation is prevalent today for animated feature-length movies, special effects, video games, and TV commercials. 3D modeling is a completely different conceptual and production model than 2D animation, due to aspects such as angles, lighting, and direction. Figure 5-7 shows examples of both 2D and 3D animation.

Depth allows for the illusion of 3D space. 2D space can have some depth, by use of shading and color gradations, but the appearance of the graphics is still somewhat flat. With 3D graphics, the distance and angle of the camera affects the way the animation is perceived and the story is conveyed. Camera shots, or *positions*, are the same for film and video as they are for 3D animation. We attribute these techniques to how well characters are presented in their environments and how they relate to their surroundings.

3D animation is very effective for educational purposes, as it has a way of simplifying complicated subjects and ideas. Different views and vantage points can be presented, and events can be re-created, such as an ancient civilization in ruins. Virtual light sources are used to produce reflections, transparencies, and shadows on objects and scenes for a hyperrealistic effect.

3D animations mathematically represent objects in three dimensions. Motion is calculated based on the x, y, and z axes. This allows for different views of the object (top, bottom, front, back, and so on).

3D animation is the basis for many popular computer action games and role-playing simulations. Such games actually create and render 3D scenes in real time. The use of modeling and rendering gives 3D animation its realistic qualities.

Modeling is the process of creating and defining 3D objects, characters, and scenes on an underlying grid containing the x, y, and z axes. 3D software utilizes modeling to provide different views and angles as well as lighting effects, so the end product appears accurate. Modeling techniques include both wireframe and solid objects.

Rendering is the last step in the 3D animation process. It provides texture and surface patterns, as well as reflections and transparency features. The rendering process can be time-consuming, depending on the complexity of the objects

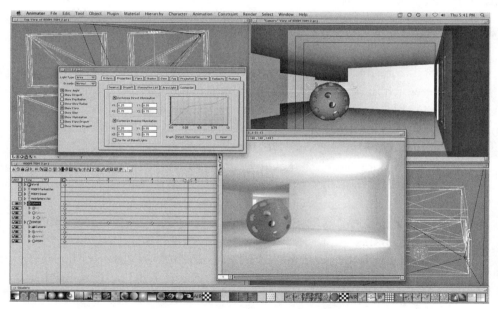

FIGURE 5-7 • A 2D animation example in Adobe Flash (top) and a 3D animation example (bottom)

and the duration of the animation. Because 3D models tend to be complex—often having thousands of separate elements, connections, and textures—a market for premade models has developed. Figure 5-8 illustrates modeling and rendering a 3D scene.

TIP   *Some high-end and widely used software programs for 3D animation are Autodesk Maya, Autodesk 3ds Max, and NewTek LightWave. Blender is a very good free open source animation program, and Google's SketchUp is a popular 3D modeling program that is also free. There are many other freeware and shareware options that can be found on the Web, but you need to check the system requirements for compatibility before downloading the software. Sites such as www.turbosquid.com provide a marketplace where a developer can find models for any conceivable object—everything from humans, airplanes, cars, and other common objects. Using a premade 3D object can save many hours of painstaking work.*

Animation Files and Formats

File compression is another important step when saving animated movies for multimedia, so that the files are not too large to be viewed on the screen or downloaded from the Web. Taking into consideration the end use will help to determine which file format to use and how much to compress the file.

Animation files need to be saved in different formats depending on the delivery device (how it will be used). Saving animation files is a twofold process. First, the file will be saved in its native software program, for instance Flash (FLA format). When saving an animated Flash movie, you typically save it as a SWF file, so that it can be played on the Web with Flash Player software. Saving files allows for compression, which is necessary for reducing file sizes so they will play on different devices and on the Web. You save in two ways so that you have the option of going back and editing the animation and resaving it for the intended media.

Animation can also be saved in QuickTime or Windows Projector format for playing on the Web or for downloading to a computer. The Graphic Interchange Format (GIF) format is designed for web graphics, and the Animated GIF format is designed for small web animations that are composed of individual frames. Animations that have interactive elements must be saved in a format such as SWF that enables the user's computer to render it on the fly in real time. Animations rendered as QuickTime or Windows video formats are essentially frame-by-frame formats, which do not allow interactivity.

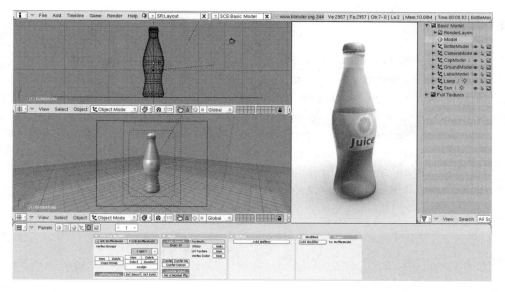

FIGURE 5-8 · 3D modeling (top) and a rendered 3D scene (bottom)

Summary

In this chapter, you learned the ins and outs of animation and how it is used in multimedia. Moving images can attract, entertain, and explain, but they can also be overdone and excessive. Planning a concept and developing a narrative sequence are key to successful animation. The technical side includes deciding whether to use traditional approaches combined with the computer or strictly digital animation, as well as determining if 2D or 3D animation will better suit the needs of the project. In the next two chapters, you will discover sound, or *audio*, techniques, and the video capabilities for multimedia.

QUIZ

1. **What is another word used to describe a narrative?**
    A. Story
    B. Nonlinear sequence
    C. Storyboard
    D. Moving images

2. **What is *not* an advantage of using animation for multimedia?**
    A. Providing feedback to users when accessing active areas
    B. Drawing attention to buttons and navigational devices
    C. Decorating the screen
    D. Demonstrating complex concepts

3. **Digital game consoles were first introduced with the Odyssey by Magnavox in what decade?**
    A. 1960s
    B. 1970s
    C. 1980s
    D. 1990s

4. **Which of the following statements applies more to attributes of 2D animation than to 3D animation?**
    A. Different camera views and vantage points
    B. Realistic re-creation of events
    C. Flat, cartoon-like
    D. Virtual reflections, transparencies, and shadows

5. **The traditional cel animation process requires how many individual drawings for each second of animated film?**
    A. 15
    B. 24
    C. 30
    D. 60

6. **What does the digital animation process of tweening refer to?**
    A. The location of individual frames in an animation
    B. The placement of the first and last frames in an animated sequence
    C. Frames that are inserted in between key frames or end frames
    D. The empty frames at the beginning of an animation

7. **Which of the following formats can be used to save animation files?**
    A. SWF
    B. JPEG
    C. TIFF
    D. EPS

8. What is *not* one of the primary purposes of using a storyboard?

    A. Sketching the sequence of events in an animation
    B. Prototyping on the computer all the frames in an animation
    C. Planning how the animation will unfold
    D. Developing the story and planning the action in the animation

9. Why did British photographer Eadweard Muybridge photograph horses?

    A. To see how fast they could run
    B. To demonstrate the capabilities of capturing fluid motion
    C. To tell a visual story
    D. To produce a feature-length animated movie

10. Which of these early animation inventions means "moving picture" and was essentially a flip book?

    A. Thaumatrope
    B. Zoetrope
    C. Phenakistoscope
    D. Kineograph

chapter **6**

Audio: Music and Sound Effects

This chapter covers the medium of sound and how to use it in multimedia projects. Sound and music are all around us, and they shape our experiences. At times, the power of sound is taken for granted, so understanding and appreciating audio is the first step in working with it. Recording and acquiring audio will be discussed, as well as editing with designated software programs. You will get some basic concepts and tips to help you understand how to work with and save digitized sound for interactive programs and the Web.

CHAPTER OBJECTIVES

In this chapter, you will:

- Discover the difference between analog and digital audio
- Become familiar with using sound effects and music in multimedia projects
- Learn what it means to customize and make improvements to audio tracks
- Distinguish between the recording of sounds as opposed to importing digital files
- Determine which file formats are best for saving different kinds of sound files

Audio Fundamentals

Audio is another word for *sound recording*, meaning the reproduction of sound in all its forms. We regularly listen to a variety of recorded audio, such as music tracks, podcasts, news stories, advertising jingles, TV soundtracks, and digital (audio) books. We tune in for all sorts of reasons: entertainment, relaxation, education, work, and so on. Online music stores, such as iTunes and Napster, offer seemingly infinite choices of music from every genre, as well as movies, TV shows, and applications of all sorts. They allow us to browse and search the database or *store*, play entire songs, listen to samples, create playlists, organize, synchronize multiple devices, and download. Pandora is another online music service that allows you to set up a personalized radio station based on your preferred music.

Audio intended for multimedia can be broken down into three primary categories: sound effects, narration, and music. Sound can be used simply to draw attention or set a mood, or it can synchronize to animation and film, explain concepts, and provide voices for character personalities. Learning how to incorporate sound into multimedia projects and web sites requires some knowledge of the physics of sound and the terminology associated with it.

Mechanics of Sound

Sound is *energy* that we perceive through our sense of hearing. Sound energy is transmitted by means of air pressure as a delivery mechanism. Tiny fluctuations in air pressure are interpreted as sound. We are able to hear and understand sounds because our eardrum vibrates when a sound is made, as illustrated in Figure 6-1. This sends a nerve impulse to the brain, similar to other sensory responses of seeing, tasting, smelling, and touching.

Auditory capabilities are universal in humans, but the quality can vary. Sound levels, or the amount of sound that can be heard, affect how we respond physiologically and how we cognitively interpret what we hear. We also experience a psychological response to sound depending on whether or not we are already familiar with it.

When transferring audio to the computer, pressure waves that result from sounds are converted electronically by means of a microphone (mic). Computer sound cards (generally built in when manufactured) convert these voltage changes into digital samples.

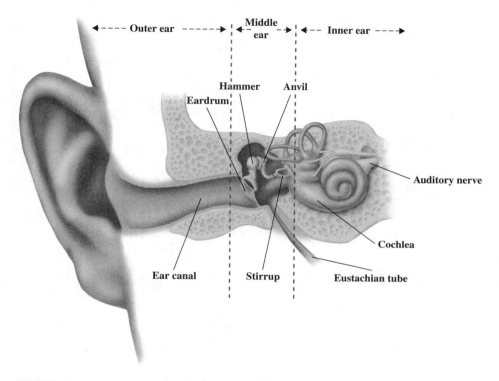

FIGURE 6-1 · The eardrum responds to sound energy

Two primary characteristics of sound are amplitude and frequency. *Amplitude*, normally called *volume*, is the power of a sound, as shown in Figure 6-2. It is the strength or loudness of a sound, so the higher the amplitude wave, the louder the sound will be. Amplitude is measured in data bits (8, 16, 24, or 32), which determine the level of sound quality. The number of bits is also called the *sample size* or *resolution*. The higher the bit depth, the better the sound quality.

The *frequency* is the number of times each second that a sound pressure wave vibrates (see Figure 6-2). Many wave peaks in one second of sound reveal a high frequency and a higher sound; fewer peaks represent a low frequency and a deeper sound. The measurement of frequency is how many cycles occur per second, which is also called *hertz* (Hz). Sound files are measured in hertz, which means "per second," so 44 Hz is 44 samples per second. Kilo is thousands, so 44 kilohertz (kHz) is 44,000 samples per second. For example, for CD-quality sound, music needs to be recorded at 44 kHz, 16-bit, stereo.

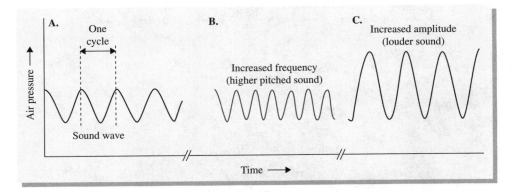

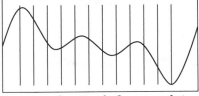

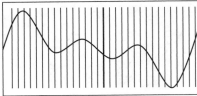

Lower sample rates take fewer snapshots of the waveform....

Faster sample rates take more snapshots....

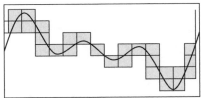

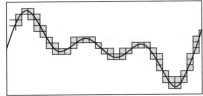

...resulting in a rough recreation of the waveform.

...resulting in a smoother and more detailed recreation of the waveform.

FIGURE 6-2 · Audio waveform showing amplitude and frequency (top) and relationship between an audio waveform and sample rates (bottom)

Still Struggling

The frequency at which you take a sample of sound and the more stored data you have, the finer the resolution and higher the quality during playback. The end result of your audio and how it sounds are based on the quality of your recording, and not the device on which it will be played. As a result, digital audio is referred to as *device-independent*.

To further understand sound mechanics, studying waveform attributes is essential (see Figure 6-2). A *waveform* is a visual representation of sound. Sound is a continuous flow, or rise and fall, of "waves" that are transmitted by variations in air pressure and converted to data bits when digitized.

Analog and Digital Audio

Any sound we hear is essentially an analog signal, whether it's a human voice, live music, or a car horn. *Analog sound* is a continuous, endless flow, as opposed to *digital sound*, which is nonlinear.

Using a microphone, sound waves can be recorded onto a physical medium, such as magnetic tape, or recorded by digital means. Sound that has been recorded onto an audiotape will play continuously, and is started, paused, rewound, and stopped by means of a cassette recorder/player. Such audio tracks can be converted to a digital signal to become data bits that are capable of being listened to, edited, mixed, and saved on a computer.

Sounds that originate on the computer (generated using a computer) or are digitally recorded automatically become digital data. Digitizing sound is the process of capturing the amplitude of a sound at a set frequency. Sound *channels* come into play. Two channels designate sounds as mono or stereo. *Mono* sound is a single channel, and *stereo* is double, correlating with the left and right speakers.

Audio is recorded by using digital audio recording devices that translate sound waves into digital code; in other words, sounds become numbers. Sound that is digitized is also called *sampled*. Sound samples are made up of binary digits, or *bits*. The computer converts these samples into bits so that it is compatible with digital technology.

Sound can be digitized using a microphone or *synthesizer*, which is an electronic device that generates sounds by directly creating digital waveforms. Sound can also derive from original recordings (either analog or digital) and prerecorded CDs and DVDs. When transferring audio to the computer, microphones electronically convert pressure waves that result from a sound being made. Sound cards built in to the computer convert these voltage changes into digital samples.

Analog-to-digital converters (ADCs) are electronic devices used to transfer an analog audio signal (as with a microphone, for instance) into a digital one, as illustrated in Figure 6-3. The audio data is then stored in the computer or on an external drive. *Sampling* is the process of converting analog sound into digital sound. A higher sampling rate will result in a higher-quality sound that closely reproduces the original with more accurate pitch and tone. A lower sampling rate alters the original sound wave, and distortion results.

FIGURE 6-3 • Analog-to-digital converter

Audio files use something called *pulse-code modulation* (PCM), which is a digital version of an analog signal that has been sampled. In each sample, the amplitude of the signal is *quantized*, which means it is assigned a digital value.

PCM is a waveform coding method that converts analog waveforms to digital wave shapes. It is the standard format used by the audio in your computer, as well as CDs, DVDs, and digital telephones. It works by the sound signal transmitting electrical pulses, which are recorded digitally using the PCM method. When these waves are quantized, they can be adjusted to different levels (sampling rates), leading to higher or lower sound quality.

The quality of digitized audio is directly proportional to the amount of data used to represent it, which, of course, affects the file size. This depends on three factors:

- How frequently the sound was sampled
- How many bits were taken per sample
- How many channels the audio has: one for mono or two for stereo

Sampling the audio consists of measuring the *volume* (size of the pressure wave) at any given moment. Using more bits for each sample allows for a greater number of intervals of volume per sample, which is analogous to measuring a board in inches instead of feet. Sampling more frequently allows for a more accurate waveform, similar to measuring rainfall every hour instead of once a day. Generally, a stereo sound is twice the size of a mono sound because it has two separate sound channels, left and right.

Still Struggling

Do not confuse the *sampling frequency*, which is how frequently samples are taken, with the *sound's frequency*, which is how frequently the sound pressure wave is vibrating. Both are measured in hertz (cycles per second). A higher sampling rate will provide a higher-quality digitization and a more accurate waveform when converted back to analog, especially with higher-frequency sounds.

Sound effects can be obtained from existing sound clip media and are saved in different formats. They range from low to high quality, which in turn affects the file size. A low sampling rate results in a smaller file size, but also a lower-quality sound. Different sizes are necessary when choosing clip media, so that you have enough file format selections from which to choose.

NOTE *Digital audio quality constitutes a number of factors, such as whether the original source is of high quality, if the equipment is adequate to record or convert the sound, and the capabilities for playing back the sound (speakers and headphones). The quality of the original sound is important in the same way that the quality of a visual image is critical. Ultimately, the end result is only as good as the original.*

Some audio files contain typical "canned" sound effects; others are more creative and unique. These can be manipulated further in audio-editing programs, such as Adobe Soundbooth and Apple GarageBand. They can be repeated, looped, clipped, reversed, and so on to suit the needs of the project. Sound effects can also be created from scratch. These are called *Foley* sounds, named after the Hollywood sound engineer who first developed ways of making credible sound effects with day-to-day objects. Figure 6-4 shows an example of equipment for digitizing and editing audio.

FIGURE 6-4 · Equipment setup for digitizing and editing audio

Recording vs. Importing Sound

Recording sound requires that you record twice the frequency (in terms of the sampling rate) to adequately capture and play back audio. Handheld digital audio recorders can be used to record meetings and interviews, but they vary in terms of quality and price. The accumulated data can be transferred to a computer with a USB cable. When recording with a microphone and a computer, plug it directly into the computer's microphone input port. If you are digitizing prerecorded audio, connect the recording device into the headphone port on the computer.

NOTE *A variety of software programs can be used to record and edit audio, as discussed in Chapter 10. For example, Adobe Soundbooth is a comprehensive, industry-standard software program that is also fairly easy to learn and use.*

Setting recording levels is vital to good-quality output. Depending on the level set while recording, you could end up with distortions, and the end result will not be acceptable. Digital meters, which allow you to view the audio-input levels, are typically included with audio-editing software, as seen in Figure 6-5. Adobe Soundbooth documentation recommends watching the meters in the

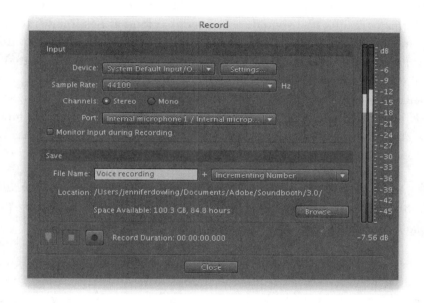

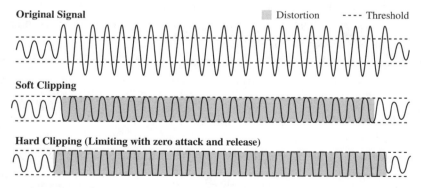

FIGURE 6-5 · Audio recording levels (top) and clipping waveform (bottom)

Record dialog box while setting recording levels. You should try to prevent the loudest peaks in the yellow range from going beyond 3 dB. If the display is in the red range, it is too loud and will result in some degree of distortion. To control this, adjust the volume by reducing (turning down) the input volume or the source output level.

Levels also need to be adjusted if a recording is too quiet, as it can pick up unwanted background noise, or if it is too loud, potentially causing sound distortion. This can be controlled by turning up the input or output volume. For good-quality results, you should record audio as loud as possible without clipping it. (Clipping is a waveform distortion that occurs when an amplifier or recording device forces an audio signal to exceed its maximum capacity.)

All recording systems have a certain level of "noise" they add to the signal. The distance between this noise and the loudest possible signal is the system's *dynamic range*. Keeping the recording loud but not clipped will minimize this inherent noise. An audio waveform that is clipped is a result of too high a level. It has broad, flat areas at the peaks, resulting in popping or clicking sounds (see Figure 6-5).

TIP *Audio can be cleaned up after it's recorded, similar to using photo-editing techniques. However, the rule of thumb in both cases is to always get the best quality possible up front and not rely on software to improve it.*

When digitizing sound, the *amplitude* (strength and loudness of a sound) is measured in data bits, and this determines how many levels of sound are recorded. The higher the bit depth, the greater the dynamic range. As a result, the sound quality is better, since it is more accurate in relation to the original. There is also a lower *noise floor* (extraneous, unwanted sounds) and higher fidelity in terms of reproduction precision.

For high-end digital recording that requires 16-bit sound with 44 kHz sampling rates, a specialized audio studio with the latest equipment is necessary to get the best results. However, this is a costly endeavor and should be considered only if having high-quality output is a necessity, and also taking the project budget into account.

Here are some suggestions for getting the best audio recording:

- Do *not* use on-camera microphones unless absolutely necessary.
- Use blimps or zeppelins to reduce wind noise when recording outdoors.
- Use shotgun mics or "booms" for recording sounds from a distance.
- Use mic pickup patterns for voice and live recordings.

- Use wireless or lavalier (lapel) mics for interviews.
- Use isolation or voice-over booths to control sound and eliminate outside noise.
- Use balanced inputs or XLR connectors.

MIDI and Digital Music

The Musical Instrument Digital Interface (MIDI) format is used to encode computer-based music. It is essentially electronically synthesized music generated and manipulated on a computer. MIDI was originally developed in 1982 by the music industry as a means of combining electronic music and computers. MIDI cannot record sounds or speech; what it does is generate *notes*.

MIDI files are typically smaller and take up less storage space than standard waveform audio because the format uses digital command sequences to describe the musical score, allowing for greater editing flexibility. Instruments are coordinated using these detailed descriptions, and each note has particular/individualized data associated with it. The difference between digital audio and MIDI is that the former is recorded digitally and the latter is a numeric form of music that is carefully timed and orchestrated.

MIDI allows you to create an original musical score for a multimedia project. It has the capability of recording audio while instruments are being played and exchanging musical information digitally. It also adds computerized effects for enhancements to the audio production process (see Figure 6-6).

Precision and sound accuracy are inherent qualities of MIDI, and data can be edited easily. However, MIDI systems differ from one another in terms of capabilities and features. For instance, lower-level systems limit the number of instrumental and percussive tracks available in a given piece of music. Higher-end systems have more options, leading to a better-quality end product. Playback hardware also factors in, since the quality of the sound depends on the particular MIDI device being used.

Digital music is recorded audio that has been sampled. It can also be created by a musician who composes and plays original music designed specifically for a project (see Figure 6-7). Digital audio is more widely used for multimedia than MIDI due to its reliability in terms of playback, as well as the availability and selection of audio-editing tools. Digital music is typically listened to with small headphones (earphones or earbuds), a computer's internal speakers, or small external speakers attached to a computer. The standard and commonly used file format is MP3, which provides good-quality sound for these purposes.

FIGURE 6-6 · Using the Musical Instrument Digital Interface (MIDI)

Music used in multimedia sets up an atmosphere and elicits emotion, as well as synchronizes with animation and film. Music can be acquired by making selections from a digital audio library, in much the same way that you can use image libraries, or from the public domain. As with images, music can be purchased from libraries, either online or CD, for a one-time use or for unlimited usage rights. The cost depends on the music and the intended use.

Music in the public domain means it is available for most uses and is not restricted by copyright law. Such music was created long ago enough (more than 75 years) to qualify, or it was never copyrighted in the first place. In any case, if music created by someone other than yourself is being included in a multimedia project, procuring the rights to use existing music is necessary to avoid a legal snafu.

FIGURE 6-7 • Digital music recording session and DJ mixing sound

NOTE *A* **mashup** *is a digital mixture of music tracks made up of portions of various songs. This popular technique blends prerecorded songs, and often the vocals of one song merge with another. It is not difficult to create these types of songs using software such as Audacity, but there are copyright protections in place to prevent unlawful use. It is important to acquire permission from the owner if any potential profit could be made as a result.*

Editing and Manipulating Audio Tracks

Digital audio allows for capturing and modifying sound data. Editing is a common procedure after digitizing audio to improve the results. If an audio track is in fairly good condition, only straightforward editing is needed for minimal changes—such as cropping, copying and pasting, deleting, and trimming—as well as adjusting volume by equalizing, amplifying, and compressing. A useful technique for blending tracks together or transitioning from the end of one to the beginning of another is *fading*. Audio software's fade-in and fade-out tools are typically easy to use, and the results are very effective (see Figure 6-8).

Adobe Soundbooth and Audacity, a free open source program available for multiple platforms (http://audacity.sourceforge.net/), offer advanced techniques. These and similar audio-editing software allow you to perform noise reduction/elimination, equalization, pitch change, reverberation, looping, stretching, echoing, and reversing. You can also repair sound files with such programs, and you can combine multiple tracks; for instance, you could create a voice-over with music along with digital mixes.

There are times you will need to resample the file if it is saved in a format that is higher quality than needed or is too large. This process is similar to image file reduction in that it lowers the resolution. It will save space, and sometimes the changes are negligible and will not be noticed. Common *downsampling* approaches are reducing a 44 kHz file to 22 kHz, or a 16-bit file to an 8-bit file, or a stereo format to a mono format (see Figure 6-9).

TIP *To learn more about digital audio and editing techniques, go to the Adobe Soundbooth reference pages at http://help.adobe.com/en_US/Soundbooth/2.0/index.html.*

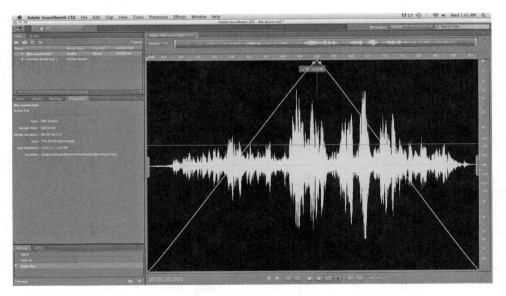

FIGURE 6-8 · Fade-in and fade-out techniques shown on a digital sound wave

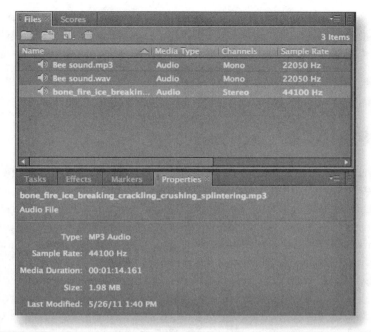

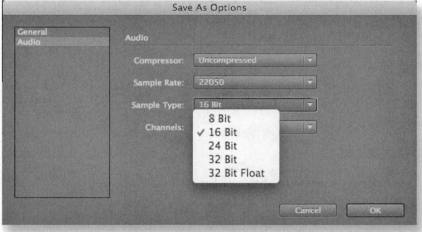

FIGURE 6-9 · Sampling rate, file size, and resolution

Audio File Formats and Compression Schemes

File formats are essentially patterns for storing sounds as data or computer code. This encoding process is similar to what happens when saving visual images and graphics files, in that they are simultaneously saved and compressed for the ultimate goal of playing back (or viewing) on different devices and platforms. Compression is typically used to reduce file sizes so audio files can be posted on the Web or sent via email, as well as for storage purposes.

Still Struggling

If you have adequate disk space on your computer and bandwidth (Internet connection speed), it is not necessary to compress audio files. If you have technological limitations, audio files should be compressed according to the purpose and intended use. To recap, sampling rates determine the sound quality, and sample size (bit rate) determines the dynamic range of the sound. Most, if not all, audio compression formats allow for setting both.

Software that both compresses and decompresses audio and video data is called a *codec*. Such methods allow for transferring, storing, and playing files. Depending on the codec used, they generally maintain the quality of the audio. Just as with image files that are saved in JPEG format, some codecs use a *lossy* compression scheme, which results in data loss leading to lower-quality results, depending on the settings used.

Table 6-1 summarizes the sampling rates and bit depths of various audio devices. Table 6-2 compares the sound duration, bit depth, and sampling rates for CD storage.

Audio File Types

Two of the more common file formats for audio are AIFF and WAV. These have been in use since the early days of Apple and Windows operating systems, and

TABLE 6-1 Sampling Rates and Bit Depths

Audio Device	Sampling Rate	Bit Depth
DVD	48 kHz	24 bits
CD	44 kHz	16 bits
Radio	22 kHz	8 bits
Telephone	8 kHz	8 bits

TABLE 6-2 Comparison of Sound Duration, Bit Depth, and Sampling Rates for CD Storage (700 Mb)

Use	Duration	Bit Depth	Sampling Rate
Voice	1,083 minutes	8–bit mono	11 KHz = 600 Kb per minute
High–quality music	61 minutes	16–bit stereo	44 KHz = 10 Mb per minute

neither one compresses the sound. They are still available and in use today due to their universality and compatibility, as well as their familiarity (they are easily recognized as sound files).

Audio files are handled differently than MIDI files when saved. MIDI files are more specialized and tend to be smaller in size compared with digitized audio. This is because they originate as digital music and are organized efficiently according to data tracks. Standard audio files can range from high quality (large files with limited compression) to low quality (smaller files with greater compression), depending on their intended purpose.

Table 6-3 lists audio file formats and their purpose. The extension listed next to the format appears at the end of a file name and indicates the type of format that was used.

The distinction between a *codec* and a *container* is somewhat confusing but important to address in relation to multimedia. Keep in mind that a codec is software used to compress media files. A container is a *file type* that is capable of storing many different formats of media, compressed with a codec, such as QuickTime (.mov). Another example of a file type that is actually a container is the Advanced Audio Coding (.aac) codec format. Containers can contain multimedia in the same codec (for example, an FLV file can contain a soundtrack compressed with the Advanced Audio Coding codec).

Storage Options

Audio CDs are used for storing sound recordings and music files, and they contain high-quality audio due to sampling rates and storage capacity. CDs are commonly used for audio files, as they are reliable and versatile for both storage and playback.

External drives are often necessary for backing up audio and video files because some computers do not have a large enough storage capacity. Standard data-storage peripherals are acceptable, as they can stockpile numerous large

TABLE 6-3 Audio File Formats

Format	Extension	Description
Adobe Sound	.asnd	Adjust fades and effects; store history to restore previous edits; supports multitrack mixes for combining multiple audio files and scores
Advanced Audio Coding	.aac	The successor to MP3; a compressed format based on MPEG4; higher audio quality than MP3 format with similar bit rates
Audio Interchange Format	.aif	The standard, uncompressed audio file format for Mac OS; 8–bit mono only; can lead to large files
AU Audio	.au	Audio format for computers using the Unix operating system; can be used on the Web
MPEG3	.mp3	Originated with the Motion Picture Expert Group; widely used for web audio and portable media players; compresses file size and optimizes audio for fast downloads
MPEG4	.mp4	Derived from Apple QuickTime and used as an alternative to MP3 on iPods and iTunes
QuickTime	.mov	Apple's audio and video compression format
Waveform Audio File	.wav	The standard, uncompressed audio format for the Windows operating system
MIDI	.midi	File format for MIDI sounds and music

files. A variety of drives are available for purchase; however, the greater the capacity, the more expensive they become. Storage drives can be connected directly to a computer, or files can be transferred via a network.

Audio files can also be transferred to a remote server for storage purposes. They can be uploaded to an FTP site on the Internet or copied directly to a networked server by using a specific server address, which is typically password-protected. There are also free and fee-based file-hosting web sites to store, organize, retrieve, and play/stream audio files. Another option is to set up your own iTunes server that can be connected to multiple computers in one location. This consolidates music and video files so they are centrally located and easily accessible.

Using Sound in Multimedia Projects and for the Web

Multimedia is not complete without audio, as it is an integral part of the product. Sound that is part of a multimedia project comes in many forms, such as ambient background music, speech/voice-over for educational purposes, and effects/noises for user feedback.

When sound is used as voice commands for tutoring or instruction, it can be helpful, but it may also be overdone. Providing a mute option is essential, since some do not appreciate the added sound (or they are trying to remain inconspicuous while using the material).

Special sound effects can be included for *feedback* when a user clicks something or to let the user know something is taking place or about to happen. Sound in multimedia is reinforcement for the user, similar to the function of animation, which is used to draw attention, explain things, and give feedback.

Sound effects should be planned carefully and used consistently. They should reflect the primary theme of the multimedia program or web site and coincide with the graphics to which they are associated. A sound that is asynchronous with a visual is confusing and inappropriate. It will not likely sustain interest or facilitate learning. Table 6-4 provides some guidelines for planning and executing sound elements.

Programming is necessary for sound files to play and function properly in a multimedia project or web site. For instance, sound files used in Flash need to have ActionScript code applied so they will start, stop, and synchronize with visual elements. For a web site to control audio, HTML code and the appropriate player, such as QuickTime (or a link to download it) will be required to open files and play sounds.

Sound files for multimedia cannot be too large, as they need to be easily stored and also to play properly. Audio files have a tendency to balloon up to unreasonable sizes due to the need for high-quality sound. For instance, mono sounds are more than adequate and are substantially smaller than stereo sounds. Similarly, 16-bit sampling is typically not needed; 8-bit may be sufficient. Also, because the voice comes from only one point, recording vocals in stereo is generally an unnecessary use of resources, and mono will work fine.

TABLE 6-4   Guidelines for Planning and Executing Sound Elements for Multimedia and Web Projects

Task/Decision	Solution
Sound selections	Figure out what *kinds* of sounds will be needed: background music, sound effects, and voice–over.
Digital audio or MIDI	Choose between digital audio or MIDI data and decide how they will be used.
Playback options	Determine the sound playback capabilities (codecs and plug–ins) of the final delivery system.
Audio arrangement	Consider *where* the audio will be included (placed) in your project.
Kind of audio (original or acquired)	Determine whether to create sound/music (using MIDI or GarageBand, for instance), purchase from a music library, or acquire from public domain/free media files.
Editing audio	Use software (such as Soundbooth or Audacity) to edit and/or manipulate sound files.
File formats	Select the appropriate file format(s) for compatibility with authoring software and delivery devices (must consider file storage and bandwidth capacity).
Testing	Test sounds so they are timed/synchronized with images and animation.
Playback	Listen to audio with headphones, high–quality speakers, and laptop speakers; assess the location and how sound will be listened to (public or private space).

Multimedia sound files use sampling rates between 11 kHz and 44 kHz. The standard sampling rate for CD quality sound is 44 kHz, but it is not necessary for multimedia. A typical sample size for a multimedia sound file is 22 kHz, and the quality is generally not compromised.

Technical components needed for audio production are microphones, recorders, speakers, players, and manipulation devices. Digital audio software allows for the following capabilities when working with sound, which are similar to controls on audio players: playing, recording, pausing, stopping, fast-forwarding, and rewinding. The performance of the sound file depends on the equipment used to both capture and play it.

Web Site Audio

Internet sound files are essentially *linked* to web sites. Including the linked web address of the sound file in the HTML code allows the file to be played. This process is called *embedding*, so that an Internet browser will download the file to the computer when the user activates a request by clicking a link. The following example uses such code with the embed tag:

```
<embed src="filename.mp3">
```

You have undoubtedly experienced playback interruptions after selecting an audio file or video on the Web. At times, you hear or see only part of it, and then it stops or pauses, or you need to wait until it has finished downloading to listen to it or view it. This delay is due to several factors, such as file size and bandwidth speed, and the process is called *buffering*, which is needed for smooth playback.

Media files can be viewed and listened to via the Internet by means of *streaming*. Streaming generally refers to files that are sent in packets with a handshake between the user's computer and the server sending the media. This enables the server to moderate the delivery of packets and, in some cases (such as Real Media), adjust the quality of the media dynamically. The performance of streaming audio or video depends entirely on the Internet connection speed.

Still Struggling

While a media file is downloading, it goes into the computer's *buffer*, which means it is being stored in active memory, as opposed to in permanent hard-disk memory. Once it has fully buffered, the file can be played back continuously without further disruptions. This type of media transfer is known as a *progressive download* (as compared to streaming).

Mobile Device Audio

Audio files designed for cell phones and other mobile devices are chiefly categorized by music and ringtones, in addition to sound that is associated with or embedded into a video and animated media. Music files on mobile devices are most often saved in the MP3 format, which is the same format as audio played on a laptop or desktop computer, as well as on portable MP3 players.

Ringtones supplied with a mobile phone are produced by MIDI software within the device or played from sound files with digital "notes" stored in the internal memory chip. You can also download ringtones from a myriad of web resources. Some older songs whose copyright has expired, or audio that was never copyrighted, are free for the taking, since they are in the public domain; others require a fee to download and use.

A relatively newer method for obtaining ringtones is to send one to your phone or mobile device via sound waves. You can send the mobile device a text message that has the ringtone program included in it. As noted in Chapter 4, text messages use SMS technology to transmit and receive. Nokia and Intel teamed up to create a "smart" SMS protocol that allows messages sent between cell phones to contain programming code that tells the device it is receiving a message other than text, such as a ringtone or graphic image.

Ringtones can also be generated directly on the cell phone by using music-composer or melody-creation programs. Volumes can be adjusted using software and hardware controls, and sounds can play on a small speaker built into the device.

Summary

In this chapter, we focused on the medium of sound and how it is used in multimedia projects. However, it is difficult to isolate audio as a single medium because it is typically contingent upon other media. Before completing Part II of this book, we will delve into video, as it is another critical element of multimedia.

QUIZ

1. **What is *audio* another word for?**
   A. Sound recording
   B. Energy
   C. Waveform
   D. Resolution

2. **What is *amplitude*?**
   A. How many cycles occur per second
   B. Power of a sound
   C. Size of a sound file
   D. Vibration of the eardrum

3. **What is electronically synthesized music that is generated and manipulated on a computer?**
   A. Sampling rate of a sound
   B. Cycles of waves per second
   C. Frequency
   D. MIDI

4. **Where does the file format .aif derive from?**
   A. Mac OS
   B. Unix
   C. Windows
   D. Mobile

5. **Which has a higher sampling rate: voice recorded at 8-bit mono or music recorded at 16-bit stereo?**
   A. Voice
   B. Music
   C. Both
   D. Neither

6. **What is the final yet most important step when working with audio in multimedia and web projects?**
   A. Kind of audio
   B. Editing
   C. Testing
   D. Audio arrangement

7. **Which of the following has the lowest sampling rate and bit depth?**
   A. Telephone
   B. Radio
   C. CD
   D. DVD

8. **What is it called when there are interruptions during the playback of audio or video files on the Web?**
   A. File size
   B. Buffering
   C. Internet speed
   D. Internal speed of the computer

9. **What is the best way to store and back up either large quantities or large file sizes of sound recordings and music files?**
   A. External drive
   B. Flash drive
   C. Audio CD
   D. Internal hard disk

10. **What is a codec?**
    A. MIDI software
    B. AAC file format for higher audio quality
    C. Software that both compresses and decompresses audio and video data
    D. Music synthesizer for creating and manipulating sound

chapter *7*

Video: Recording and Manipulating Moving Images

This chapter focuses on all things video—one of the more powerful media elements used in interactive multimedia and the Web. You need to first develop an understanding of how video works before embarking on a project that requires it. The next step is planning ahead so you can budget costs, organize equipment, and create high-quality video clips. You will gain a foundation in how to capture and edit digital video, as well as learn about special imaging effects using end-user software. The chapter also covers the file formats for compressing, transferring, storing, and displaying video for different purposes.

CHAPTER OBJECTIVES

In this chapter, you will:

- Learn what video is and the tools that are needed to record or acquire it
- Discover compression schemes and file formats for saving, storing, delivering, and playing back digital video
- Get an idea of the differences between analog and digital video
- Find out about capturing, editing, and adding special effects to video for a high-quality end product

145

Video Mechanics

So what is video and how is it recorded? Video begins as a form of light, similar to photography. The lens inside a video camera captures this light, which is then converted electronically using a *charge-coupled device* (CCD), as shown in Figure 7-1. The CCD is a sensor that detects the light energy and splits it into different components of brightness and color.

A camcorder contains three distinct CCDs for processing each of the additive color primaries: red, green, and blue. For digital video, this color information is sampled, digitized, and saved in the camera's internal memory or to an external storage device. Having three CCDs is beneficial, as using multiple mechanisms to represent color improves the video resolution and image quality. However, such cameras are more costly to manufacture due to the added components. Some of the less expensive cameras have only one CCD, where all colors are recorded simultaneously. This is an alternative if the budget is tight and especially if high-end equipment is not needed.

Video in Multimedia

Video is powerful in its impact to engage and influence audiences. It is also an effective educational medium for instruction in schools and training in professional situations. However, like other multimedia components, video can be overdone and not beneficial to the audience when it is used excessively or for the wrong reasons. Poorly executed video can be detrimental to the success of a project. Proper planning and setting clear goals are crucial to having your video serve its function for the end user.

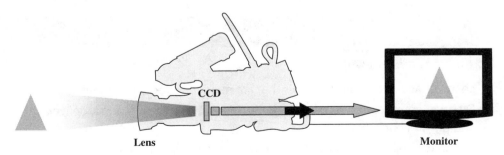

Lens   **Monitor**

FIGURE 7-1 • Mechanics of video: Light passes through a video camera lens and is converted into an electrical signal using a charge-coupled device (CCD)

Video is defined by captured motion—a recording of events—and can be obtained in a variety of ways (see Figure 7-2 for some examples). It is the live-action complement to animation and computer graphics.

TV and movies are *forms* of video; they are unique kinds of media in their own right. Segments of TV programs and movies can be copied and used as video clips for multimedia projects.

Some purposes of video are entertainment, documentaries, news, art, story-telling, teaching, training, and recording personal events. This is by no means an exhaustive list, but it includes the major categories of which there are a myriad of subcategories.

Now for a bit of video history. Starting in the 1970s, before the widespread use of digital technology, the term *video* referred to the physical medium of magnetic videotape or videocassette tape. The dominant video format was

FIGURE 7-2 • Capturing video using different cameras: a camcorder and digital video camera

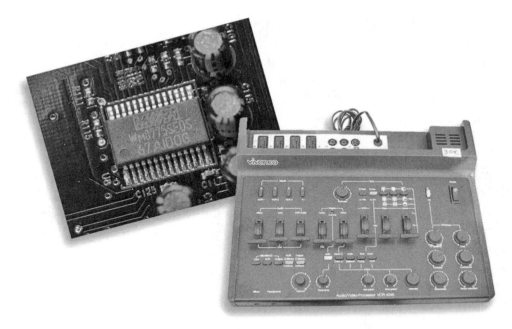

FIGURE 7-3 · Analog-to-digital video conversion equipment

Video Home System (VHS). Depending on the recording and playback device, image and sound quality varied. This type of video is referred to as *analog*, which can be converted to a digital format using an *analog-to-digital converter* (ADC) (see Figure 7-3 for an example). ADCs are discussed further in the next section. Videotapes and VHS systems for the consumer market evolved over the years until digital video devices, such as DVD players, became affordable and more widely accessible in the mid-1990s.

Analog and Digital Video

Analog video derives from a nondigital signal, and it is not recorded on a computer. Video cameras record the analog signal and either transfer or record it. This type of video can be captured live or copied from a TV signal or a film clip. It can be written onto magnetic videotape or made into a digital file by means of an ADC. Video that has been previously recorded onto tape that will end up being transferred to tape again can be edited on computer-controlled editing systems.

Today, most video is *high definition* (HD) and is taken with a digital video camera (or *camcorder*) with high pixel resolutions and quality results. Whether you are an amateur or professional, you will be working with digital components and processes in all aspects of video-making.

Figure 7-4 shows some examples of analog and digital video equipment and media.

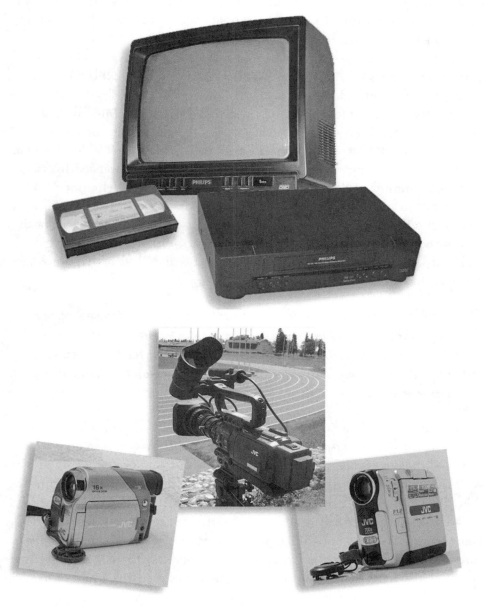

FIGURE 7-4 • Traditional analog video equipment and media (top) and digital video equipment and media (bottom)

Composite vs. Component Signals

Most consumer analog video devices send the video signal as a *composite*, where each frame is represented by fluctuating voltage signals called *analog waveforms*. Composite video, which is used for analog TV, has color, brightness, and synchronization combined into one signal. Quality is relatively low compared with separate signals as with a CCD, and reproductions of the original are typically not very good.

The standard analog TV composite signal in the U.S. is National Television Standard Code (NTSC). This has also been referred to as Never The Same Color, due to monitor discrepancies.

TVs now have ports for composite video, S-Video, and HD Multimedia Interface (HDMI) for Internet or other digital connections, so they are compatible with a number of devices and formats. The digital standard for TV, developed in the 1990s and implemented nationwide in 2009, is digital Advanced Television Systems Committee (ATSC), better known as HDTV (high definition TV).

Composite video typically uses 525 scan lines drawn every 1/30 second with an aspect ratio of 4:3. The *aspect ratio* represents the width and height of the viewing area. Figure 7-5 shows some examples of different aspect ratios, which will be discussed further in the "Display Standards and Playback Options" section later in this chapter.

TIP *For illustrations comparing different aspect ratios for TV and theater screens, go to the Turner Movie Classics web site. The links for Valentino and Lawrence of Arabia are www.tcm.com/tcmdb/title/94624/Valentino/theatrical-aspect-ratio. html and www.tcm.com/tcmdb/title/4455/Lawrence-of-Arabia/theatrical-aspect-ratio.html, respectively.*

Scan lines that draw image frames on a TV screen are completed in two passes, which are called *fields*. With *interlacing*, the first pass of scan lines is even lines and the next is odd lines. Interlacing is measured in cycles per second, of which there are 60. Progressive scans for computer displays, on the other hand, draw lines of a video frame that are 1-pixel thick. It is done in a single pass without interlacing or any resulting flicker. If a video you are working on is going to be viewed on both a digital display and a CRT or TV monitor, make sure that any lines created are at least 2 pixels thick, so there is no flickering. For titles, use fonts that are not too thin; otherwise, the strokes and serifs will most likely get lost during the scanning process.

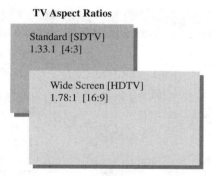

TV Aspect Ratios

Standard [SDTV]
1.33.1 [4:3]

Wide Screen [HDTV]
1.78:1 [16:9]

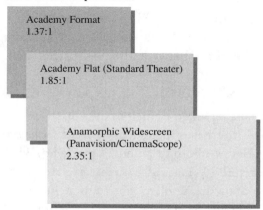

Movie Theater Aspect Ratios

Academy Format
1.37:1

Academy Flat (Standard Theater)
1.85:1

Anamorphic Widescreen
(Panavision/CinemaScope)
2.35:1

FIGURE 7-5 · Different aspect ratios for TV, computer, and movie screens

Table 7-1 lists the four different analog video standards used around the world.

Composite video has no color separation. Since it combines the RGB color channels into one signal, and is not split like *component* video, it results in the lowest quality video due to the lack of color detail.

Component video results in a higher quality than composite, as does S-Video. It splits the different components of color and luminance (brightness) into three separate signals (S-VHS, for example). Like composite video, component video still degrades somewhat when copied, but it yields a better result in general.

HDTV began with the Federal Communications Commission (FCC) in the 1980s when the digital TV standard was established. It is based on 1,125 scan lines at 60 cycles per second and a 16:9 aspect ratio. This results in a much

TABLE 7-1	Analog Video Standards for Broadcast Media Adopted by Different Countries	
Video Standard	**What It Stands For**	**Who Uses It**
NTSC	National Television Standard Code	US and Japan
PAL	Phase Alternating Line	Europe and Australia
SECAM	Sequential Color and Memory	Eastern Europe, France, and the former Soviet Union
HDTV	High–Definition Television	Universal US standard

higher image quality with considerable color accuracy. To recap, older analog TV that uses composite video has a resolution of 525 scan lines with a 3:4 aspect ratio, so the difference between the two is significant.

Analog-to-Digital Conversion

When you convert analog video to digital, the conversion device will read the scan lines and break the video into separate *data packets* (small packages of digital information, like a photo or an email message), which is similar to the process of digitizing audio. When video is converted to the computer, the vertical resolution depends on the number of horizontal lines that are present. ADCs are used to convert an analog stream to a digital one that is made up of bits/bytes representing the image frames in a video sequence. From a technical standpoint, an ADC receives a continuous signal of voltage or electrical current and transforms it into discrete binary numbers/digits.

NOTE *Analog and digital video are complex topics with many facets. There are four different analog video standards (see Table 7-1), a number of different analog videotape standards (for example, Beta, Beta SP, and VHS), and several different broadcast transmission formats (such as RGB, YUV, S-Video, VGA, HDMI, and DVI). We will only scratch the surface here, but you can find a lot of information on the Web. To begin learning more about analog and digital signals, go to Through the Wires web site, at http://library.thinkquest.org/27887/gather/fundamentals/analog_and_digital.shtml.*

Video Resolution

Video resolution is the number of scan lines that fall within a square area on a screen. The two types of resolution are horizontal and vertical. Resolution is defined by the number of scan lines within a region on a screen. There are fewer horizontal lines than vertical lines, because displays are wider than they are tall.

Analog and digital resolutions are inherently different because they use completely different storage and transmission paradigms. *Analog video resolution*, with respect to older TVs with CRTs, refers to the horizontal scan lines. Each scan line represents color and brightness measurements, similar to audio signals. The signals converted by a CCD are recorded onto magnetic tape. Higher-end equipment will create more discrete separations between color components (color information), leading to better-quality video output. Each color channel is transmitted as a separate signal using its own conductor. This is called a *component*, and each color has its own. Figure 7-6 illustrates some equipment for working with analog video.

Digital video resolution, with respect to computer displays and digital TVs, uses pixels instead of scan lines. Each pixel has a color and brightness value associated with it. This is the digital representation of an analog video signal, and there are four channels: red, green, blue, and luminance.

Digital video does not show the generational loss that you find with analog video, as its binary data stays intact and does not degrade when copies are made.

FIGURE 7-6 • Analog video equipment for editing frames from videotape

High-quality digital video is expected for TV viewing, and video professionals use it exclusively.

Digital Video Characteristics

There are distinct advantages to using digital video (DV) rather than analog:

- The quality of digital video is higher than analog video.
- It can be accessed at any time.
- It is easily and quickly stored, transported, and edited.
- It can be compressed using different file formats.

A number of desktop computers come with FireWire ports that allow for connecting to digital video cameras, and they are capable of operating digital video-editing software. Some video-editing products are easy to learn and use. In addition, flat-screen TVs (LCD and plasma) that accommodate HDTV signals have replaced traditional CRTs. The image quality has improved considerably, and the screen format is typically wider, allowing for more viewable content.

Digital video is not simply clips taken from other sources. Just like traditional tape-based video, it is live-action recordings. The technology of digital video is the output of the CCD in a video camera that is digitized (converted to a computerized format) into a sequence of individual frames.

Digital video files can be fairly large, so you will need to have ample storage. For example, one minute of high-quality uncompressed digital video takes up roughly 7GB of disk space. Video designed for multimedia projects and the Web typically needs to be shorter and have a lower resolution for sufficient downloading and streaming, so files will not surpass the size of those destined for TV. Of course, this all depends on how the video data is compressed. You will discover that compressing files to a reasonable size becomes a necessity. You will also need to prepare ahead for storage options.

NOTE *The subject of digital video is quite vast. There are dozens of different video codecs and containers, as well as several different digital video tape formats. For more information, go to http://en.wikipedia.org/wiki/Digital_video and http://en.wikipedia.org/wiki/Digital_Video_(DV).*

You may be curious about what determines the size of a digital video file, how long it takes to render and process, and what the quality will be. Primarily, the following play a role in the answers to those questions:

- **Frame rate**   The frame rate is a specified amount of time and it determines how many frames are shown at a given second. The video frame rate is 30 FPS, film is 24 FPS, and the Web is often 12 to 15 FPS.

- **Frame size**   This is the height and width of a video frame. Smaller frame sizes are faster to process since there is less data, but the quality and viewing area are reduced.

- **Color depth (resolution)**   This is the amount of colors displayed on the screen at one time. Each video frame is made up of pixels, and a color is assigned to each pixel: 8-bit = hundreds of colors, 16-bit = thousands of colors, and 24-bit = millions of colors.

Still Struggling

There are some differences between the computer and TV in terms of saving video and the viewing quality. Screen dimensions for various devices differ, and this will determine how the video is shot, edited, and saved. For instance, the widest mobile screen is 320 pixels, so video should be set no larger than 320 wide by 240 high.

Table 7-2 lists the video display standards on various digital devices.

TABLE 7-2 Video Display Standards on Digital Devices

Display	Format/Size	Aspect Ratio	Pixel Dimensions
HDTV	Standard	4:3	1,280 × 1,024
HDTV	Widescreen	16:9	1,280 × 720
Desktop computer	15 inch	4:3	800 × 600
Desktop computer	17 inch	4:3	1,024 × 768
Desktop computer	19 inch	4:3	1,280 × 1,024
Mobile devices (such as iPhone)	1.9 inch	3:2	480 × 320
Larger mobile devices (such as iPad)	9.7 inch	4:3	1,024 × 768

Shooting or Obtaining Video

The first question to ask yourself is "What is the final goal for using video?" In other words, how will the user be viewing or interacting with it? Is it for a web site, a presentation, or a DVD that will be mass-produced and distributed commercially?

Next, you will need to decide if you want to shoot video on your own, hire someone (if the budget allows), or acquire video from existing sources. These three options are discussed in the following sections to help you, regardless of the route you choose to take.

Recording Raw Footage

The process of recording video is also referred to as *capturing*. Although recording to videotape is not a common practice anymore due to the ease of capturing with digital technology, it is helpful to have a comparison to clarify the distinction between the two. When capturing video directly to tape, the analog signal superimposes long, diagonal stripes onto the surface by means of a spinning recording head. Each stripe contains information for one *field* of a single video frame, and each frame has two interlaced fields. As previously mentioned, interlacing is building a single frame from two fields, or scan passes, and this helps prevent flickering when a video is viewed.

Digital video refers to video that will be created, edited, and viewed on a computer. Digital video recordings are directly converted to data bits, and each frame is composed of pixels, so it is not interlaced like analog video. Digital video can be recorded to tape, to disk (CD or DVD), or to a hard drive.

Some essential equipment is needed for shooting video and translating it into a digital format: a camera with a tripod, a microphone, a fast computer processor, large storage capacity (hard drive or external disk), speakers, video editing software, and a nonlinear editing (NLE) system. You can choose from a number of excellent digital cameras, which vary in terms of expected ability level, features, and prices.

Digital still cameras (DSC) are intended for taking photographs and not shooting video, even though many of these cameras also have video capabilities. However, the photo quality tends to be higher than the video quality. Digital camcorders are specifically designed for video capture, but also have picture options. The quality is much better for video, but still-image output tends to be average. For broadcast-quality video—meaning video that will be presented on

TV—you need high-end equipment with adequate storage and data-processing capabilities, and software with a variety of compression options.

TIP   *A free software program for creating your own video demonstrations and screen-based tutorials is CamStudio (http://camstudio.org). This software captures video and audio directly from your computer monitor to produce streaming videos for the Web.*

A high-end, professional video setup, or editing suite, could include hardware and software for recording, importing, converting formats, copying, editing, adding special effects and graphics, and working with audio for the soundtrack and sound effects. (Figure 7-7 shows an example of a digital video-editing suite.) With an arrangement such as this, it is not just one piece of equipment that does everything, but many connected devices that provide a multipurpose and efficient work environment. Costs for such equipment can mount quickly, and so such a setup may not be financially feasible for an independent multimedia developer. A variety of reasonably priced digital video equipment is available for use with a desktop computer, as will be discussed in Chapter 9.

FIGURE 7-7 · Digital video editing suite

Video-input boards were once the hardware that needed to be installed in desktop computers in the mid-1990s, and digitizing cards were necessary to convert video to digital data. Much has changed! Many mobile devices—such as the iPhone, DROID, and BlackBerry—have built-in video-capturing capabilities that allow you to record short, small-format videos. These video files can be sent and received using the Multimedia Message Service (MMS) text message format that includes multimedia content. This configuration extends Short Message Service (SMS), which is used for standard text messaging and has a 160-character limit, without any multimedia allowances.

TIP   *The old yet accurate adage "garbage in, garbage out" applies to digitizing video, audio, and images. The end result is only as good as the original.*

Capturing Directly from TV

Transferring video clips from the TV to a computer is called *digitizing* the TV signal. Digital video recorders (DVRs) allow you set a scheduled program to make a digital copy of TV programs so they can be viewed at a later time. One of the first recording devices of this kind to hit the market was TiVo in 1999. It is still a popular brand, but there are many other options available. DVRs mainly use the MPEG4 video codec for saving and compressing video clips.

Importing Video to Computer

Importing video is similar to capturing video, and there are a few ways of going about it. One technique uses hardware in the form of a capture card that transforms a video signal into a digital one. Both analog and digital video can be imported to the computer. Importing analog video can be done from videotape by means of a videocassette recorder (VCR). A configuration using a FireWire connection from the VCR to the computer allows for the conversion of analog to digital video. FireWire provides a digital link between the camcorder and the PC, so the transfer itself is digital.

Digital files can also be moved to and from different devices, and are easily imported and exported using software that accepts video formats. Importing is a technique that involves transferring video from one source to another, so you can edit it or combine it with other digital media (adding sound effects or music, for instance), and then output or export it as a digital file. This can be done using a variety of techniques, from editing with nonlinear digital video software (such as Adobe Premier) to simply inserting the video file into a presentation (such as with Microsoft PowerPoint).

Acquiring Video Clips

When shooting new video footage is not an option due to tight budgets, time constraints, or lack of experience, you can acquire existing video clips. You can obtain video using clip media (like image and sound libraries) or from the public domain, either for free or for a fee. Older, archival footage is worth considering, as it can be cheaper to use than more current video.

Clip libraries typically provide different resolutions and sizes of royalty-free video, which you can find online or buy on CD. This means they are free or can be purchased for a fee, either for one-time use or unlimited usage. Remember that using copyrighted video requires prior permission. Procuring the rights ahead of time will spare you hassles and potential legal action from the copyright owner. (For more information about copyright laws, go to www.copyright.gov.)

Video from the public domain can be reproduced without permission, which means it can be copied freely. However, you still must do research to find out if it is actually available for use free of charge (don't assume anything). The rule of thumb is, for any works not in the public domain, request permissions.

Still Struggling

Fair-use provisions in the law allow for limited copying and distributing. Educators can use copyrighted material for teaching purposes, with some restrictions imposed. For a class project, students can use media elements created by others, but it is important to keep track of web sites where the media was found, and always credit the owner and/or source in the same manner, as a footnote or bibliography citation.

If something created with copyrighted material is then used for commercial purposes, such as selling the project or promoting yourself for the job market, or if it is placed on the Internet in any form (because anyone can copy it), then the owner needs to be contacted to grant permission or charge a usage fee. If that's not possible, it is best to use something that is not copyrighted or that is an original creation.

Display Standards and Playback Options

Display differences translate as distinct aspect ratios, which are dimensions based on ruler measurements and the number of pixels. Aspect ratio is the width-to-height ratio of a video frame, or the ratio of the length of the horizontal scan lines to the distance covered vertically. For example, the aspect ratio for feature-length movies is 2:1; for TV, it is 4:3. These ratios are used to determine sizes for enlarging or reducing videos with respect to displays for different viewing options, such as TV versus mobile devices. Figure 7-8 shows some examples of video aspect ratios.

In terms of display requirements, you have a number of options. For example, if you are working with broadcast-quality video for TV, you will need a large, single computer monitor with a TV connected for viewing the final product. If you are working with digital video exclusively (for input, output, and playback), dual monitors are needed to have the controls and timeline on one screen and the video screen on the other. Both of these scenarios assist the workflow by providing adequate displays for editing and previewing the video.

Widescreen Theater
1.85:1

Standard TV
1.33:1 [4:3]

HDTV Letterbox
1.78:1 [16:9]

Widescreen HDTV
1.78:1 [16:9]

FIGURE 7-8 • Examples of different video aspect ratios

Playback options for video are quite varied. Mobile devices, such as the iPad, allow for face-to-face video calls with two cameras, so you can talk to someone as well as switch to the video camera on the back to record live action on the spot. The videophone capability is made functional with Apple's FaceTime software.

QuickTime is Apple's proprietary software used for capturing and playing video, as well as converting and saving to different formats. It was first announced in 1991 and was instrumental in introducing video to desktop computers. QuickTime can be used as a full-fledged program to play and edit video, or simply as a free player, which can be downloaded from the Web (see Figure 7-9 for a screen capture). As discussed in Chapter 6, QuickTime is technically a *container* format or file type, which can be used to store numerous types of media, such as audio, video, MIDI, text, chapter markers, sprites, and scripting capabilities.

TV is primarily cable-fed, but Internet protocol TV is in the works (also referred to as an Internet-based television platform). This is where the TV signal will go through your Internet connection rather than your set-top cable box. Comcast, one of the largest cable companies in the United States, delivers TV programming by means of digital TV, but it is not connected to the Internet. Comcast is intent on providing live programming to its customers to make it possible to view TV on any device that has an Internet connection. Its technicians are testing this video-delivery technology at the Massachusetts Institute of Technology (MIT) and then expanding to Comcast employees, to determine its viability.

FIGURE 7-9 · QuickTime screen capture

With an Internet-ready TV and a Blu-ray player or Xbox unit, you can access the Internet simply by connecting an HDMI cable from the device to the TV. Through your TV, you can play music on Pandora, view YouTube videos, select and watch movies instantly on Netflix, download and play video games, and so on. Each of these scenarios operates the same way as if you were viewing or listening to media on your computer, where the video or audio signal is streamed through the Internet. Companies in media, cable, and technology are working out what can be shown and when it can be shown, and whether it is accompanied by commercials.

TV programs can be watched online with a desktop or laptop computer, or on a mobile device with services such as iTunes, Netflix (video streaming), and Hulu. Playback depends on the software used, whether it is viewed on its own in an individual video window or embedded within another application, and the bandwidth speed and Internet connection (Wi-Fi or 3G). Controls are similar to a DVD unit for playing, stopping, pausing, and rewinding, so the end user can take command over playback features.

Mobile handheld devices can display TV programs using ATSC—Mobile/Handheld (ATSC–M/H), a digital standard that differs slightly from that of HDTV. The following are some application software for mobile devices that allow for TV viewing by means of the Internet (requiring a Wi-Fi or 3G connection):

- Netflix is an app for watching TV shows as well as movies and documentaries.
- Hulu Plus provides streaming services, similar to Netflix.
- HBO GO is similar to other cable networks that provide a streaming service for TV programming.
- DIRECTV is an app that also lets you set your DVR remotely.
- ABC Player is an app for watching streamed TV shows.
- TV.com is a CBS app for viewing TV programs.
- SPB TV is an Android phone app for watching TV.

Editing and Manipulating Video

As with audio, video footage typically needs to be edited into a coherent narrative and to improve the overall structure. A primary feature of editing is removing frames and sequences that are either unnecessary or that extend the piece too much.

Adobe Premier and Apple Final Cut Pro are two examples of nonlinear digital video-editing software programs. At a basic level, with minimal training, you can use these programs to import footage, place transitions between scenes, layer multiple video and audio tracks, and so on.

You can enhance video with creative treatments using programs such as Adobe After Effects. This is a powerful postproduction editing program, with a fairly steep learning curve, and due to its complexity, is time-consuming to use. However, the results are impressive and worth the extra effort in the end.

Still Struggling

Software for digital video captures, edits, saves, compresses, and plays back video. You would either need to purchase end-user software or rely on built-in operating system drivers. Other video drivers can be added as the technology evolves.

Video-capture software controls the hardware used to capture the video. It also controls video-input settings (color, brightness, and so on), as well as compression schemes, frame rates, frame size, color depth, bit rate, and audio sampling. The final output is a data file of the video.

Video is essentially just image frames arranged in an order and played at rapid speeds, giving the illusion of motion. So, video editing produces finished videos in the following ways:

- Cutting, pasting, deleting, and copying individual frames
- Combining frames from different video sources
- Changing frame sizes (dimensions) or changing the frame rate
- Editing audio in conjunction with video
- Placing digital images and graphics on top of video using editing software
- Adding special effects (transitions, rotoscoping, alpha changes, transparencies, and so on)

Here are some of the more common software program options for video editing:

- **Apple iMovie**   This package has basic features and is easy to learn. It provides for multitrack audio editing. You can record or import video and music. Video, titles, photos, and sound effects can be added.

- **Adobe Premier and Apple Final Cut Pro**   These are standard professional nonlinear digital video-editing programs. Figure 7-10 shows an example of working in Final Cut Express HD.

- **Adobe After Effects**   This is postproduction software used to apply special effects and add motion graphics to video. You can merge animation, photos, graphics, and type effects with video. Figure 7-11 shows an example of working in After Effects.

- **Avid**   This is a high-end professional system with proprietary software and hardware.

- **Apple Xsan 2**   This is video postproduction software used to apply effects and add motion graphics.

- **Camera and iMovie apps**   These applications allow basic editing to videos taken by a mobile device.

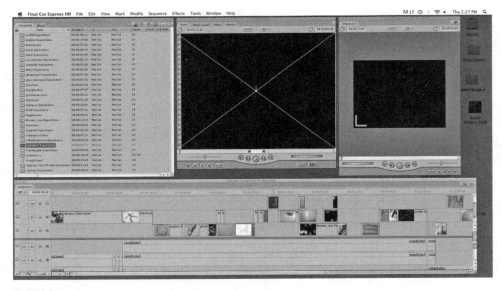

FIGURE 7-10 · Working with Apple Final Cut Express HD

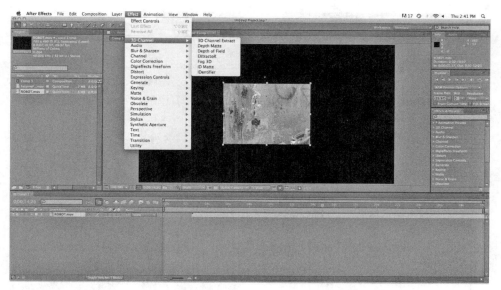

FIGURE 7-11 · Working with Adobe After Effects

Video Compression Schemes and File Formats

Video files need to be compressed for multimedia and web projects so they can be saved, stored, transferred, delivered, and played back quickly and easily. Uncompressed files are typically too large and become unmanageable.

The process of compressing files occurs in a few different ways. Typically, when a video file is being saved, there is a list of formats from which to choose, and this selection determines how much a video will be compressed. Compression methods vary, just as hardware for playback does, but the overall goal is to reduce the amount of data.

As discussed in Chapter 6, similar to audio compression/decompression schemes, video uses a *codec* for the transfer and playback of video files. A codec compresses video so you can deliver it on the Web or DVD, and then automatically uncompresses it in real time so it plays back quickly. However, video files are large, so codecs often require more time to compress than the length of the content.

Table 7-3 lists the amount of video saved by various storage devices.

Video compression uses mathematical algorithms to calculate reductions in data. Video is compressed by eliminating or grouping similar data in the video

TABLE 7-3   Storage Devices and Amount of Video Stored

Device/Media	Storage Capacity	Video Length/Duration
CD	650–900MB	1 hour
DVD single–layer	4.7GB	2 hours
DVD double–layer	8.5GB	4 hours
DVD double–sided	9.4–17GB	8 hours
Blu–ray	25GB (single–layer)	9 hours
Blu–ray	50GB (double–layer)	23 hours
100GB Blu–ray	Up to 128GB (triple–layer)	130 hours
Internal hard disk	Wide range	Varies depending on disk size
External removable drive	Wide range	Varies depending on disk size
RAID or disk array	Wide range	Varies depending on disk sizes
Online storage	Wide range	Varies depending on service

signal. Only one algorithm is used for an entire file, which determines compression for capture as well as playback. These step-by-step procedures manifest themselves in the form of compression formats.

Video File Types

File formats for video are similar to audio in that they compress data so that files will be a reasonable size for transferring and playing. The more compression used, the lower the image and sound quality, and the smaller the file. The compressed data is called a *container*. Some common formats are FLV (Flash Video), MP4 (QuickTime), WMV (Windows Media Video), RM (Real Media), and WebM. Table 7-4 describes some of the common video-compression formats.

A *compression ratio* is used when compressing video. This is the size of the uncompressed file compared with the compressed file. The more a file is compressed, the higher the ratio and the greater the difference between the two numbers. For example, 200:1 means the initial video setting is 200 times as large as the compressed file. This ratio results in lower-quality video than if the ratio were 200:50. Another way of looking at it is a 20MB file reduced to 2MB has a compression ratio of 10:1.

TABLE 7-4 Some Common Video-Compression File Formats		
Format	**Extension**	**Description**
Motion Picture Expert Group	MPEG–1–MPEG–4	Lossy format that saves and compresses for digital video; used for streaming on the Web, distribution on CD, voice (phone), and broadcast TV
MPEG–4 Advanced Video Coding	MPEG–4 AVC (same as H.264 MPEG)	Codec for video on Blu-ray player disks; HD digital video
Flash Video	FLV and F4V	Flash video formats; need to have Flash Player to view
QuickTime	MOV	Apple's file format, which provides multiple tracks of media data
Windows Media Video	WMV	Proprietary video codec
Audio Video Interleaved	AVI	Microsoft's video container format for Windows video
3rd Generation Partnership Project	3GPP	Multimedia container format for mobile devices

As with still images and audio, compression for video can be *lossy* or *lossless*. Lossy compression is the loss of quality between the original and the compressed video, once it is decompressed for playback. Some quality is lost regardless of the method used, but lossy compression files are smaller than those created with lossless methods. During the lossy compression process, a video frame (*keyframe*) is compared with the one before and the one that follows, and the compressor assesses the image to determine whether there are similar attributes of both. If they are similar, the frame is deleted. If not, it becomes the keyframe. The frames in between are reconstructed frames based on similarities between keyframes.

Lossless compression, on the other hand, means there is little or no degradation of quality in the final video file. The file is reduced in size, but the original data is left intact. Lossless formats compress data within a single frame rather than between frames, as with lossy compression.

Remember that the more compression used, the longer it takes to process the file for compressing and decompressing. Try to use the most up-to-date codecs in your multimedia projects, but bear in mind that they may not work on all computers. Common codecs (see Table 7-4) can be selected from the saving options in most video software programs, as shown in the example in Figure 7-12.

Video *bit rate* has to do with the number of kilobits played per second, which is dependent on the bandwidth of the playback system. Bit rate settings are also based on a computer's processing speed and available memory, so that adequate amounts of data can be processed in a limited period of time. The bit rate ultimately affects how a streaming video plays on the Internet and a local area network (LAN).

You can set up video for the Web with Flash Player or with HTML5, which uses the <video> tag to embed video in web pages. Three formats are supported by most web browsers: Ogg, MPEG4, and WebM. Since not all formats are viewable in all browsers, it is a good idea to save video in all three formats, along with including controls and the frame dimensions. The HTML code looks like this:

```
<video width="320" height="240" controls="controls">
  <source src="movie.ogg" type="video/ogg" />
  <source src="movie.mp4" type="video/mp4" />
  <source src="movie.webm" type="video/webm" />
</video>
```

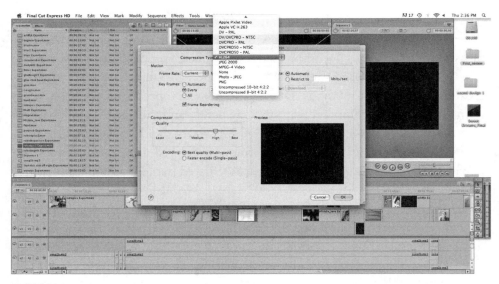

FIGURE 7-12 • Different compression formats in Final Cut's save file dialog box

Storage and Memory

Video files need to be stored for backup purposes so you won't lose all that precious footage, and so that you can access them later when you are working on projects. You can store large video files using an external hard drive, computer network storage, or an online storage server (also called *cloud computing* or *cloud storage*).

One major advantage of using online storage is that you can access files from any computer that has an Internet connection. Google Docs is a popular low-cost option for creating and storing spreadsheets, word processing documents, and presentation files to retrieve later or share. Apple's iCloud is in development for online storage for all data files (e-books, photos, music, and video). Some free or reasonably priced storage providers are Dropbox, Mozy, and Box.net.

CAUTION *A word of caution when using online storage: Uploading to an Internet server makes your personal and professional information available online, which can be accessed or distributed if it falls into the wrong hands. It is best to go with a reputable company with security provisions built into their services to safeguard your data. Look for providers that use protection, such as encrypted file transfer, and have safety measures in place to protect passwords and privacy. If online storage is not your cup of tea, as it leaves open the possibility of loss or theft, consider synchronizing multiple hard drives with regular file backups.*

Using Video in Multimedia Projects

As with the other multimedia components, it's extremely important to consider how video will be used in your multimedia or web project. Will it be an online video embedded within a page or linked to another web page, part of a stand-alone kiosk, video on demand, live feed, real-time streaming, or buffered?

Video can be used for purposes such as education/training, entertainment (movies, TV, art films, and musical performances), speeches, conference presentations, recordings of historical events, and advertising. Video can be a component of a multimedia project or the primary element.

Video games are another significant aspect of interactive multimedia, as they are widely used for entertainment purposes. Referring to them as "video" games is a bit of a misnomer, since they are mostly animated with computer-generated characters and rendered scenes. They are still referred to by this term due to the original association with moving graphics on a screen that the player interacted with by pushing buttons or manipulating a controller.

Some of the more popular and impressive home console systems are Xbox 360, Sony PlayStation, and Wii. Handheld devices such as Nintendo DS have products with Internet and 3D options. There are many online multiplayer role-playing games, as well as single games for individual use on a desktop computer. Regardless of the kind of video game or system, they all require a video display or screen of some sort to play. With HD display quality, the graphics are so realistic that they appear to be video, even though they are created with 3D computer graphics and animation.

The following are some ways that video can be viewed:

- Internet (videos need to be uploaded to a server first; when a link is clicked, the video will either stream directly off the Web or buffer while downloading to RAM)
- Camera connected to display such as a computer or TV
- Directly on a recording device (camcorder)
- Mobile devices and cell phones
- Desktop computers (view on the Web or download to the hard drive to view using QuickTime or Media Player)
- TV using Netflix or OnDemand
- Online video-access services, such as YouTube, Hulu, and Netflix

Summary

In this chapter, you learned what video is, the different kinds of video, the distinction between analog and digital video, and the standard signals for broadcasting on TV and the Web. You now have a basic understanding of video recording and editing, file compression, and the various formats in which to save digital video. You know about transferring and storing video for use in multimedia and web projects so it will play back quickly without sacrificing quality.

QUIZ

1. **What is a compression ratio?**
   A. The size of the uncompressed file compared with the compressed file
   B. A mathematical algorithm used to calculate reductions in data
   C. The width and height of the viewing area
   D. The number of pixels in a video frame

2. **What does DVD stand for?**
   A. Digital Versatile Disc
   B. Digital Video Device
   C. Digital Video Disc
   D. Digital Virtual Disc

3. **Analog video is composite. What does that mean it has?**
   A. A larger composition or frame than digital video
   B. Three different signals for red, green, and blue
   C. High-quality output similar to component video
   D. Color, brightness, and synchronization combined into one signal

4. **What is *not* a viable option for storing large quantities of video?**
   A. CD
   B. DVD
   C. Blu-ray
   D. RAID

5. **Which file format is most commonly used for video compression?**
   A. 3GPP
   B. AVI
   C. FLV
   D. MPEG

6. **What is a codec?**
   A. Compression scheme for video files
   B. Container
   C. Coder/decoder method used for saving video files
   D. Compression ratio

7. **What does lossy compression mean?**
   A. Loss of quality between the original and the compressed video
   B. Files reduced in size
   C. Video files that can be transferred and stored more easily
   D. All of the above

8. **What is cloud computing another term for?**
   A. Server providing online data storage
   B. Viewing streamed video on the Web
   C. Video used in an interactive multimedia project
   D. External storage device

9. **What is the digital standard for TV in the United States?**
   A. PAL
   B. HDTV
   C. NTSC
   D. SECAM

10. **What is the aspect ratio for widescreen HDTV?**
    A. 3:2
    B. 2:1
    C. 16:9
    D. 4:3

chapter 8

Authoring for Multimedia Functionality

This chapter covers the inner workings of multimedia projects and web sites. In order for interactivity to take effect, programming must happen. There are a number of different approaches and methods to creating the functionality for multimedia, and this chapter will give you a clear picture of what is involved. You will also learn about designing the user interface and what kinds of rules to follow for successful results.

CHAPTER OBJECTIVES

In this chapter, you will:

- Discover what it means to add functionality to multimedia
- See what it takes to create an effective, well-organized, logical, and aesthetically pleasing interface design
- Learn about programming languages and HTML
- Find out about software tools for creating web pages and authoring multimedia

Programming and Scripting to Create Interactive Environments

Once the media elements are selected and tweaked, the text is fleshed out, and the animation, video, and audio are complete, it is time to bring everything together to make it work as a unified multimedia piece. The process of integrating these interface elements is one of the last stages in the production of a functioning interactive program. Then you choose an authoring tool and employ it to make the program fully functional and work out any kinks. This phase in the development process provides the framework for the end product. It is this fundamental structure that allows everything to coexist and work together in unison.

What does *authoring* mean? It sounds as though it has to do with writing a book, but in terms of multimedia, it is the *programming* side of the development process. The person who writes the code to make a multimedia project interactive is the *author*. Authoring is what provides multimedia with its interactive functionality. It allows users to click screen elements and move through the program.

Multimedia development is not dissimilar from designing a newsletter or creating a sculpture out of clay. You follow a required procedure that leads to an end result. The step-by-step process is akin to baking a cake: Begin with the recipe, gather the ingredients, prepare them in the correct order and manner, combine them, cook the food, test for doneness, and enjoy.

Multimedia authors, also referred to as *developers*, are those who program multimedia projects so that they work. Authoring pulls together all the multimedia elements and makes them interactive. Authors incorporate various media types for a harmonious and well-orchestrated final product.

Authoring tools can assist in the creation and editing of a product, as well as in the preparation of it for delivery. Such tools are also referred to as *authoring* programs. The kind of programming needed depends on a variety of factors.

Tools for Authoring

Authoring tools are software programs that help you to write the code that provides functionality to an interactive program. Authoring tools typically have dual purposes: They allow for creating and editing the interactive program, and they also serve as a delivery device for the end result.

At a base level, graphics and presentation software and word processors can serve as simple tools to create and program multimedia projects. At the next level are programming tools that are equipped with graphic, text, and animation-creation capabilities, such as Adobe Dreamweaver and Flash. Even more complicated authoring tools provide developers with extensive control over the coding of interactive features, using programming languages such as Visual Basic and Java. End-user authoring programs are typically easier to learn and use than most programming tools, since they facilitate the process by not requiring in-depth technical knowledge.

Authoring software assists in the development of a multimedia production by coordinating media types. These tools allow you to implement significant control over the interactive environment. The more basic authoring tools, such as Microsoft Word, offer simple, easy-to-use techniques for HTML web page development. Adobe design software—such as Illustrator, Photoshop, and InDesign—have built-in features for converting layouts to web pages. A more advanced industry-standard option is Adobe Dreamweaver, which allows for web page design as well as HTML editing and JavaScript imports.

Other programs offer multimedia capabilities that can be organized by the creator. For example, with Microsoft PowerPoint, photos, graphics, and text can be imported, and videos can be embedded into the presentation. Animation and transition features allow for movement, and the program comes installed with numerous preset background templates and color options. You can open other files and software applications from within PowerPoint, and insert web links as well.

NOTE *One of the more high-level authoring programs for dynamic web sites is Adobe Flash, which uses ActionScript as a scripting language for multimedia. This is industry-standard software and worth learning, but it requires time and instruction to get up to speed with it. However, some premade scripts that reduce the time involved considerably are available from the Web. Actions can be placed in the timeline or applied directly to a button or graphic on screen. With ActionScript 3.0, scripts that control the entire project are placed in a* **movie clip,** *to consolidate them and allow for seamless edits and updates.*

An alternative to an authoring tool is a programming or scripting language. This approach provides more options for authoring multimedia applications. For example, Visual Basic and C++ are general-purpose programming languages that allow for a good amount of control and flexibility in interactive environments. They are well suited to video games because the level of coding assists the processing and executing of commands. They are more powerful in that they can be programmed for a wider range of functionality than an authoring tool, but they are also more complex and typically take longer to develop the same functionality.

Tool Selection Considerations

How do you select the appropriate authoring tool to use? The primary determinant is the function of the product. In other words, how will it work and how will users interact with it? The following are some crucial factors that come into play when choosing an authoring tool for a multimedia product:

- Location/environment
- Hardware (platform)
- Software (operating system)
- Web browser
- Media content
- Functional goals
- Interface
- Maintenance plan
- Budget
- Timeline/schedule
- Skill set of the team

These will determine what needs to be done to get everything up and running.

The hardware for user interactivity is also an important factor to consider, as it will affect the interface design as well as the programming. For instance, will the program be used on a touchscreen, or will the user be interacting with the screen with mouse clicks? Costs can quickly mount when making technological purchases for the final end product, so the hardware must be carefully planned and budgeted.

You also need to take into account which versions and kinds of operating systems and web browsers will be used. Most users are familiar with a few common browsers, such as Microsoft's Internet Explorer, Apple's Safari, and Mozilla's Firefox. Browsers can store web pages as *bookmarks* or *favorites*, so they are easily accessible at a later date. They keep a history to track Internet usage, and these pages are *cached*, or stored for quick retrieval. Browsers can also customize home pages such as iGoogle or myYahoo! for easy access to preferred web sites.

Still Struggling

The eventual purpose and functional goals of the multimedia program or web site will dictate how the *user interface* is designed. The interface has to do with what the user will interact with on screen, such as buttons, menus, audio controls, images, links, input boxes, etc. If the potential audience is not known or if it is designed for the general public, it should be simple enough to use so it is accessible to a wide range of people of varying levels of ability.

The project may also require platform-centric or device-specific programming. For instance, a game system such as Sony PlayStation requires high-level programming, since speed is crucial. With multiplayer games that involve fast action, the animation sequences and responses to interactive commands must happen quickly, so the experience runs smoothly and meets the expectations of the user. Video games have a variety of uses, and they can be intended for individual consoles, online use, or desktop computer applications. They need to be designed and programmed with specific system requirements in mind so that they function properly.

Bandwidth for Web Projects

Programs and games that are designed for use on the Web rely heavily on bandwidth speeds for acceptable performance. *Bandwidth* is the amount of data that a device can transmit or receive over time. It determines the rate at which information is transmitted via the Web, and it is dependent on the type and size of data files. Text files tend to be small and are quick to transfer. Video files are large and can be slow to transfer, depending on the user's bandwidth capabilities.

Bandwidth speed is measured in kilobits or megabits. For instance, *Kbps* is kilobits per second, and *Mbps* is megabits per second. Bits refer to transfer of data; bytes have to do with data storage. Table 8-1 lists bandwidth speeds for different Internet connection devices. The information in this table is based on the charts at http://intouch-2000.net/seniornet/bandwidth_chart.html and http://support.summersault.com/bandwidth_chart.html.

TABLE 8-1 Bandwidth Speeds (Bit Rates)

Device	Description	Average Data-Transfer Speed
56K modem	Dial-up using a regular/standard phone line	40–56 Kbps
ISDN	Stands for Integrated Services Dedicated Network; dedicated phone line with router	64 Kbps–128 Kbps
Cable/Ethernet	Coaxial cable	1.5–20 Mbps
DSL	Stands for Digital Subscriber Line; delivered through the regular phone line	128 Kbps–8 Mbps
Satellite	Signal is transmitted over airwaves	6+ Mbps
Wireless	Connects to a high-speed cellular communications system to transmit and receive signals	30+ Mbps

Web Authoring with HTML

The way pages and multimedia elements are linked on the Internet depends on the type of authoring. The Web was originally designed to provide hypertext capabilities for sharing and accessing information. We are able to access this information using a URL, or web address. The transfer of web documents is accomplished by the Hypertext Transfer Protocol (HTTP).

HTTP is the conduit by which information is exchanged between computers, primarily the client and server. The *client* is the user who makes a request, by typing a URL in an address field or a keyword in a search engine field, to access a document or web page from a server. The *server* is the computer that houses the document that sends the information to the client in response to the request. The same holds true for linked pages—when the user (or client) clicks an active link on a web page, the browser will retrieve and display the page within the same window, or in a new window on top of the original one.

Hypertext Markup Language (HTML), introduced in 1990, is a markup language for web page development. HTML defines web page content, and it allows us to see and interact with what is on the page. It was intended to be used to *mark up* text on a web page in order to specify headlines, subheadings, and paragraphs in terms of the font, size, placement, and treatment (underline, italics, lists, indents, and so on). The underpinnings of all web pages are essentially documents written with HTML. These use an encoding scheme that combines text, graphics, animation, and links to other HTML documents and external files.

HTML is limited in terms of web design, so additional scripts such as JavaScript add interactive functionality that is not available with HTML alone. The following are some expanded versions of HTML that provide further interactive and multimedia capabilities:

- Dynamic HTML (DHTML) is used for interactive and animated web sites. It combines HTML, JavaScript, and CSS to liven up static HTML pages.
- Extensible Markup Language (XML) is similar to HTML, but it allows you to define your own web page elements in a creative manner. XML is more flexible than HTML, making it preferable when organizing large amounts of data.
- HTML4 has been updated to HTML5 for added functionality.

HTML Tags

HTML is made up of *tags*, which tell the web browser how to present the document. These tags are brackets that contain words, phrases, and numbers.

The first tag on any web page starts with `<html>` and ends with `</html>`. The / indicates the end of tagged information. The brackets are like slices of bread in a sandwich; you need one at each end to hold it together. What is in between the `<html>` and `</html>` tags is the meat of the web page. For instance, the following shows a web page with a heading (`h1`) and an unordered bulleted list (`ul`):

```
<html>
<body>
<h1> Multimedia Demystified Features</h1>
<ul>
<li> Comprehensive and detailed overview of basic multimedia
concepts </li>
<li> Tools, tips, and techniques for learning how to use
different kinds of digital media </li>
<li> Technical information on hardware and software </li>
</ul>
</body>
</html>
```

TIP *The HTML tags are fairly simple to learn and use, but they are limited in the control they give you over the appearance of the page. For an HTML tutorial and a list of common tags, visit www.w3schools.com/html/default.asp.*

As of this writing, HTML5 is the most current version of the HTML standard for web page structure. It was developed in response to the need for combining

HTML and XHTML. Developers have been picking up steam with this version for use with mobile devices, primarily to allow for transferring and viewing video. HTML5 opens up greater possibilities for playing synchronized/simultaneous video, drag-and-drop capabilities, canvas-drawing elements, geolocation, and more. In HTML5, changes have been made to basic tags—such as `header`, `nav`, `article`, `section`, and `footer`—as well as to multimedia tags, providing more support for embedded media elements.

The number of tags in an HTML document can get extensive and also include embedded or linked scripts, such as Javascript and Flash SWF files, for greater functionality. However, HTML5 is a drawback for Adobe, as it is replacing Flash ActionScript as the standard programming used for viewing videos and interacting with dynamic web sites. Flash is not fully supported by Apple, and the iPhone and other handheld devices cannot view and interact with Flash-based sites as intended. The question remains as to whether different browsers for computers, phones, and handheld devices will perform properly since HTML5 and Flash function differently.

Still Struggling

To get an idea of what makes up authoring for the Web, it is important to understand the distinction between the following: web pages that are based on HTML, Flash content that is embedded in a web page and played by means of a plug-in, and compiled executables (generally compiled Objective C, and now Flash compiled to bytecode).

The following are examples of HTML4 and HTML5 pages, which are also illustrated in Figure 8-1. The first is HTML4 with `div` tags:

```
<body>
  <div id="header">...</div>
  <div id="nav">...</div>
  <div class="article">
    <div class="section">
      ...
    </div>
  </div>
  <div id="sidebar">...</div>
  <div id="footer">...</div>
</body>
```

The next example is HTML5 with new elements identifying common constructs:

```
<body>
  <header>...</header>
  <nav>...</nav>
  <article>
    <section>
      ...
    </section>
  </article>
  <aside>...</aside>
  <footer>...</footer>
</body>
```

HTML4 Example

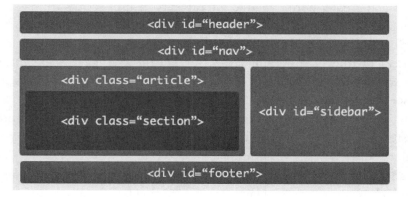

HTML5 Example

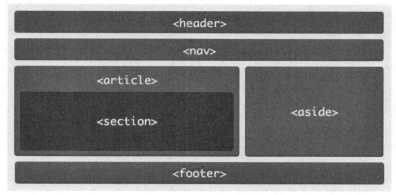

FIGURE 8-1 • How HTML5 differs from HTML4

HTML5 is currently considered a draft, although it was first introduced in 2004. While some web developers have embraced the latest version, not all browsers (especially older versions) support HTML5. As a result, many developers have steered clear of HTML5, waiting for it to become more widely accessible. (For more information about the differences between HTML4 and HTML5, visit www.w3.org/TR/html5-diff/.)

TIP *A number of web sites offer free HTML browser tests or downloadable tools so you can check how your browser is performing. Try The HTML5 Test site at http:// html5test.com/ to see if your web browser is HTML5-ready.*

JavaScript Programming

JavaScript is a *scripting language* used in many web designs to enhance user interfaces and create more dynamic interactivity. It uses scripts to make a web site more functional.

Most web browsers are *JavaScript-enabled*, which means that you can view and interact with web sites using JavaScript. The browser may also be *JavaScript-ready*, which means that JavaScript needs to be enabled by the user with the browser's preference settings.

Many scripts are already written and available to use for free. This code can be pasted into the tags of an HTML document and will then become embedded in it.

JavaScript is not the same thing as HTML, which is a markup language, or Java, which is a programming language. A scripting language is geared toward a specific purpose (such as manipulating the elements and interactions of a web page), so it is not as widely useful as a general-purpose programming language. Scripting languages are simpler and less robust than programming languages. JavaScript is known as a *client-side scripting language* because the user's web browser takes care of the loading and performance of the embedded script.

Like HTML, JavaScript uses beginning and ending brackets. The following is an example of what a basic script with a text message looks like:

```
<script>
 document.write("<h1>Hi there!</h1>");
</script>
```

In this example, the user types a URL (web address) and the browser locates the page and opens it. Some JavaScript will load immediately, if that is the way it is programmed; other scripts will specify user interaction to make something happen.

Web Page Formatting with CSS

As mentioned in Chapter 4, Cascading Style Sheets (CSS) is a technique used to format page layout and text. Before style sheets became more common, HTML was the standard method of formatting web pages. Typically, tables and frames were used. These became cumbersome, and they did not always appear the way they were intended between browsers.

The CSS styles are technical specifications that allow web designers greater control over the appearance of text. You can assign exact parameters to type—such as style, size, font, color, and spacing—which can be applied to the entire web site. Figure 8-2 shows an example of using CSS.

HTML specifies the content and structure of the data or information of a web site. CSS provides the visual presentation of the page layout. Style sheets are external files attached to the HTML document in order to specify and control the visual and text elements for the overall *style* of the page. CSS changes the appearance of HTML and XML elements by assigning styles to them.

Not only does CSS assist the design process for the web designer, but it also benefits the user, in that pages with CSS attributes load faster due to their greater efficiency. The number and size of images dictate the amount of time it

```
1  /* GENERAL STYLES
2     *------------------------------*/
3  html, body, form, fieldset, img, img a {
4      margin: 0;
5      padding: 0;
6      border: 0;
7  }
8  body {
9      color: #414141;
10     background: url(../images/bg.jpg) repeat-x #ebe8df;
11     font-family: Arial, Helvetica, sans-serif;
12     line-height: 120%;
13     font-size: 12px;
14 }
15
16 a:link, a:visited {
17     color: #685966;
18     text-decoration: underline;
19 }
20 a:hover {
21     color: #2b212c;
22 }
23 .article_separator {
24     line-height: 5px;
25     height: 5px;
26     font-size: 5px;
27 }
28 /* SITE WIDTH
29    *------------------------------*/
30 .rht_container {
31     width: 1020px;
32     margin: 0 auto;
33     margin-top: 25px;
```

FIGURE 8-2 · CSS example

takes for a web page to load. The first time someone opens a web page with CSS, the images and style sheet load simultaneously. When the user requests other pages associated with the web site, the HTML file (which is just text) is all that needs to load, because everything else is cached or stored in the computer's memory. This speeds up the process, since each page does not need to download images multiple times.

CSS also separates the actual information in a web page from the visual presentation of that information. This has important implications in how the information is stored, generated, indexed, and searched. So, CSS can also be a critical aspect in managing and administering large web sites.

 Still Struggling

Styles are saved as external files with the extension .css, so you can easily open, edit, and save the styles of a web page. It is faster to update web sites that use CSS because you need to change only the style sheet, and that change will be applied to all of the web site pages. Without styles, each page would need to be updated individually, which is very time-consuming.

CSS complies with web standards, which provides for consistency between web browsers. "What are web standards," you may ask?

Web Standards and Guidelines

There are specific technical guidelines that need to be followed when designing for multimedia and the Web. Web standards are set by the World Wide Web Consortium (W3C), which is an organization that originated with Tim Berners-Lee in 1994. Groups were formed from major companies and universities to assess how the Web operated and which applications would be used for the Web. They accepted and examined recommendations so that the Web would be widely accessible.

The W3C has established an Open Web Platform (OWP) for application development. A number of companies have joined the consortium to partake in the effort, as they see the potential for widespread interactive media. Dr. Jeff Jaffe, the CEO of W3C, said the following about the Open Web Platform (from the press release announcing the platform, at www.w3.org/2011/05/membership-pr.html):

"W3C's Open Web Platform is emerging as the platform of choice for the delivery of services and the development of rich applications across a broader set of industries, including mobile, television, publishing, and advertising. The immediate impact of new Web standards will result in more innovation, more powerful Web-based products and services, and economic opportunities for businesses and consumers alike."

TIP *Go to the W3C web site (www.w3.org) to learn about compliance standards and how to implement them. The site also offers free tools to detect noncompliant use, such as the CSS Validator, which can be found at www.w3.org/QA/Tools/.*

Another consideration is content accessibility. We assume that what is created for the Web and how we use it is generally acceptable for a wide range of users. However, those who have vision and hearing impairments and other physical limitations will not be able to view, listen to, or interact with images, text, menus, audio, buttons, and video. The W3C provides guidelines for web content accessibility for those with disabilities, at www.w3.org/TR/WCAG20/. It is important for web site designers, authors, and programmers to adhere to the guidelines, which allow multimedia content to be more accessible to a wider audience.

Interactive Design

Effective interface design requires research, planning, organization, and testing. This process saves time and money in the long run. Design considerations include the following:

- Screen layout
- Font selection
- Type treatment
- Consistency between pages associated with the same web site
- Multiple categories and subcategories
- Navigation
- User interface
- Color
- Moving images
- Backgrounds (such as photos, patterns, illustrations, and animation)

"Form follows function" is a common expression that was coined by architect Louis Sullivan, who was Frank Lloyd Wright's mentor. This is a valuable lesson to adhere to when designing anything—from houses to appliances to cars to multimedia.

In essence, the saying translates as the way something works is more important than how it looks. The final design should come after carefully planning the functionality. The initial appearance may be very appealing and attract users, but if it doesn't lead them where they want to go—if it is confusing, has bugs, or just plain doesn't work—they will walk away and not return. Designing with functionality in mind *just makes sense*.

The following are some important considerations before beginning the design of any interactive program:

- Theme, concept, and underlying idea that runs throughout the project
- Selection and use of graphics, illustrations, and photos

FIGURE 8-3 · Good design: what works for screen layout

- Layout of the screens: placement of headings, subheadings, graphics, photos, text blocks, and images
- What will be emphasized or dominate
- The way elements will be treated
- Choice of color scheme and the correlation of colors with the concept/theme
- Selection of the typeface(s) and how the type will be arranged, or treated

Figure 8-3 and Figure 8-4 show examples of both good and bad screen design for web sites.

Designing multimedia for small screens, such as iPods or smart phones (also called *mobile technology*), requires using small file sizes, as well as reduced dimensions (height and width). Yet, the design must have enough detail to maintain interest and relate the elements visually. These small interfaces need to accommodate touchscreens and scroll bars. This is a challenge for the designer who is familiar with standard computer display dimensions. It is never an easy task to create designs in miniature and have them appear properly on numerous types of devices that are manufactured by different companies.

FIGURE 8-4 · Bad design: what to avoid for screen layout

Existing web sites need to be converted so that they can be readable on both large and small size displays. Conversion typically results in removing visual elements to optimize the existing screen space and download speed. There can be delays, distortions, and font discrepancies that can render a web site unusable, leading to reduced traffic to the site. The organization of information and the interface elements become paramount as the *screen real estate* (the amount of space on the screen) is minimized; more must fit in a smaller area and still communicate clearly and be functional. Some web sites offer services called *mobile simulators*, which allow you to view your web site in a mobile device format. Figure 8-5 shows examples of different mobile screen sizes.

Graphical User Interfaces

User-interface designers craft the experience a person will have with a multimedia program or web site. This involves page/screen layout of all elements, including the following:

- Appearance, treatment (static, animated, or rollovers), and placement of navigational elements, and/or hot spots, and/or links (text, images, buttons, or a combination)
- Menus and/or lists
- Text fields
- Images and graphics

FIGURE 8-5 · Comparison of different mobile screen dimensions

If an interface is designed effectively, it is seamless and effortless to use; it is functionally intuitive.

In the early days of multimedia in the mid-to-late 1980s, the programmers who wrote the code also designed the user interfaces. Software engineers used the programs, so they were designed in a way that was logical to them, but, unfortunately, not to the average person who would be using it. The user interface at this time was not as important as the functionality.

As access to software grew, as a result of the increased popularity of the desktop computer, the necessity for *user-centered design* became greater. In other words, the needs of the user had to be considered. However, the appearance and the way the user would interact needed to be intertwined. This was a difficult task when designers' skills were rooted in graphic design for print; they needed to learn the ins and outs of interactive design. The programmers then needed to learn about visual design so that they could work with the graphic designers.

Today, the responsibilities of designing and programming often rest on the shoulders of one person. This is due to the accessibility of software for web design and multimedia that allows for both designing the interface and programming the code. Two programs that allow for creation and authoring are Adobe Flash and Dreamweaver. These provide web site design capabilities as well as access to HTML, which is commonly known as an HTML editor. Dreamweaver uses *round-trip HTML*, which means that changes made to the design and layout will automatically be updated in the underlying code and vice versa. Graphics software, such as Adobe Illustrator and Photoshop, allow for the preparation of graphics and text elements, as well as the design and layout of web pages.

While Flash and Dreamweaver allow designers to create virtually any kind of interface, other tools—such as Adobe Flex and Runtime Revolution—include a predesigned palette of interface elements, in addition to buttons, sliders, and other controls. These elements are designed to comply with user-interface guidelines regarding how buttons should look and behave. They also have built-in functions that enable them to slide and scale as the user resizes the interface. Unless you are developing a program that is meant to creatively challenge design expectations, you are well advised to stick to these standard interface elements.

You can take many different approaches to designing for a multimedia program or web site, and some methods are clearly better than others.

The following sections outline some user-interface design approaches, with suggestions of what to include and what to avoid.

Screen Layout

- Place navigational items in accessible and obvious locations (left, top, or somewhere nearby). These items should remain consistent from screen to screen.
- The title of the program or company name should be prominent in terms of color and size, but the placement and size on each page can vary.
- When you place text on top of photographs or illustrations, make sure the text is readable. Create a semitransparent box over part of the underlying image so that text is more readable. Alternatively, fade out, blur, and/or desaturate underlying images.
- Make sure screens are not cluttered to the point of having no focal point—no place for the eye to rest (negative space) or no visual interest.
- Balance screens so the elements that need emphasis to attract the user's attention are set apart from other less important parts (like decorative elements).

Color

- Use colors that are harmonious with one another.
- Create a balance between strong and soft hues and color contrasts.
- Don't overuse color so that the main information gets lost; use it selectively.
- Use contrast, especially with text. Make sure the text color stands out against backgrounds so it is readable.
- The color scheme should relate to and reflect the general theme or concept. For example, tie text color in with colors in photographs/illustrations so there is consistency.
- Be aware of cultural norms regarding color and meaning, as well as physical limitations to viewing color, such as color-blindness.

Images

- Images and graphics should be large enough to be clear, smooth-edged, and detailed, but not so large that they overpower other elements on the screen and download slowly.
- As with text, keep images relevant to the topic and consistent with the rest of the pages/screens.

- Allow enough negative space between images and text, and avoid crowding the screen.
- If photographs or illustrations are used, select them carefully. They should be appropriate for the subject matter. Make sure they do not create ambiguity or weaken the design concept.
- Keep a record of where images were found by saving web site addresses. This will help if you need them again later and if you need to obtain permission from the owner.

Text

- Keep descriptive text brief (one or two short paragraphs), if used at all.
- Limit the number of top-level menu items or categories to six or less to keep choices focused and simple. You could provide subcategories using drop-down menus.
- Make sure the message being communicated is easily understood.
- Keep text uniform throughout and maintain consistency with placement and treatment from page to page or screen to screen.
- Sans serif fonts are preferable to serif fonts for screen readability.
- Alignment for body text should be left-justified, unless there is a need to center it. Don't use right-justified, as page resizing could cut off the text.
- Use pop-ups, tooltips, and callouts to organize and present information.

Typography

- Use one or two fonts so that the design is clean and the readability is not compromised. One font should be simple and readable (for body text or text blocks), and the other font can be more expressive/decorative (for headings or titles).
- Choose fonts, styles, and sizes that are legible on the screen.
- Type for body text should be no larger than 12 points and no smaller than 10 points (depending on the font chosen and the subject matter/audience). Less than 10 points is too hard to read; more than 12 points takes up too much screen space.
- Type for categories/navigational items should be no larger than 11 or 12 points. It can even be 9 or 10 points, if accompanied by an icon or a picture.

- Type size for headings/titles can vary depending on font choice, placement, and color choice.
- Make sure type is anti-aliased, readable, and appropriate for the subject matter.

Video and Animation

- Video or animation can be used for entertainment or to capture attention, but keep it nonobtrusive and informative.
- Use it for explanation of concepts and to draw viewers in.
- Do not randomly place animations or video for effect only.
- Consider size, duration, and amount when including video and/or animation.

Links

- They should look like a *link*, and not just text or an image. (Just as an image or graphic should not look like a link or button if it isn't one.)
- Make sure links are relevant to the content.

Navigational Items (Buttons and Menus)

- Navigation should not be too large or confusing.
- Navigational items should be organized and categorized logically.
- Make sure it is clear what the navigational items are and where they will take you.
- When using icons for navigational items, make sure they are simple and clear, and that text accompanies them (even as a rollover effect), so their meaning does not confuse users.

General Guidelines for Design

- Keep compositions balanced and unified by utilizing the *principles of design*.
- Establish a hierarchy of design elements (largest and/or what is noticed first should be the most important).
- Make cohesive and comprehensive screen designs that immediately reflect the subject matter of the program.
- Don't make users guess what they should do next or how to make choices (unless exploration and searching are part of the concept of the program, such as with games).

Screen Layout and Arrangement of Elements

Navigating around a multimedia program or web site can be easy, clear, and enjoyable (designed well) or difficult, confusing, and frustrating (designed poorly). The goal of any multimedia designer is to create an interactive environment that facilitates the *way-finding* process. This all starts with careful organization of the material/content.

Navigation takes many forms, with interface elements such as menus, buttons, images, animation, and type. Navigation can be nested within other primary elements, or it can be spread out so all choices are available at once. The former is preferable, as it conserves precious screen real estate, generally makes it easier for users to find information, and is faster overall.

Applying another CSS style or template can easily change the graphics and overall layout associated with an HTML document. The content of a web site will remain unchanged, but it can readily sport a new look. Free web templates are available online if you are low on time or lack the creativity. The style or theme used for the interface are predicated on the primary message that needs to be communicated. For example, the presentation can take on a serious tone if it is for a medical facility, or a more playful feel if it is an art center for children.

As a multimedia designer, you need to understand that there are numerous browsers operating on several different computer platforms and hardware configurations, with different sets of installed plug-ins. When designing multimedia for the Web, it is especially important to test how your design is rendered on various configurations. While you will never be able to test for every anomaly, you should be able to check on the most commonly used browsers, platforms, and screen sizes.

Summary

In this chapter, we focused on how to make multimedia function, using terms such as *coding, programming,* and *authoring.* We covered authoring tools as well as HTML tags, CSS, and JavaScript programming. The importance of user-interface design was stressed, as this is what people interact with and it also reflects the content of the program or web site.

This concludes Part II of the book, which covered the essential components of multimedia and the various media elements. Part III delves into the hardware and software necessary for creating multimedia projects.

QUIZ

1. Who is the author when it comes to designing web sites and multimedia projects?
   A. The person who writes the code to make a multimedia project interactive
   B. The person who designs the user interface
   C. The person who writes the content for multimedia
   D. The person who tests how the program or web site works

2. What is it called when changes made to a web design and layout are automatically updated in the underlying code?
   A. HTML editor
   B. Round-trip HTML
   C. HTML tag
   D. Dynamic HTML

3. Which organization sets the standards and provides guidelines for web content accessibility?
   A. HTML
   B. CSS
   C. XHTML
   D. W3C

4. What is the difference between JavaScript and Java?
   A. One is a markup language and the other is a programming language.
   B. JavaScript uses brackets similar to HTML tags.
   C. Java is a full-fledged programming language and has more features and options than JavaScript.
   D. All of the above.

5. What are HTML tags?
   A. A scripting language used to enhance user interfaces and create more dynamic interactivity
   B. Brackets that contain words, phrases, and numbers to tell the web browser how to present the document
   C. ActionScript for interactive menus and buttons
   D. A technique that is used to format page layout and text

6. What is *not* a suggestion for selecting and using color when designing interactive multimedia programs?
   A. Create a balance between strong and soft hues, color contrasts, and so on.
   B. Don't overuse color so that the main information gets lost.
   C. Color contrast should never be used, especially with text.
   D. The color scheme should relate to and reflect the general theme or concept.

7. **What does designing multimedia for small screens, such as mobile devices, require?**
    A. Large file sizes
    B. Expanded screen dimensions compared with standard computer displays
    C. Limited or minimal detail
    D. Interfaces that accommodate touchscreens and scroll bars

8. **What is a CSS style?**
    A. A diagram for laying out web sites
    B. A template that provides modifications to an overall layout associated with an HTML document
    C. An unordered list within an HTML document
    D. A format for saving web files

9. **Which of the following applies to navigational items on a multimedia screen?**
    A. They should be clear to avoid confusion.
    B. They should be placed in a random manner to encourage curiosity and exploration.
    C. They should be categorized alphabetically.
    D. They should be varied in terms of size and treatment to add visual interest.

10. **Which is the fastest device in terms of bandwidth speed?**
    A. 56K modem
    B. Cable
    C. Satellite
    D. Wireless

Part III

Tools for Creating Multimedia Projects: Hardware and Software Needed to Make It Happen

chapter 9

Hardware and Equipment Options

Now we will launch into Part III of the book, which covers the all-important "tools of the trade." These include both hardware and software for making multimedia projects and web sites that use media components.

This chapter covers the gamut of options, ranging from input and output equipment, storage solutions, and computing platforms. It is a concise, up-to-date primer for helping you set up your multimedia production studio.

CHAPTER OBJECTIVES

In this chapter, you will:

- Discover the differences between various input devices for creating multimedia, such as scanners, digitizing tablets, cameras, microphones, speakers, and headphones

- Learn about computer display distinctions when interacting with multimedia in different environments, such as public kiosk, Web, and personal uses

- Get a handle on the various types of storage options for all the media files you will be generating

- Find out what it means to prepare multimedia for different computing platforms, including mobile and desktop purposes

Multimedia Project Equipment Setup

When designing and developing multimedia for a presentation, computer kiosk, or web site, a number of pieces of equipment are essential to get the job done. A modest setup is ample for web design and simple multimedia projects. This would include a computer, display, camera, and speakers. For a more involved project, such as a public museum kiosk, more advanced equipment is necessary. In either case, an organized, well-equipped work environment is vital for productivity.

You will need to outfit yourself with both hardware and software to create graphics and text, capture and manipulate images, record and edit audio and video, render animation, and write programming code. At the very least, you should have a fast CPU for processing video and rendering animation, as well as a large hard disk for storing files.

You also will want to work with the technology intended for the end user. If this is not possible due to financial limitations or space constraints, then it is imperative that each of the media elements and the final project are previewed and tested for proper functionality, image color accuracy, and display output, so that edits can be made prior to launching the project.

If the prospect of purchasing all this equipment seems daunting, then renting or borrowing is a viable option. Here are some tips:

- Team up with professionals who have particular technical skills in the field so you can share the workload.
- Ask other people about the equipment. They may have hardware and software that you need and let you use it.
- Use the client's resources if possible (it can't hurt to ask).
- Rent time at a high-end video- or audio-editing studio.
- Rent equipment.
- Do not re-create the wheel if original media elements are not required. Acquire the media you need from existing sources (such as clip art and stock libraries) when you are unable to create it yourself.

Developing interactive multimedia involves many steps, a variety of equipment, and different kinds of software programs to make it all happen. In a nutshell, you need media, and this must be *input* or acquired in some way (*hardware*). You will then need to edit, combine, author, and save media elements (*software*). Lastly, you must present or deliver everything on a screen-based device (*output*). This chapter deals with hardware requirements and options. We will focus on software for multimedia in the next chapter.

Input Devices

Input is an all-encompassing term for bringing media elements into the computer. Once they are available in a digital format, media can be treated separately or blended together for a unified, interactive product.

Initially, if you do not already have the necessary media elements, you will need to create the media yourself, get some help, or acquire it. The next step is to transfer everything to the computer that will house all the myriad parts of the multimedia project, and then open or import the files into software programs so you can begin working with them. After editing your media, you will combine elements and author for functionality, and then *output* the data in a visual form with which users can interact.

Mice, Digitizing Tablets, and Trackpads

Many tools are available for the input of media, ranging from the standard mouse and keyboard to touchscreens and scanners. For navigating around a screen and clicking active elements and links, the mouse is commonly used. This is the manner in which people first interacted with GUIs on personal computers; however, the keyboard came first.

Before the mouse was widely used, the keyboard was the primary means by which data was input. Computer illustrations were done using a keyboard. When I worked in the field of computer graphic slides in the late 1980s, I input key commands to indicate where a point would be placed on the x and y axes, and then connected them and applied color using typed commands. I used arrow keys to move the vector graphics around and to adjust placement on the screen.

The mouse was originally sold with early Apple computers. When Microsoft developed Windows in the late 1980s, it used the same design, but modified it slightly to complement the interface and functionality of Windows. The mouse was tethered to the computer with a cable, as some still are today.

The wireless or cordless type of mouse became available in the mid-1990s, providing flexibility as to positioning on the surface or desk. (Today, a number of brands have a scroll wheel to move up and down a page or a tilt wheel allowing the user to scroll in all directions on a page without moving the mouse.) One downside to wireless mice is that the battery can run out while you are working, and you will end up with missing keystrokes. This can be a problem, especially when calculating numbers, since accuracy is essential. The unreliability of this style of mouse is something to consider. A solution is to have on hand some replacement batteries or fully charged rechargeable batteries.

The mouse for Apple products once differed in design from the type made for Windows-based computers. The Apple mouse had only one primary button—one click highlighted or selected an item on the screen, and two clicks (a double-click) opened a file or folder. The Windows mouse was designed with two buttons, so the user could click to select items with the button on the left side, and the right button brought up submenus, providing a handy shortcut. Apple eventually followed suit due to consumer support and a growing demand for this style of mouse.

However, the older style mouse posed complications for lefties, as the buttons were backward for them, or at least did not work in the way they were intended. In 2005, Apple did away with this mouse style and introduced the Mighty Mouse, which offers a track ball on top, similar to a tilt wheel, as well as a left and right sensor for versatile clicking and selecting.

Apple also offers the Magic Mouse, which is designed to be multitouch and versatile for right-handed and left-handed users alike. You can either move the mouse to navigate around the screen or scroll a page, or you can move your fingers to select and activate elements on the screen, as well as advance through documents. Like other models, the mouse can be customized to suit your needs.

NOTE *Computer mice work best when designed in an* ergonomic *fashion* (ergonomically), *meaning the product design facilitates natural handling and coincides with how the human hand conforms to its shape, as well as taking into consideration fatigue and strain. Hands, wrists, and fingers can tire out quickly when using a poorly designed mouse, which can lead to injury and low productivity. Logitech's MX line of mice is more ergonomic than others.*

Digitizing tablets, such as the Wacom line of products, serve as a substitute for the mouse. They are accompanied by a stylus pen that responds to the amount of pressure used. Tablets are referred to as *pressure-sensitive* for that reason, and are very intuitive to use, as they are analogous to a pen or pencil. The Wacom Bamboo tablets give users the option of using their fingers or a stylus pen to interact with what is on the screen. These devices are the epitome of ergonomic design, but they take a little practice to use. Figure 9-1 shows an example of a tablet with a stylus, as well as a wireless mouse.

FIGURE 9-1 · Wireless mice and tablets with stylus

Trackpads, also called *touchpads*, are an alternative to using a mouse. They work well if you like how a trackpad operates; however, some laptops have trackpads that are unresponsive and hard to use. Apple's Magic Trackpad boasts a multitouch surface that mimics the trackpad functionality on laptops and can be used with any desktop computer in place of a mouse.

Using a mouse—wireless or connected to the laptop—is an alternative to the trackpad. Swiftpoint produces a versatile mouse for laptops that can be used directly on top of the trackpad, whereas most often the mouse must be placed beside the laptop, on a flat surface. This is a good alternative when on a plane or in a car. Some Wacom digitizing tablets have a similar feature, which allows the stylus pen and mouse to be used on the tablet surface interchangeably.

Trackball devices are an alternative to a mouse. They have a ball encased in a socket, along with buttons to allow quick access to software functions and greater control over the user interface. Wireless trackball products give the user even more flexibility in terms of location and proximity to the keyboard and monitor. Trackballs and joysticks are commonly used for video games, since they provide precision and quick movements. Another benefit is that trackballs (and other specially designed input devices) can assist those with mobility impairments.

Keyboards

Keyboards are essentially designed for typing. Most English keyboards are set up with the QWERTY format, which is the most widely used today. The arrangement of keys may not appear logical, but when learning to touch-type (typing without looking at the keys), the keyboard layout is more efficient than if the letters were arranged alphabetically. The keys are placed in locations that are paired with commonly used letter combinations.

Clearly keyboards are an indispensable part of any computer setup. You can find wired, wireless, and on-screen varieties. Each type takes a little getting used to when switching to a new model or a different size or format. There are also some keyboard models that sport an iPhone dock, such as Omnio, LifeWorks, and iHome, if you are looking for added features.

As with a mouse, ergonomic design is important in terms of how it feels to type on the keyboard and if the design facilitates the process or impedes it. Comfort and ease of use are priorities when typing, as fatigue can quickly set in, which can lead to making mistakes. Wireless keyboards are convenient because they can be positioned for comfort, but they have a similar battery issue as wireless mice. You may want to consider purchasing a keyboard with an indicator that alerts you when the power is getting low.

TIP *Most cameras, laptops, cell phones, and handheld mobile devices must be recharged regularly, as the battery life is relatively short. So, regardless of whether you need to install batteries or the equipment comes with a rechargeable battery, make sure you plug in and charge your equipment every night, so the batteries will not expire during production.*

Laptops have keyboards attached with built-in touchpads in place of a mouse. On the whole, these keyboards are much smaller than the standard-size keyboards used with desktop computers, and it is easier to press incorrect keys due to their proximity and size.

The same holds true for on-screen, or *virtual*, keyboards. Since they are software-based and not tangible hardware, they work differently in terms of how you type on them. Due to the small size of the keys, people typically tap with their fingers in a somewhat unnatural manner. Once the format becomes familiar, the process tends to speed up; however, they are unlike traditional keyboards and an adjustment period is inevitable. For this reason, frequent virtual keyboard users prefer to purchase a supplemental physical keyboard and mouse to use with a laptop, iPad, or game controller. A keyboard and mouse controller can be purchased for the Xbox 360, for example, and Apple sells a wireless keyboard to use with the iPad.

Scanners

Scanners are the primary mode of digitizing images and text, and they are essential pieces of equipment in any design and multimedia setup. Standard desktop scanners will capture flat, 2D images, as well as 3D objects in some models. They can also be used for scanning film negatives and slides when outfitted with additional features, but it is best to purchase a dedicated scanner that is designed exclusively for digitizing film negatives and slides. These produce better-quality results than a scanner that is intended primarily for flat, reflective media or one that is promoted as an all-in-one solution. The recommendation is that you use a scanner that suits your project goals; for example, if you have a lot of slides to scan and want the best output, use a film scanner. Figure 9-2 shows examples of several types of scanners.

A decent-quality flatbed scanner with a transparency adapter will be capable of scanning the following types of media: photos, artwork (paintings, drawings, illustrations), photo negatives, slides, overhead transparencies, small 3D objects,

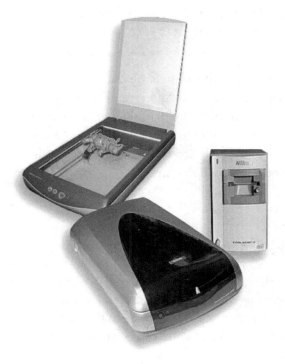

FIGURE 9-2 · Flatbed and film scanners

and 2D printed material (newspapers, magazines, books, brochures, flyers, posters, and so on). A scanner without a transparency feature can reproduce only *reflective*, or opaque, material.

Some attributes to look for in a flatbed scanner are resolution (or PPI), color depth, density range (shadows and brightness), page dimensions, scanner speed, and scanning software options. Low-end, inexpensive flatbed scanners are more than adequate for preparing images for multimedia, as they do not need to be very large in terms of dimensions and file size. A basic scanner is adequate for minimum resolution, since the images will be presented on the screen, not in print. If images need to be scanned for both screen and print, use a high-quality scanner to obtain the highest quality possible at the required size for the project.

Still Struggling

Optical resolution is the highest number of pixels the scanner can produce with built-in optics. There is also something called *interpolated resolution*, which is a much higher number because the scanner will guess to add pixels to the final digitized image. When purchasing a flatbed scanner, look for the highest optical PPI compared with the interpolated PPI.

Scanners often come with optical character recognition (OCR) software. OCR software analyzes an image and attempts to re-create text by comparing the shapes it finds with mathematical models of characters. This can be very helpful if you need to be able to edit the text from a document and you have only a printed version. Such conversion is also available online with services that read text from uploaded documents.

Still Struggling

Do your research and consider both your needs and budget when selecting a scanner. Scanners serve a variety of purposes, and they vary in terms of quality and price. The bit depth is also something to think about—the higher it is, the better the results in terms of obtaining color correctness and accurate image reproduction.

Image and Motion Capture

Digital still cameras (DSCs) are essential for photographing images for multimedia projects. The cameras and setup you need depend on the purpose of the photographs. You might work in a studio arranged with professional lighting or in an outdoor setting for a more natural environment, for example.

Most cameras have both automatic and manual options for taking photos, as well as interchangeable lenses. The more advanced digital cameras are the single-lens reflex (SLR) type, which closely mimic traditional 35mm film SLR cameras. The advantage of these cameras over lower-quality products is that they provide the photographer with a preview that accurately matches the output.

As mentioned in Chapter 7, camcorders record video and can be analog or digital. Most digital cameras designed for photographing images come equipped with video-recording features, but the quality ranges depending on the type of camera. When capturing video specifically for multimedia and the Web, you only need small formats and file sizes. Despite this, it is best to purchase a digital video camera or camcorder for video capture, as the quality of the results will be much higher, and you will have more options while recording. The best option is an HD-digital video camera, so it is compatible with the latest Web, mobile, and TV technology. You should also have a tripod for stability and steady camera work, so your photographic and video results look professional. Figure 9-3 shows some examples of digital cameras and camcorders.

When a scanner is not available, digital cameras and cell phones are often substituted for taking quick photos, but they are inferior when it comes to matching the sharpness, resolution, and color precision. However, smart phones come equipped with both photo and video cameras that provide adequate output for on-the-fly multimedia purposes, such as posting on Facebook or a blog. The iPhone, Android, and BlackBerry are popular mobile brands with a variety of features for taking images and capturing motion. Some of the better-quality small HD camcorders are the Kodak Zi8 and the Flip Video. They are as compact as a cell phone, and also affordable, lightweight, and easy to use.

Portable tablet computers, such as the Apple iPad and the BlackBerry Play-Book, take very good photos and video, and you can download apps that allow you to edit and compress video clips. These are additional options for taking and sharing images and video on the Web.

Microphones

The kind of microphone used to input audio is central to the quality of the sound file. Built-in microphones are installed in cameras, computers, and mobile

FIGURE 9-3 • Digital camera for photography and camcorder for video

devices to record sound. External varieties can be wired or wireless. The wireless type is a good option when conducting interviews, since these microphones are portable and unobtrusive. Often, the kind of microphone that is built into a camera is fine for low-end video, but it is generally not acceptable for recording high-quality audio.

Some microphones are small and connect directly to your computer with a USB cable. These can be handheld or positioned on the desktop for recording voice-overs and sound effects. Other microphones are higher-end podium-style versions for voice recording. Figure 9-4 shows some examples of microphones.

Larger, external microphones can be held or attached to a camera. These are often preferential over smaller microphones when you need to pick up subtleties and discrete nuances, and minimize distortion and ambient noise. If you're recording outside, such microphones can be assisted by the addition of a windscreen.

Because the electronic signal produced by a microphone is very small, it needs to be amplified significantly before being digitized. Built-in audio cards come with preamplifiers (*preamps*), but generally the quality of such preamps

FIGURE 9-4 · Microphones

on most consumer-grade PCs is somewhat poor. For best results, you should use a high-quality preamp card or an external preamp before digitizing the signal.

The recording of live music will require special microphones to pick up tone and pitch, because they are complex. Another factor in selecting a microphone is whether the sound recording is done in a studio or in a natural setting. Some microphones are connected to portable audio-recording devices so they can be carried while recording; others connect externally to a camcorder that is attached to a tripod for stability and signal constancy.

Recording audio should typically be done in stereo format, because humans have two ears. In terms of recording the human voice, it is usually best to record it in mono as opposed to stereo, because the human voice comes from just one point.

Touchscreens and Fingerprinting Technology

When designing the interface for your project, you should take into account the type of multimedia display that will be used, as there are different approaches depending on how the users will interact with the screen. Touchscreens are not practical for designing multimedia, but they are commonly chosen for interactive displays because they give a more tangible quality to the user experience.

When it comes to choosing a touchscreen, the more responsive the better, because it will require less effort on the user's part and speed up the process. However, a touchscreen should not be selected simply because it is the most up-to-date technology and what everyone is using. Your highest priorities should be the purpose of the multimedia project, the subject matter, the environment in which it will be used, and the user interface. These will dictate which kind of technology will be needed, not the other way around.

Still Struggling

As an example, if you are designing an interactive kiosk for the lobby of a bank, you would most likely want to include a combination of touch-sensitive screen and keypad, as there needs to be a Braille option for those with vision impairments, as well as a physical number keypad for those who prefer it over a touchscreen. In other cases, the size and type of monitor to be used will determine how the screens and user interface are designed.

Fingerprint-detection mechanisms are necessary in companies or government offices that emphasize tight security for their data. They are also helpful for identity confirmation in large public venues. For example, Disney World has a system that scans customers' thumbs when they enter and exit the park. It is a way to keep track of the number of visitors and determine if people have actually left once the park has closed. Figure 9-5 shows examples of devices with a fingerprint-detection mechanism.

Digital Audio Recorders

Digital audio recorders are accompanied by a microphone and serve the purpose of recording conversations, lectures, notes, songs, music, and interviews for note-taking, music composition, journalism, and documentaries. These recorders are also helpful if your multimedia project will include voice recordings that need to be accompanied by text for hearing-impaired users or those who prefer to read rather than listen to stories or instructions.

Like most kinds of digital media, recorders that create high-quality sounds also produce large files. Make sure you have a place to store and back up the files for duplicate copies, so that they are secure and readily available when you're integrating the sounds into your multimedia project.

FIGURE 9-5 • Touchscreens with a fingerprint-detection device

Some audio recorders have liquid-crystal displays (LCDs) to show you what is being recorded in text format. Another handy feature is audio detection (also called *voice activation*), which will start and stop the recording process with the presence or absence of sound input.

Transferring audio files should be hassle-free. Look for those with USB cables or built-in connectors so you can easily transfer files to your computer or external storage device. As an essential time-saver, you will need a means of converting the recording into a typed format so you won't have to transcribe it on your own. You can purchase transcription software if the recorder is not already supplied with it.

Digital voice recorder systems (see Figure 9-6) use voice-recognition software, which means the recorder recognizes audible words. The spoken word is immediately translated into a digital format and saved as a text file that can be edited in software such as word processing programs. Multimedia projects that require voice input for answers to questions posed, for instance, will benefit from this type of system. The key feature to look for when purchasing this technology is *accuracy*.

FIGURE 9-6 • Digital voice recorder

Output: Displays and Screens

Computer monitors, or displays, come in a variety of styles and sizes. Flat-screen LCDs are the dominant technology for screen viewing. Color pixels that are visible on the screen represent images, text, video, and animation, and these pixels contain liquid crystals, which are displayed as a result of a light source placed behind them. The LCD components in the back of the display allow light to emit, appearing as the additive primaries of red, green, and blue. There are also LCDs back-lit by light-emitting diodes (LEDs), which are used for TV. Brightness or luminosity, contrast, and color vary in both computer and TV displays. The more expensive the LCD, the greater the number of colors.

Organic light-emitting diode (OLED) is a newer type of display that emits a higher-quality image with increased contrast. Plasma displays are designed for TVs and use the equivalent of fluorescent lights to generate color, brightness, and contrast. The plasma (or gases) makes the pixels on the screen glow.

The older, more boxy models are CRTs, also referred to as *video display terminals*. Unlike flat-screen LCDs, CRTs are heavy energy hogs that leave an afterimage on the screen, such as elements on the desktop, if they remain on the screen in the same location for long periods.

Small, portable mobile devices are not necessarily limited to a reduced screen format. For example, the iPad can be connected to a TV, computer display, or LCD projector for a larger screen-viewing format.

Regardless of which brand, model, and size display you choose for desktop computing and TV viewing, it is important to test all the images, video, and animation used in your multimedia project on a variety of display devices to see how colors and motion will reproduce.

Dual Monitors

Figure 9-7 shows an example of a work setup with two monitors. Dual monitors are advantageous for a number of reasons. Additional attached displays with a shared interface provide a more effective and productive work environment for developing multimedia. You must have a TV attached to your computer when working with broadcast video. As discussed in Chapter 7, this allows you to test the video in the intended viewing format.

Using two computer screens is worthwhile for designing, authoring, and editing. One screen can be used for tool palettes, controls, and menus. The other screen can be used for previewing web sites, interactive screens, animation, and video. Multiple displays give an all-important increase in screen real estate so

FIGURE 9-7 · Dual-monitor display

that you are not overwhelmed by software components, and you can more easily separate the design and development side of things from the final product.

In the 1980s, the Wacom Company initiated input devices in the form of graphics tablets. Wacom products now use ergonomic tablet-and-pen technology, and they range from stylus pens for the iPad, to touchpads of various sizes, to larger displays that can be drawn on and edited in the same way as touchscreens. The Wacom Cintiq differs from the stylus tablets mentioned earlier, as it has a dual function: It is a large input device (or tablet) and also serves as a monitor. The advantage of this type of display is that the dimensions are sizeable and the surface can be drawn on directly using a stylus pen.

Speakers and Headphones

Stereo speakers and headsets (see Figure 9-8) are necessary pieces of equipment when creating and testing audio (music, voice-overs, sound tracks, and sound effects) and video for multimedia. As with microphones, there are wired and wireless varieties. You can connect speakers to most desktop and laptop computers by plugging the audio cable into a headphone jack.

FIGURE 9-8 · Headphones and speakers

Speakers used for preparing multimedia differ from those that are part of the presentation or distributed product. You will need stereo sound as opposed to mono to be able to play music or sounds that emit from both or one side. Speakers for a multimedia kiosk, for instance, need to be loud enough to accommodate ambient noise and built into the structure or casing, so they are not damaged or stolen and will remain intact for the duration of the contract.

Your target platform will also impact how you mix and equalize your audio. For example, if you know your presentation will be heard using high-quality speakers, you should listen to it using similar speakers. Conversely, if your users will be listening on laptop speakers, you should test for that as well, and adjust the sound accordingly.

Headphones or headsets allow for quiet, focused listening and editing, and they will not disturb others if you are working in a group or office environment. Some of the more expensive types come in both headphone and earbud varieties. For personal music listening, some headphones cover the entire ear and have external noise-cancellation features. These should not be used for studio mastering, however, as the cancellation processing will change the sound of the source material.

Data Storage

Saving and storing media files is an important part of developing a multimedia or web project. The files can get rather large, and there will inevitably be many of them, so make it a priority to have a place to store them for secure archiving and retrieval. There are many data storage options for organizing your files and, regardless of which type you choose, it is essential to duplicate your work in case of loss or damage.

Internal Drives

Internal drives are hard disks installed inside a computer or laptop. You will automatically have *native* storage or disk space built into the computer. However, this is not always adequate for the size and quantity of files you will accumulate for multimedia projects. You will also need a backup device so you always have two copies of your files in the event something happens to your computer (and it always does at that inconvenient moment when you are nearing the end of a project!).

Additional storage drives can be installed inside your computer or laptop, as most have expansion slots for this very reason, as well as room for additional memory chips (RAM). This is a good option if you prefer a consolidated computer system without the bother of yet another device to connect. The downside, however, is that if something happens to your computer, you cannot access the files without repairing it.

External USB Drives and Large-Capacity Hard Disks

Another option is to use an external drive that can be connected to a USB-compatible port on your computer, which are called *flash drives* or *jump drives*. These are widely used because they are so convenient, affordable, and reliable. The smaller-capacity drives range from 2GB to 64GB, and the larger-capacity drives hold up to 256GB. Figure 9-9 shows some examples of data storage options.

Larger drives with a USB 3.0 interface, as opposed to the smaller varieties that use USB 2.0, are not as compact as the jump drives and are less portable as a result (they can't easily fit in your pocket). However, they provide even more disk space for storing and backing up media files, and the data transfer rate is generally much faster.

Iomega and Toshiba are reputable companies that manufacture large external drives for backing up files. There are models with up to 500GB of disk space, which is more than ample for storing your media files. Some large drives are not all that portable and can weigh over 3 pounds. There are desktop models that provide 1.5 terabytes (TB) of storage and use USB 2.0, so they have a substantial amount of storage but are slower at transferring data. External hard

FIGURE 9-9 · Data storage media

drives may be USB but can also be eSATA or FireWire. The bottom line is that the larger the capacity and faster the transfer speed, the more you will pay for the drive.

NOTE   *Manufacturers of internal hard disk drives will be converting to a different format that provides significantly more space and uses less power than in the past. These 4K drives will lead to greater data security and reliability, as well as a more efficient user experience. Many current operating systems are already compliant with this newer technology.*

Online and Networked Storage

Other alternatives for storing files include online storage services, of which there are many. This alternative is convenient, as it can be accessed anywhere you have an Internet or Wi-Fi connection, and you will not be bogged down with additional equipment.

As mentioned in Chapter 7, online storage is a better option to use as a *backup*, rather than a primary storage location, because it is vulnerable to viruses, damage, and replication, despite the security measures that are in place.

Computing Platforms

Your multimedia project may be designed for operation on a desktop computer or a mobile device, such as a smart phone or tablet. You will need to be able to view your interactive screen designs and test the project's functionality on standard desktop computers, laptops, tablets, and mobile devices.

Desktop Computers

For creating multimedia, it is necessary to have a computer setup and peripheral equipment with the following capabilities:

- Recording and editing video and audio
- Photographing and editing images
- Preparing web pages
- A lot of computing power with a fast processor

Many PCs are available for this purpose, and they can be customized to exact specifications. Researching products and getting assistance from knowledgeable technicians are crucial to making wise purchases.

The most widely used computing platforms and operating systems are Mac OS, Microsoft Windows, and Linux (see Figure 9-10). These differ somewhat in terms of how files are handled and stored, and what they offer in terms of multimedia development.

For end users who want to fully experience multimedia with a desktop computer, a system that will not be outgrown quickly is paramount. The computer needs to be fast and up-to-date with a current operating system. It should be capable of running multiple simultaneous functions, such as watching movies or TV, listening to music, surfing the Web, viewing photos, conferencing with video, playing games, and reading email. Adequate disk space and memory will be needed for running and storing files. Speakers and a large monitor are also vital to enhance the viewing and listening experience.

FIGURE 9-10 • Desktop platforms

Mobile Devices and Operating Systems

Handheld mobile devices (see Figure 9-11), such as smart phones, are essentially minicomputers where the viewing, interaction with, and creation of multimedia are expected.

Some of the more popular mobile operating systems are Apple iOS, Android, BlackBerry, Windows Mobile and Phone 7, webOS, and Symbian OS. These vary in terms of functionality and features, but a number of models can take photos and video for viewing, playing, editing, and sharing. Mobile Internet Devices (MID) are specifically designed for multimedia entertainment and use a wireless internet connection (the Medfield platform is the most current).

4G is a cellular wireless standard for mobile broadband. This capability is available with a number of smart phones as an optional feature. 4G allows for making phone calls, texting, emailing, and web surfing when there is no Wi-Fi or cell phone coverage. It comes with a cost, but it is worth the investment if you always want to stay connected, for instance in a car or train.

FIGURE 9-11 • Mobile platforms

Along with cost, sorting through the service plan options is another factor when purchasing such a device. You may be able to borrow a mobile device to test your work if you do not own one. If you are looking to buy a mobile device, you will want to access full multimedia capabilities, so your plan should include a minimum of phone, data, email, and texting, preferably with 3G or 4G capabilities.

Summary

Now you have a good handle on the technology needed for producing and displaying multimedia. The bottom line is that you should purchase the best you can within your budget because the adage "you get what you pay for" is very true when it comes to the quality of output. However, since multimedia and web files are typically on the small side, you can often get by with the less pricey, mid-range hardware for some tasks, and spend more on those pieces of equipment required for tasks whose quality cannot be compromised.

QUIZ

1. **What is meant by optical resolution when it comes to scanners?**
   A. The lowest resolution a scanner can have
   B. The highest number of pixels a scanner can produce with built-in optics
   C. The number of colors in the final scanned image
   D. The scanner's interpolation of pixels

2. **What is the best kind of microphone to use for recording high-fidelity sound?**
   A. Larger, external microphones to hold or attach to a camera
   B. Microphones built into digital cameras and camcorders
   C. Podium-style for added stability
   D. Digital voice recorder microphones

3. **Why is it important to have a backup of your media files?**
   A. For storage and later retrieval
   B. For archiving purposes
   C. For security measures in case the original files get lost or damaged
   D. All of the above

4. **What does ergonomic mean when referring to a computer mouse?**
   A. The style is oriented toward left-handed users.
   B. The product design facilitates natural handling.
   C. There is a low comfort factor with extended use.
   D. This describes wireless varieties, rather those those attached by wire.

5. **What is a technology that substitutes for a mouse and uses a pressure-sensitive pen?**
   A. Digitizing tablets
   B. Touchscreens
   C. Trackballs
   D. Touchpads

6. **Which of the following is the most portable and convenient file-storage option?**
   A. Large-capacity hard disk
   B. Online or networked
   C. Jump drive
   D. Internal hard disk

7. **Which kind of computer display is currently the dominant technology?**
   A. CRT
   B. LCD
   C. Plasma
   D. OLED

8. **What is the most important requirement when choosing a digital voice recorder?**
   A. Accuracy
   B. Portability
   C. Voice activation
   D. Color LCD display

9. **Which of the following is a commonly used computer connection for peripheral devices, such as microphones, cameras, and scanners?**
   A. SCSI
   B. USB
   C. FireWire
   D. HDMI

10. **What is one disadvantage of using wireless keyboards?**
    A. They are not as fast as wired keyboards.
    B. They are too small.
    C. They are not ergonomic.
    D. The battery can run out while you are working.

chapter 10

Software for
Multimedia

The focus of this chapter is on software and how to make everything come together. Software and hardware go hand in hand. When designing multimedia, it is nearly impossible to separate the hardware from the software, so this chapter in many ways is a continuation of Chapter 9, and references the technology we discussed in that chapter. We will cover high-end industry-standard products, as well as freeware, shareware, and open source options that can be downloaded from the Web.

CHAPTER OBJECTIVES

In this chapter, you will:

- Learn about the software needed for multimedia production
- Distinguish between high-end and free software programs
- Discover what to look for when purchasing or downloading software
- Find out what it means to capture and record from the screen
- Get an overview of media player applications

Multimedia Software Options

When undertaking a multimedia project, you will undoubtedly need software programs that can handle all the necessary design and development tasks. For a successful end product, you should have a variety of software.

Some software options are do-it-all programs; others are dedicated to a particular task. Some products you should consider investing in are the better-known and highly recommended workhorses that will inevitably set you back more in terms of cost; other options are freeware, shareware, and open source programs that will cost little or nothing to obtain. These may not have all the bells and whistles of the industry-standard programs, but you should be able to find one among the many available that will do the job, or you can pair programs together for greater efficiency and productivity.

Software allows you to design, edit, and control the media elements. The three main categories for the kinds of software you will need for your multimedia toolkit are creation, editing, and authoring tools.

A wide variety of software programs are at your disposal to help develop multimedia, such as the following:

- Vector graphics programs
- Image-editing programs
- Office packages for scripting with word processing tools
- Spreadsheets for tracking assets and organizing data
- XML editors
- Script editors/integrated development environments (IDEs), such as Eclipse
- Other utilities for batch-processing and renaming files

Some examples of software with programming capabilities specific to interactive multimedia development are Adobe Director, SMIL, Adobe Flash, and HTML5. Each one possesses different attributes for developing dynamic multimedia.

Still Struggling

You will face many choices and have a lot to learn when it comes to software. Planning and setting firm goals will help you. Too many tools can become overwhelming. Select a program to focus on and allow time to practice so you can build skills to develop a level of comfort with it. Educate yourself with whatever training resources you can get your hands on, such as software manuals, third-party books, videos, online courses, workshops, friends, colleagues, and instructors.

The following are some good software web resources worth looking into:

- Lynda.com (Lynda Weinman is an author and authority on all things related to design, the Web, and video software)
- Adobe TV (many video tutorials on the Adobe products)
- YouTube videos (these range in quality, so select them with caution)
- Message boards and blogs focused on specific programs and techniques
- Software company web sites
- Software *Help* files (usually found in a dedicated menu selection within the program)

NOTE   *For an extensive list of free open source software for the Mac, see http://downloadpedia.org/Open_Source_Mac. For open source alternatives to proprietary software, visit http://whdb.com/2008/the-top-50-proprietary-programs-that-drive-you-crazy-and-their-open-source-alternatives/.*

Vector Graphics: Illustration and Line Art

Creating vector graphics is a frequent task when developing a multimedia project. As discussed in Chapter 3, vectors are object-oriented, line-based graphics with anchor points and curves. Examples include logos, illustrations, maps, signs, posters, and typographic effects. Figures 10-1 and 10-2 show examples of vector graphics.

FIGURE 10-1 • Object-oriented graphic: camera lens

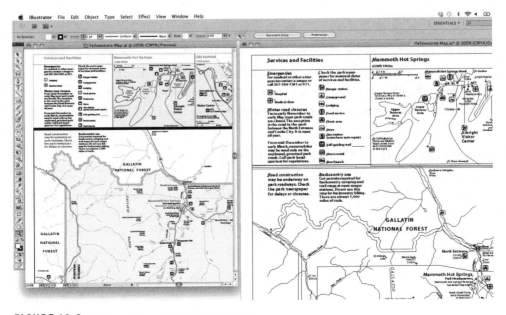

FIGURE 10-2 • Color and line art: Yellowstone map

Some common features of vector graphics software are tools to create lines, shapes, and text with anchor points and curves; fill and stroke colors; color palettes and swatches; art boards with crop marks; and tools for manipulating, intersecting, overlapping, merging, and aligning shapes. You will need at least one software package that can handle vector graphics when developing multimedia, as they are scalable and not dependent on resolution as bitmapped graphics are.

Adobe Illustrator is an industry-standard vector graphics software program that provides tools for creating illustrations and graphics (see Figure 10-2). Although it is complex—with many panels, menus, tools, and levels—it can be learned relatively quickly if you use step-by-step tutorials.

When creating vector graphics, you work with curves with anchor points to build endless, layered shapes. The software attributes may appear awkward at first, as the tools don't always do what you want them to do. My students find that with practice it gets easier, and they are able to produce good results within a few weeks.

Aside from Illustrator, there are other professional illustration programs, such as Adobe Freehand and CorelDraw. Adobe Flash allows the capability to modify vectors directly, without using Bezier handles, which is more intuitive for some users. Flash is also able to work directly with vector artwork, as well as import layered Illustrator artwork.

You can download a free 30-day trial of the most current Adobe software programs, and some illustration programs can be obtained from the Web for free. For instance, the Serif company distributes DrawPlus and a number of programs for photo editing, desktop publishing, and web design. Inkscape is a free open source vector graphics program with features similar to those of Illustrator and CorelDraw. SmoothDraw NX and InsightPoint are free programs for Windows worth considering.

Some basic features of Illustrator—and most Adobe products—are page/document parameters, menu commands, tools, layers, as well as palettes for editing colors, swatches, gradients, text, and line widths.

TIP *You can download free plug-ins for Adobe Illustrator from http://dzineblog .com/2010/09/10-popular-free-plugins-and-shareware-for-adobe-illustrator.html.*

Digital Imaging: Photography and Bitmapped Images

Digital imaging refers to pixel-based or bitmapped images. Typically, these are photographs taken with a digital camera or images that are scanned into the computer. Examples are artwork; drawings; illustrations; printed material from books, magazines, and newspapers; and small 3D objects.

The majority of images included in multimedia projects are bitmapped graphics because they are viewed on digital displays, which are composed of pixels, and therefore are limited by screen resolution (see Figure 10-3). These images consist of photo sequences, collages, web page designs, menus, and navigational items.

NOTE *You may want to refer back to Chapter 3 for more information about raster graphics. There are specific software programs dedicated to manipulating pixels, and some have a combination of raster and vector capabilities rolled into one.*

Adobe Photoshop is the industry-standard software for photo editing. It is referred to as a *digital darkroom* due to its tools and image adjustments that mimic traditional photographic techniques. Photoshop is a bitmapped program that imports, edits, layers, and montages pixel-based images.

Some of the primary characteristics of Photoshop—and of other image-editing software—are RGB color, pixel resolution, cropping, layering collages, red-eye removal, cloning, transformations (rotate, flip, distort, and so on), and image adjustments (retouching, color correction, tonal changes, painting, cloning, special effects, and so on).

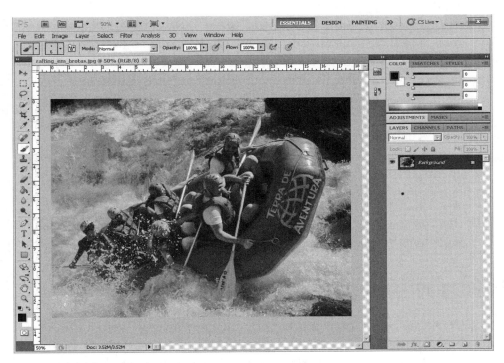

FIGURE 10-3(a) · Photoshop bitmapped image: 100% view (*Continued*)

When it comes to bitmapped or raster images, the higher the image quality, the more pixels there are, and consequently, the larger the file size. When working with photos on a project, it is not uncommon to have many image files. They typically start out large, so that they can be cropped and reworked. Make sure you have enough active memory (or RAM) and some type of storage or backup option, as discussed in the previous chapter.

Images used in multimedia are screen-based, so they reflect the resolution of the output device (72 DPI for a monitor, as opposed to 300 DPI minimum for print). Therefore, the resolution of images targeted for multimedia does not need to be as high as for print images.

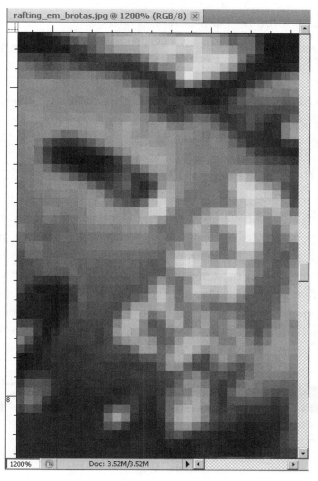

FIGURE 10-3 (b) · Photoshop bitmapped image: 1200% view

TABLE 10-1 Image-Editing Programs

Operating System or Type	Software
Windows	Paint.net, Photoscape, Pixia, Ultimate Paint
Mac	iPhoto, Photoshop Elements, Preview, Photo Booth, Google Picasa (free), Pixen (donation-ware), Acorn, ACDSee
Mac and Windows	GIMP (open source), Serif PhotoPlus for photo editing, Serif PanoramaPlus for making photos into panoramas (free), AMS Photo Art Studio, Zoner Photo Studio
Art-creation programs	Corel Painter, Synthetik Software's Studio Artist (Mac only)
File-conversion software for multiple platforms	Apple GraphicConverter

Table 10-1 lists some free or inexpensive image editors.

A number of mobile apps allow you to accomplish a substantial amount of photo editing and special effects on a small screen using photos you have just taken with the device or those you transfer or download, as listed in Table 10-2.

Screen Captures and Recordings

Capturing a screen image, or a *screenshot*, allows you to take a picture or a recording of what is displayed on a computer monitor or TV. Another type of screen capture is a screen recording referred to as a *screencast* or *video-screen capture*, which creates a movie of what is happening on the display and is accompanied by narration or some type of audio. Software that allows you to record the screen is beneficial because you can speak as you are demonstrating, so audio and video are combined. Both of these are useful for a variety of purposes, such as training and instruction, demonstrating software, recording errors, and saving screen information.

TABLE 10-2 Mobile Image-Editing Apps

Device	Software
iPhone	Photoshop Mobile, Photoshop Express, Pixelmator, Photonasis
BlackBerry	Picture Magic, Doodle, MiniPaint
Android	Photoid, PicSay, FxCamera, Vignette, Camera Illusion

TABLE 10-3 Free Mac Screen-Recording Software for Screenshots and Screencasts

Program	Description
Capture Me	Resizing and saving options
Copernicus	Exports in different formats; makes screen movies in QuickTime format
Snapper	Screen capture and recorder; saves in JPEG format; can add titles to screenshots
Screen Movie Recorder	Single-click for screenshots; makes QuickTime movies of screen recordings
Jing	Captures and records computer monitor screen

Some built-in tools for screen capturing are already installed on your computer. For instance, on the Mac, you can press COMMAND-SHIFT-3 on the keyboard to take a picture of the entire screen, or COMMAND-SHIFT-4 to select a portion of the screen. For Windows, press the Print Screen key (PRTSC) on the keyboard, and the screen image will be captured and placed on the clipboard or RAM. You could then paste the image into Paint or Word (or OpenOffice, a free open source program) to quickly save it, and then import into other programs to edit.

Tables 10-3 and 10-4 list some free screen-recording software for screenshots and screencasts for Mac and Window systems, respectively.

On mobile devices, such as Mac iOS, you can press the Home and Sleep/Wake buttons, and the screen image will be saved in the photos folder. Other software programs that can be downloaded and used for screenshot purposes include Grab, which comes with the Mac (in the Utilities folder). Grab allows you to take a timed screen or a single window, in addition to standard screen

TABLE 10-4 Free Windows Screen-Recording Software for Screenshots and Screencasts

Program	Description
BB Flashback	Can add text, sound, images, and special effects; saves in many movie formats
Capture Fox	An add-on for the Mozilla Firefox web browser
Windows Media Encoder	Converts screen recordings to Windows Media format
FLV Player	Makes Flash movies of your screen for animated tutorials
CamStudio	Open source screen and audio recorder; creates AVI video files and SWF Flash movies

captures. For Windows, there is Capture Assistant and Window Clippings. These can be readily shared by email, Facebook, Twitter, or a blog.

Screen readers are for those who need *assistive technology* (AT). These allow for text-to-speech and Braille conversions of what appears on the computer screen. Some screen readers come with the operating system software, such as Microsoft Narrator for Windows and Apple's VoiceOver for the Mac. Spoken-Web is a software program designed to read web page content for those with compromised vision.

Page Layout and Typography

Page layout or desktop publishing (DTP) software has numerous functions in multimedia design. These programs are traditionally used for designing print pieces, such as brochures, menus, books, magazines, and newsletters. Since most print design ends up in a digital form on the screen at some point, it is a good idea to have some kind of DTP software.

Arranging elements on a page that can be used for print or the Web is a common practice, as it makes the work more versatile. For instance, a brochure layout designed for print that is laid out in Adobe InDesign (see Figure 10-4) can be transferred to the Web by saving it in a web-ready format. It can be saved as a PDF file or made into a web page. In both cases, it can include active links.

Although relatively recent innovations for web page design, such as CSS standards, have improved the way that visual elements are displayed in browsers, when exporting web pages from DTP software, you must be cautious. DTP programs typically create bloated web pages that are slow to load and rarely render correctly across various browsers.

Some features that DTP software is known for are multiple pages; typographic treatments; CMYK or process color; tools to arrange photos, graphics, and type; and CSS for consistent stylistic treatments. DTP software allows you to create *digital magazines* (also called *webzines* or *e-zines*) for standard web display, mobile devices, and tablets such as the iPad. Often, they are mirrored in a print form, but many are intended for screen display. Using a DTP program with a grid, tabs, columns, and guides for arranging page elements will provide the structure needed for organized, consistent pages.

You can also use DTP software for e-book creation and authoring, including video and audio tags. Digital books are used with e-book readers (or *e-readers*), such as Barnes and Noble's Nook and Amazon's Kindle, as well as mobile devices and laptops. The e-books are primarily made up of words, as they are

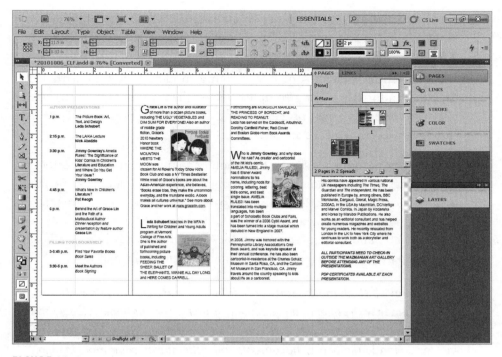

FIGURE 10-4 · Adobe InDesign page layout example

intended to be read as digital books, but some include hyperlinks and illustrations, especially those geared toward young readers.

Your page designs can be exported to the EPUB format, which stands for
"electronic publication" and is an e-book standard. They can also be converted
to HTML. Both cases allow for web page transfer.

Some free open source and low-cost DTP programs worth looking into
include Scribus, PagePlus, Pages, PagePublisher, Canvastic, and iCalamus.

Animation and Motion Graphics

Computer animation was discussed at length in Chapter 5. Here, we'll go over
the software options for both 2D and 3D animation. First, here is a recap of the
differences:

- 2D animation is similar to traditional cel animation and uses frame-by-
  frame and tweening techniques with keyframes, in addition to layering
  and onionskinning. The look is typically flat shapes outlined in black, with
  an illustrated or cartoon-like appearance. Although this look is common

and hearkens back to hand-drawn animations where the outlines were drawn in ink, many animators have used innovative approaches with numerous visual styles made possible by the software.

- 3D animation is made up of wireframe models rendered with light, shadow, and texture using complex vector shapes (see Figure 10-5). 3D software requires a fast processor and a generous amount of RAM and storage space, as the files are large.

Creating motion graphics is similar to computer animation in that the intention is to make things move. Motion graphics combine text, video, graphics, and audio for use in movie titles, advertising, short videos, news graphics, and animated billboards. Motion graphics programs include Adobe After Effects, Camtasia, 123 Video Magic, and Silhouette FX. A plug-in for After Effects called particleIllusion creates visual particle effects (emitters) for images, animation, and video.

TIP *The speed at which animation software can be learned is relatively slow. The process can be eased with patience and adequate training, such as books, videos, and online resources. Some programs are easier to master than others, and once you have used animation software, the concepts and techniques become more familiar. Regardless, to be successful, you will need to set aside a considerable amount of time to learn and become proficient with the animation software you've selected.*

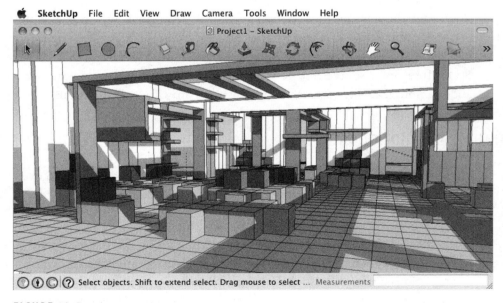

FIGURE 10-5 • Google SketchUp 3D example

TABLE 10-5 Computer Animation Programs	
Type	**Software**
2D programs	Flash, Toon Boom, After Effects, Animation Workshop, Pencil, CreaToon, Anime Studio
3D programs	Maya, Autodesk 3ds Max, LightWave, Swift 3D
3D programs for beginners	Poser, 3D Canvas, Xara 3D
Free 3D programs	Blender (open source), Google SketchUp, Anim8or

Table 10-5 lists some of the better-known and widely used animation programs.

Audio and Video Recording and Editing

Some software programs that are widely used for audio editing are Adobe Soundbooth, Adobe Audition, Apple GarageBand, Sound Forge, and Audacity (a free program; see Figure 10-6). WavePad and Cool Record Edit Pro are both

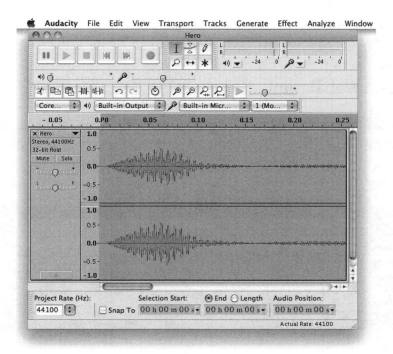

FIGURE 10-6 · Audio editing using Audacity

low-cost options with a good amount of features. With these programs, you can use audio techniques such as noise adjustments, fading, equalizing, making pitch changes, adding reverberation, looping, stretching, echoing, and reversing. Audio software can also easily create *mashups*, or music blends, which are combinations of prerecorded music tracks.

Still Struggling

Whether creating a score for a movie, adding sound effects for an animation, or including a voice-over for a tutorial, you will need software that specializes in audio recording and editing. Another essential component when recording audio is a good-quality external microphone, as discussed in Chapter 9.

Video editing is one of the more complex kinds of software with a steeper learning curve than photo editing, as there are many facets to video. You must record or acquire tracks, import them into the program, edit them with a time-line, and add and manipulate audio tracks. Finally, the audio is compressed, stored, and transferred. Some better-known video editor programs are Apple Final Cut, Apple iMovie (see Figure 10-7), Adobe Premier, and Avid.

Authoring and Web Design

Authoring for multimedia ties everything together, and it can be learned at a fundamental level. However, you may want to team up with or employ a programmer to do more advanced coding if the project calls for it.

FIGURE 10-7 · Video viewing and editing in iMovie

Basic authoring for multimedia and the Web does not require advanced software, as a web page can be created using a simple text editor such as TextEdit or WordPad, or a word processing program such as Microsoft Word and Apple Pages. These programs can translate text into HTML tags, which is helpful for those new to web design. Adobe products, such as Photoshop and Illustrator, allow you to save images and page layouts for the Web (see Figure 10-8).

Creating HTML using text editors is fine; however, other non-HTML formats typically require additional components. For example, it is possible to write MXML, which is a markup language for interface layout, using a text editor, but you will need a compiler to create an app.

Authoring software includes features such as design tools for working out the user interface, methods for combining media, and functionality controls.

For web site design, an HTML editor is necessary. The industry-standard software is Adobe Dreamweaver, as it is a WYSIWYG (*what you see is what you get*) program, so your page designs appear as they would in a web browser. It also has round-trip HTML, which means you can edit the code and page layout simultaneously so changes made to one are reflected in the other.

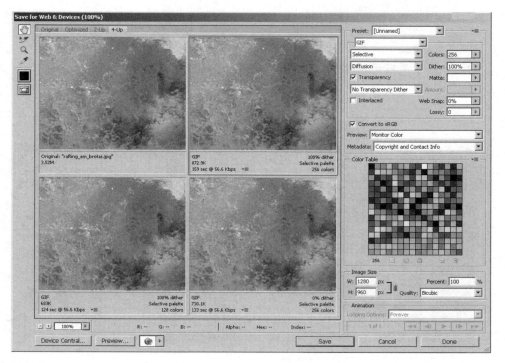

FIGURE 10-8 · Photoshop Save for Web & Devices window

NOTE *Dreamweaver requires that you are very organized with file names and folders. If you move anything out of a folder or change the name of a file on the desktop, Dreamweaver will lose the link to the image. This creates problems for the whole web site, so you will want to make any edits to files and folders within the program in the Files palette.*

Another program that has been in use since the late 1990s for web page layout and design is Microsoft FrontPage (see Figure 10-9). Although there has not been a new version since 2006, it is still widely used. BBEdit is professional computer programmers' text-editing program that is also used for web page development.

Flash is a popular professional software program by Adobe that is used for web design by means of ActionScript. Flash allows for browser-capable multimedia applications (meaning that it lets you create multimedia programs that are compatible with web browsers). The program creates compiled formats that can be played by stand-alone media players, played in browsers using plugins, or compiled with players to create executable files (flash.exe).

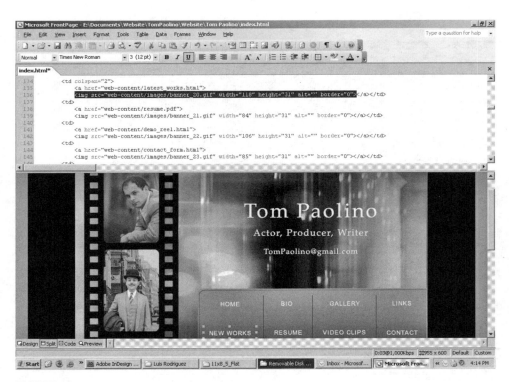

FIGURE 10-9 • FrontPage web design example

Flash is more dynamic than Dreamweaver, as you can create animated roll-overs with sound effects for buttons and menus. Dreamweaver can become more interactive with supplemental code by incorporating HTML5 and JavaScript, as well as by importing SWF files from Flash.

Flash and Shockwave players are software *plug-ins* needed by the user to view the content in their web browser. When creating web sites, you will want to include a link so the necessary plug-in can be downloaded in case users do not already have it installed on their computers. Adobe Acrobat Reader is another widely used plug-in for PDF documents, which is typically installed on the end user's computer along with the operating system software.

Dozens of authoring programs have tried to enable multimedia. Prior to the Web, such programs typically created stand-alone or player-based presentations. However, the emergence of web-based multimedia centered on the web browser led to plug-in based players. Ultimately, Flash became the primary delivery platform for interactivity and multimedia. Currently there is a debate as to whether HTML5, with its comparatively strong multimedia capabilities, will replace Flash as the tool of choice for multimedia delivery.

A number of free and inexpensive web-authoring programs can be down-loaded from the Web. A few worth looking into are Serif WebPlus, NetObjects Fusion, Nvu, KompoZer, and Trellian WebPage.

While creating web designs, you should regularly preview your work in a browser window throughout the duration of a project, and preferably more than one browser for comparison purposes (see Figure 10-10). Test your designs on different displays (desktop, laptop, and mobile) and various operating systems to view how the pages will look on different computers.

TIP *Newer Macintosh computers use the Intel processor so they are able to run Windows as well as the native operating system. This enables cross-platform testing on one computer. The Windows operating system is built in such a way that it is difficult to have two different versions of Internet Explorer installed on the same computer. However, the free IETester program (www.my-debugbar.com/wiki/ IETester/HomePage) enables several different versions of the HTML and JavaScript rendering engines to be used on the same computer.*

You can use a variety of methods to upload web files to a File Transfer Protocol (FTP) site so that they are available on the Internet. If you're working with Dreamweaver to design a web site, you can upload files directly to an FTP

FIGURE 10-10 · Firefox web browser with different iTunes displays

site from within the program. FileZilla and Cyberduck are free FTP client programs for the Mac; another low-cost option is Fetch. For both Mac and Windows, Classic FTP is free; CuteFTP and CrossFTP are inexpensive, if you want more options.

Presentations

Although multimedia end products are typically thought of as web pages and interactive kiosks, presentations often include many different types of media, such as video, animation, typography, photos, graphics, sound effects, narration, and music.

A few better-known software programs for creating dynamic presentations are Microsoft PowerPoint, Adobe Acrobat, Google Docs, and Apple Keynote. For instance, PowerPoint allows you to import, edit, compress, and embed video; import and edit photos; add templates and animated transitions; and customize typographic effects.

TIP   *There are a number of free downloadable media resources from Microsoft Office, which you can find at http://office.microsoft.com/en-us/images/??Ori gin=EC790014051033&CTT=6&ver=12&app=winword.exe. SmartArt graphics for PowerPoint are free to download from http://office.microsoft.com/en-us/ powerpoint-help/free-new-smartart-graphics-available-HA010211779.aspx.*

Media Players

In order to watch video, animation, and audio files, you need a *player* application. Media players are software programs for listening to music and watching video. Such programs allow you to control the playback with start, stop, pause, fast-forward, and rewind options. Some of the more widely used players are Apple QuickTime, Apple iTunes, (see Figure 10-11), Windows Media Player, Adobe Media Player, Flash Movie Player, and Miro 4.

FIGURE 10-11 · Apple iTunes media player

These programs are typically installed with the computer's operating system, but player applications can be downloaded or upgraded from the Internet. There are also a number of free YouTube players, which let you play videos and listen to music directly on your desktop, as well as save them to your computer without opening a web browser.

Media players that can be downloaded from the Web that will let you organize and play stored media files are Songbird, Winamp, MediaMonkey, and Banshee. You should have all of these player applications to test different files and formats. GraphicConverter is a free converter for graphics files. Adobe Media Encoder is designed for converting audio and video files into a variety of formats for distribution purposes.

TIP   *Multimedia files can be saved and played in numerous formats, whether for the Web or to be stored on a computer. Go to http://multimedia.cx/formats.html for a list of formats used to transport multimedia data.*

Summary

Now you have a fairly good idea of what you need to create multimedia from both a software and hardware standpoint. Read up on existing and new software to find what works best for both your style and the project at hand. It is important to remember that when downloading software from the Web—regardless of whether it is free or has a cost—you must first check the system requirements to make sure it is compatible with your computer and operating system.

QUIZ

1. Which company produces most of the industry-standard software for professionals working with illustration, print production, photographic imaging, and web design?
   A. Apple
   B. Adobe
   C. Microsoft
   D. Corel

2. What is Adobe Illustrator software best used for?
   A. Vector graphics
   B. Photographic images
   C. Animation
   D. Video

3. What is a free converter program for graphics files?
   A. Photoshop
   B. GraphicConverter
   C. Flash
   D. After Effects

4. Screen captures on the Mac can be done using which technique?
   A. A camera
   B. Pressing COMMAND-SHIFT-4
   C. Using screen-recording software
   D. All of the above

5. What are pixel-based images, like those in Adobe Photoshop, also called?
   A. Bitmapped
   B. Vector
   C. Object-oriented
   D. Lines and shapes with anchor points

6. What do media players allow you to do?
   A. Watch video, animation, and audio files
   B. Control the playback with start, stop, pause, fast-forward, and rewind options
   C. Test different files and formats
   D. All of the above

7. Digital magazines, or e-zines, can be created with which kind of software?
   A. Vector graphics and illustration
   B. Desktop publishing
   C. Photo editing
   D. Digital video

8. **Audio-editing software can create mashups. What are these?**
   A. Music blends
   B. Individual songs
   C. Mono sound effects
   D. Music scores

9. **What are media players primarily used for?**
   A. Recording songs
   B. Exporting music
   C. Playing video and audio files
   D. Recording and editing video

10. **FTP sites are intended for what purpose?**
    A. Sending email
    B. Blogging
    C. Transferring files to and from the Internet
    D. Recording music

Part IV

Multimedia End Products: Putting It All Together

Multimedia Projects

This chapter covers how we use multimedia. Bringing it all together for different purposes is what makes interactive multimedia so interesting, entertaining, and captivating. You will get an overview of various kinds of multimedia end products, along with some how-to information for gathering and preparing all your media elements. By the end of this chapter, you will be ready for the final stage of delivering your project to the intended audience, which is covered in Chapter 12.

CHAPTER OBJECTIVES

In this chapter, you will:

- Learn about different kinds of multimedia projects and their uses
- Find out how to prepare multimedia for diverse outcomes
- Know what it means to organize and plan for a complete multimedia project
- Discover the ways in which interactive multimedia programs and uses are similar and how they differ

Categorizing Multimedia Uses

We use interactivity all the time, even without our full awareness. When we cook, make phone calls, wash laundry, and drive, we are physically and intellectually relating to an interface of some sort. Currently, we are living in a realm of interactive multimedia due to the digital nature of all our high-tech appliances, tools, and gadgets.

All of these multimedia uses can be broken down into several broad categories: education and training, entertainment, information, business, and personal. Whether you are an end user who wants to understand what multimedia is and what goes into making it, or you are a designer or developer who is entrenched in the process of creating it, you can benefit from an overview of what it means to consolidate media into a cohesive, functional package. This chapter provides that overview, discussing the approaches for the following types of multimedia uses:

- Presentations
- Video and animation
- Educational and training programs
- Web sites
- Apps and mini software programs
- Video games
- Other gadgets and devices

When interactive multimedia is designed well, the experience is seamless and requires little thought. However, when a project is poorly designed and executed, it interferes with our lives and intrudes on our time and efficiency. The following sections provide some tips for preparing well-designed projects of each type.

Presentations

Presentations provide information to an audience on a topic or idea. They are widely used in education, business, and the medical field. Multimedia presentations help to reinforce a concept or demonstrate a procedure (see Figure 11-1).

Many presentation programs are referred to as *authoring tools* because they allow you to author (write) and build presentations. Microsoft's PowerPoint is one of the better-known presentation software programs. PowerPoint presentation

FIGURE 11-1 • A presenter on stage

files can be made into movie sequences to play using QuickTime or RealPlayer, saved in PDF format for handouts, and exported for web delivery to reach a wider audience (see Figure 11-2). A similar program is Apple's Keynote, which is frequently updated with new features that make it much more of a multimedia staple than it once was.

PowerPoint allows you to create text, insert hyperlinks, add animation and video, apply transitions between screens, and incorporate sound effects and/or music. These capabilities help to make what were at one time boring slide lectures come alive. Audiences become more engaged, and associations can be readily drawn when various media elements are used to explain and demonstrate abstract concepts and ideas.

With Adobe Flash, you can create simple animated slide show presentations, which are commonly used for portfolio photo galleries.

Table 11-1 outlines the basic steps for preparing presentations that include multimedia elements.

FIGURE 11-2 • PowerPoint presentation in development mode, as a movie sequence, a web page, and a PDF handout

TABLE 11-1 Preparing Multimedia Presentations

Task	Presentation Consideration
Create or acquire media elements and import them into the presentation software.	Different kinds of media need to be saved in formats that are compatible with the software.
Organize the content: create, duplicate, edit and rearrange slides, place multimedia in appropriate locations, and add notes.	Successful presentations rely on careful planning and organization, as well as a logical sequencing.
Preview and test the presentation. Make necessary changes.	This step will confirm whether the presentation is organized and flows.
Save the presentation in the following manner: source format (in the original program), a stand-alone executable (so it will play even if a user does not have the program), a file that can be played with a plug-in or with a media player (so it will play automatically as a sequential screen show), a document (PDF format), and a web page.	Saving presentations in multiple file formats assures versatility on different platforms and devices.

Video and Animation

Whether it is designed for the Web, TV, or the theater, digital media are incorporated into just about every facet of what we view. Including animation and video makes the subject interesting and intriguing, adds entertainment value, and keeps us glued to our screens. We watch moving images in many formats, with cell phones, tablets, laptops, and desktop computers.

Video, animation, and film are usually considered time-based linear media, and they are not complete without sound. Such media are often accompanied by text for titles and credits, graphics, and cartoons added to live action. A number of media elements are mixed in to bring video and animation to the level of multimedia. It is this combination of media that makes a richer experience (see Figure 11-3). If it is a nonparticipatory movie, for instance, then it is viewed passively. If 3D digital movies are watched with 3D glasses in a theater, the experience is closer to active participatory viewing (see Figure 11-4). When interactivity

FIGURE 11-3 • A meteorologist using an animated computer program to track weather patterns

FIGURE 11-4 · Audience watching a 3D movie; feature movies with live action and computer animation

is added, the users can control their experience. Interactive animation and video can be game-oriented or have an educational or professional focus.

Table 11-2 outlines the basic steps for preparing animation and video with respect to multimedia.

TABLE 11-2 Preparing Animation and Video for Multimedia

Task	Animation and Video Consideration
Determine how many video or animation sequences are needed and how long they should be.	The amount of video or animation is determined by the underlying purpose and goals of the project (why it is being used).
Plan the progression with storyboards.	Storyboards help to visualize the animation or video and show the narrative sequence.
Record or acquire video and create animation. Incorporate and edit audio and music, and add special effects.	Timing and synchronizing both movement and sound are crucial to communicating an effective message.
Preview the movie files within editing software.	This step will confirm if it plays correctly.
Save and compress files as needed. Perform quality assurance (QA) testing.	Testing on different media players and web browsers verifies performance.
Link or embed movie files.	The media files need to be coordinated within the multimedia project or web site.

Educational and Training Programs

Most schools, colleges, hospitals, medical centers, businesses, and homes use some form of interactive multimedia for educational and training purposes (see Figure 11-5). Because students are actively involved in the process, interactive multimedia assists them in learning concepts more readily. Users can also go at their own pace, which is essential for the learning process. For instance, providing timed quizzes with immediate feedback reinforces learning by having users adhere to a schedule.

Simulations are also very useful multimedia formats for the medical field and the military, such as virtual surgery and flight simulators

Table 11-3 outlines the process of developing interactive educational multimedia.

FIGURE 11-5 · Interactive programs used in the military, the medical field, manufacturing, and education.

TABLE 11-3 Preparing Educational Multimedia

Task	Educational Consideration
Determine the scope of the project. Create a flowchart for a project overview.	Asking questions and making a clear, logical plan will assist with project development.
Research the subject and write the content.	Consulting a content expert is important for accuracy. Make sure the content has been proofread and edited before incorporating it into the project.
Choose which authoring program will be used.	The type of authoring program and platform should be based on the rationale behind the project.
Record, create, or acquire media (graphics, photos, audio, video, and animation), add audio (music and sound effects), and make necessary edits.	Media elements should be age-appropriate and geared toward the particular subject.
Design screens—including the layout, type, colors, buttons, and menus—using image-editing programs.	GUIs should reflect the concept of the project.
Author or program to add functionality.	Using programming code allows for a variety of interactive capabilities.
Perform user testing to ensure functionality.	QA tests address performance issues so bugs can be fixed.

Web Sites

Interactive web sites are the very essence of the Web (see Figure 11-6). Web pages are fundamentally based on HTML tags, as discussed in Chapter 8. Multimedia rich web sites are the norm today. They can be created using HTML and extending it with XML, JavaScript, and Java programs (also called *applets*), which are inserted into HTML documents or Flash ActionScript for animation and interactivity. Audio and video files can be embedded into HTML pages, and animation and interactivity can be created in Flash for dynamic menus and other navigational elements.

Web 2.0, a term coined by Tim O'Reilly, is considered the second generation, or *wave*, of the Web. The notion behind it was to combine full interaction and

FIGURE 11-6 · Interactive educational web site used on a desktop computer

collaboration on the Web. Web sites that adopt Web 2.0 instill more of a sense of community. Users engage in social networking, blogging, wiki creation, and file sharing, so that no one is left out of the loop and the interaction is live.

A few key factors affect the end-user web experience:

- Bandwidth speed
- The speed of the server providing the information that the user requested by clicking the link to the web page
- The user's own connection (hard-wired Ethernet or wireless)

If a web site is slow to load, or not all media come up on the screen, people are less likely to return to that site.

Still Struggling

A *browser* is software that lets you view and interact with the Web. Not all browsers are created equal. A number of different web browsers come into play when designing for the Web, such as Safari, Internet Explorer, Firefox, and Google Chrome. Media files on the Web can be played while using a browser or downloaded and played locally on a user's computer using player software.

As previously discussed, certain plug-ins are used to play media files within a web browser. However, unless a media file is a Multipurpose Internet Mail Extensions (MIME) type, browsers are not able to display multimedia. MIME types are media file types that can be played and viewed on the Internet. (MIME types were originally created so that text messages could be sent over the Internet.) Web browsers support MIME type media files, so media that is not in HTML format can still be displayed on the Web. A number of web sites list MIME types and their corresponding file extensions.

TIP *The W3Schools page at www.w3schools.com/media/media_mimeref.asp breaks down the MIME types into media categories.*

Table 11-4 explains how to prepare web sites that utilize multimedia.

TABLE 11-4 Preparing Multimedia Web Sites	
Task	**Web Site Consideration**
Plan goals, create flowcharts, and organize the content.	Decisions at this stage should be web–specific.
Gather media elements and make edits.	For fastest loading, graphics should be optimized and compressed.
Lay out pages with menus and user interface elements in an image–editing program or a web design program.	GUIs should reflect the concept or theme of the project.
Apply CSS to pages for structure and consistency.	Add interactivity with HTML, JavaScript, and Flash ActionScript.
Test pages in different web browsers.	Testing confirms that the user interface and media elements are functional.

Apps and Mini Software Programs

The use of multimedia is synonymous with apps. These are mini-applications, or small computer programs, that do everything from calculating taxes to stepping through recipes. They allow us to make and listen to music, translate phrases, manipulate photos and video, record and transmit/share audio, play games, and so on (see Figures 11-7 and 11-8). It seems there is an app for everything.

Using apps has the following advantages:

- There are many to choose from (more than 60,000 iPad apps and more than 350,000 iPhone apps).
- They are either free or rather cheap.
- They are easily accessed, as well as portable and convenient.
- Most apps do not need Internet access once they have been downloaded.

FIGURE 11-7 · App used on a cell phone

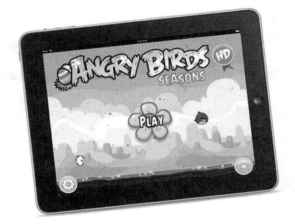

FIGURE 11-8 • Angry Birds game on the iPad

When computers first became multimedia-capable, they had limited hard drive space and screen real estate, so creating multimedia typically involved making files as small as possible. Then, with the emergence of the Internet, bandwidth limitations likewise required the same discipline. Now, with mobile apps, these same problems of small screen sizes and limited storage require a similarly disciplined approach.

Table 11-5 covers the creation of multimedia apps.

TABLE 11-5 Preparing Multimedia Apps for Mobile Devices	
Task	**Mobile Considerations**
Decide on the mobile app platform.	The app needs to be platform–specific so it will be functional.
Download the appropriate software development kit (SDK).	Each app platform has particular developmental requirements.
Plan the program within the context of its intended purpose.	The purpose of the project should be appropriate for a mini–application.
Design for mobile devices and reduced screen sizes.	Depending on the app, use gaming software, programming languages, or app development software.
Author or program to add functionality.	Interactive capabilities should suit small touchscreen devices.
Test on various devices (cell phones and/or tablets), and update as needed.	QA tests address performance issues.
Sign up as a developer for the specific platform (such as Android).	The app needs to be made available for download and purchase.

Video Games

Video games are the epitome of interactivity, as the user is inherently engaged, actively involved, and participating in every facet of the experience (see Figures 11-9 and 11-10). For instance, with the Nintendo DS and Wii game systems, the game controllers allow users to make quick, realistic movements of the characters on screen. They can jump, punch, run, fly, and move forward and backward. Sound effects and music reinforce the gameplay.

The *controller* is the interactive device that responds to the user's input and affects what is happening on the screen. Some games do not require a handheld device to interact with the system. With the Xbox Kinect and PlayStation Move, the user makes full-body physical movements or small hand gestures and facial expressions in front of a sensor to alter the characters' actions on the screen.

FIGURE 11-9 • Children using the Nintendo DS

FIGURE 11-10 · People using the Wii

A number of games originate as 3D movies, such as *Avatar* and *Tron: Legacy*. These film-based video games fulfill two types of entertainment purposes, as they tie together the passive experience of theater or home viewing with the active participation of interactive gaming.

There are a number of approaches to gaming. Some are computer-based games that can be downloaded from the Web or purchased on CD and installed. Some can be used with a mouse on a desktop computer or laptop, or with a more intricate trackball device that has sensitive input capabilities. Others are simultaneous role-playing games against live opponents via an online connection.

Developing blockbuster action video games such as Call of Duty or The Sims is a specialized skill that uses specific programming tools. While they fall into the category of multimedia, they generally require a different development approach than that of most multimedia.

Table 11-6 lists game development strategies.

TIP *More on the game development procedure can be found at http://en .wikipedia.org/wiki/Video_game_development - Development_process.*

TABLE 11-6 Preparing and Developing Video Games	
Task	**Game Development Consideration**
Decide which format to use (online, CD, or game system).	Choose the gaming platform that will be used to develop the game (Microsoft, Sony, or Nintendo).
Work on concept development.	Determine the game plan, goals, characters, and setting, including user input and available controls.
Select a game design program (development software) or 3D animation software to design a prototype for testing and demonstrating features. Add audio (music and sound effects).	Design, render, and animate objects, characters, scenes, and props, keeping in mind the theme and player usage.
Produce the game by adding functionality.	Using programming code and game development tools allow for interactivity.
Perform user testing.	The game's functionality needs to be tested on the platform that will be used.

Noteworthy Gadgets and Devices

Developers continue to come up with new multimedia devices and features to enrich users' experiences. 3D TV is an example of technology that was once reserved for the movie theater and is now distributed to the consumer market for home use (see Figure 11-11). Some TVs require the use of 3D glasses, while others, such as Philips 3D Max, do not require glasses due to a 3D polarizer integrated in the TV screen.

Another noteworthy device is one that Nintendo developed called Wii U that uses a controller in conjunction with a Wii console and is a multiplayer game system. It has a multipurpose use for interactivity with surface controls, a stylus pen, and a touchscreen. When you move the controller, it interacts with the graphics on the TV display. Others playing can use handheld controllers for interacting with the TV, which in turn affects the play on the Wii U device. This is offering multiple *everything*—screens, players, controls, and movements—for a fuller interactive experience.

Another interactive multimedia feature intertwined with print that is increasingly used for advertising, promotion, and other purposes is the *quick response*

FIGURE 11-11 • People watching 3D TV

(QR) code. The QR code is a matrix (or 2D) barcode that can be read using a QR reader app by means of a phone camera (see Figure 11-12). Once scanned, the data in the code will take you to a landing page on the Web or provide information with a text message. For example, a QR code may be printed in a newspaper as part of an article about food. Users can take a photo of the code with their cell phone, and use it to visit a web site that supplies a virtual coupon for a product that was highlighted in the article.

The QR code capability is interactive on many levels, because it involves a physical medium on which the code is printed (poster, book, sign, business card, clothing, and so on), which is then embedded within digital data, and that must be triggered by the individual user.

QR codes provide product, event, and contact information, as well as discounts, videos, reviews, and promotions. Marketers can use QR codes to track consumer interest based on how many people scanned the code.

FIGURE 11-12 • QR code used in a museum exhibit

Summary

In this chapter, you learned how to distinguish between different multimedia formats and products. Multimedia takes on countless forms and serves endless purposes, so categorizing the types of projects in this chapter was necessary to simplify the extensive list of uses. This topic leads us to the following chapter, which describes how to deliver multimedia.

QUIZ

1. **What are some advantages of using apps?**
   A. Inexpensive or free
   B. Many to choose from
   C. Easily accessible
   D. All of the above

2. **What is not one of the primary factors affecting the end-user web experience?**
   A. Web browser
   B. Bandwidth speed
   C. Speed of the server
   D. Computer connection to the Internet

3. **Which kind of multimedia is best for learning?**
   A. Apps and mini-applications
   B. Interactive educational programs
   C. Video games
   D. Presentations

4. **What is one of the key components for interactivity when playing a video game?**
   A. Display
   B. Animation
   C. Controller
   D. Sound

5. **Of the following software programs, which one is primarily designed for creating presentations?**
   A. Photoshop
   B. CorelDraw
   C. PowerPoint
   D. Illustrator

6. **What does the *QR* in QR code stand for?**
   A. Quality response
   B. Quick reader
   C. Quantity reader
   D. Quick response

7. **What is the focus of Web 2.0?**
   A. Collaboration and community
   B. Connection speed
   C. Greater access to multimedia
   D. Text-based web pages

8. **Which three companies develop (manufacture) the most established video game platforms and consoles?**
   A. Apple, Adobe, Corel
   B. Sony, Nintendo, Microsoft
   C. Nintendo, Adobe, Corel
   D. Nintendo, Microsoft, Apple

9. **Multimedia rich web sites can be created using HTML and extended with:**
   A. XML
   B. JavaScript
   C. Java
   D. All of the above

10. **What kind of programming does Adobe Flash use for animation and interactivity?**
   A. Java
   B. JavaScript
   C. ActionScript
   D. HTML

chapter 12

Delivery Systems

We have come a long way on our path to understanding multimedia. This final chapter explores how multimedia is delivered to the end user. After all that has gone into a multimedia project—the planning and preparation, recording and editing, programming, and finalizing—it needs to be brought to fruition and made accessible. There are a variety of options for delivering multimedia, which will be discussed here.

CHAPTER OBJECTIVES

In this chapter, you will:

- Learn what it means to deliver a multimedia product to the intended audience

- Discern between portable and permanent displays, as well as single versus multiple displays, and when it is best to use each one

- Figure out the distinction between the preparation of files for the Web compared with that of discs, such as CDs and DVDs

- Understand how multimedia projection is used as a more effective means of presenting to larger audiences

- Find out about multimedia projection and interactive whiteboards as a means of presenting to groups

- Discover several aspects of web site maintenance and updating multimedia titles

Multimedia Product Maintenance

Multimedia needs to remain current by keeping pace with technological advancements and consumer demand. In particular, factoring in web site maintenance is an important part of any web development project. Users expect up-to-date information and will return regularly if satisfied with their experience. You cannot expect to create it, deploy it, and be done with it.

Making sure everything continues to work requires ongoing assessments of content and functionality, as well as performing updates and making repairs. This is similar to maintaining your car so the engine keeps running smoothly.

Multimedia can become obsolete over time due to outdated technology, or it may contain content that needs to be restructured, such as news or other time-sensitive information. Also, if a title is successful, there are valid reasons for upgrading to newer versions. When designing and developing multimedia, you must be able to recognize how titles become outdated and know how to update them.

TIP *Many companies offer web site maintenance. This is a worthwhile price to pay if you are not planning to do it yourself.*

Table 12-1 lists some maintenance issues to keep in mind.

TABLE 12-1 Maintaining Multimedia Products	
Area	**How to Check**
Browser compatibility	Test the web site on different browsers regularly.
Links	Check for dead or broken links.
Web site visits	Obtain activity reports.
HTML standards	Check on markup validity at http://validator.w3.org/.

Troubleshooting and User Testing

The first step in finalizing and preparing a multimedia project is troubleshooting and testing. User testing is a crucial part of the process, as it rules out any issues before the product is shipped. Companies refer to this procedure as *quality assurance* (QA).

As discussed in Chapter 2, there are two phases for testing multimedia projects: alpha and beta. The alpha testing phase is done early on after the project is completed to see if there are any obvious bugs to address. The beta test phase is completed last to verify the functionality with the intended audience.

Performing QA procedures will confirm the program is free of programming errors. If a multimedia title is released with functional problems, users will face problems when interacting with it. For instance, they may not be able to get to the next page or level, the program may freeze, or the navigation may not work correctly. Any of these issues would most likely deter people from using the product again.

The remedy at this point would be to pull the product and fix it, which could affect the credibility of the product as well as the company. Needing to do this will require a lot of extra work, as well as costing more in the long run. Prior testing is vital for the success of the product and the reputation of the company or developer.

NOTE *It is better to wait until a product is completely ready to deliver, rather than rushing it out the door to meet an arbitrary deadline. The bottom line is that you should allow for testing and troubleshooting in the planning stages, so you will have a realistic time frame to meet your project goals.*

In the best-case scenario, a multimedia project should be tested on the intended platform, which should be decided at the beginning of the project. This test will affect how the program is designed. For instance, if you are aware it is to be used on a computer station in a museum, you can more readily predict the outcome of the user's actions and therefore plan the functionality accordingly.

It is difficult to know *exactly* how a multimedia program will be used and how it will perform, as there are many different types of hardware and computing platforms. Also the software programs—such as operating systems, web browsers, and media players—can vary. The solution is to test it on as many platforms using as much different software as possible (or take your chances). For an additional cost, you can hire a company to test it for you.

TIP   *A couple of QA companies are www.utest.com and www.a1qa.com. These companies will perform QA for your software and multimedia projects, and even provide documentation for the user.*

Unlike projects permanently fixed in a nonvolatile medium, such as CD or DVD, web-based projects are subject to several different issues:

- Users typically expect new or updated content.
- Links to external content often change or disappear.
- Servers do get corrupted, and in that case, online files will no longer be accessible.

In effect, due to the dynamic and fluctuating nature of the Web, deploying a web-based project is often an ongoing maintenance task.

Disc vs. Web Preparation

When a multimedia project is intended for web distribution, files and folders need to be moved to the Internet using FTP. This process of *uploading* to a server is a way of transferring files online so they can be viewed on the Web. Your server choices are as follows:

- The client's server
- A server that requires a fee to use
- A free, yet somewhat limited, server, such as a Google Gmail account

The product should be accompanied by a Help document with instructions on how to install and use it, as well as hardware and software compatibility information.

Files that are destined for disc can be copied to a CD, DVD, jump drive, or other storage media. Similar to web-deployed projects, you should provide documentation. Discs frequently include a README file that explains system requirements, installation procedures, and any documentation updates.

CDs and DVDs are ordinarily used when the software or game is not going to be downloaded from the Web. This is typically to control access to the product, as well as to manage marketing and distribution channels (such as purchasing a game from a store). DVDs hold much more data than CDs (more than 4GB compared with 700MB), so more complex multimedia titles with larger files can be included on a DVD.

When the production phase begins, a *master* disc is made that contains all the files needed for installing the program on a computer. As previously mentioned, the project must work flawlessly prior to mastering. Regardless of whether it is intended for a large or small production, the master is needed to replicate copies.

Lastly, packaging and documentation also must be designed and printed. The extent of this will vary depending on how large a distribution is planned. The marketing of a product is essential to how it sells—whether from a brick-and-mortar store, online, or both. Consumers make quality judgments based on the images and text used on the outside cover and overall appearance of the packaging.

Presentation Options

How a multimedia title will be presented to users is at the crux of the design. Regardless of whether it will be used publicly or privately, it is important to address presentation options in the planning and development stages. You must identify the way in which a multimedia program will be used and displayed at the beginning of the project because these are directly tied to the technology that will be needed to create it. Table 12-2 lists the presentation options available.

Portable or Permanent Displays

Two primary categories for presenting multimedia are portable and permanent (or more likely, semipermanent).

Multimedia can be movable, which means it is transported by the presenter and set up for an individual or group (see Figure 12-1). With portable multimedia, the presenter can show the display directly on a laptop or tablet computer, or connect it to a larger screen. Users can also interact with the program individually using a tablet computer, mobile device, or laptop. These are considered portable, as they are not locked down or secured to one location.

The mobility of a portable presentation affords flexibility and immediacy, and it is well suited for direct interactivity by the user. If it is to be used by a small group or an individual, it can be shown on whatever size display it is capable of being viewed on. However, when a large group is viewing a multimedia presentation, a portable device would need to be projected to a larger screen with an LCD projector or attached by cable to a large computer display or TV monitor (see Figure 12-2).

TABLE 12-2 Presentation Options for Viewing and Interacting with Multimedia

Category	Description
Portable or permanent displays	Temporary, movable displays (portable) or long-term setups (permanent) of a multimedia program
Kiosks	Stand-alone computer terminals or public information displays that use touchscreen technology
Projection	LCD unit mounted on the ceiling, placed on a cart, or located above or behind a whiteboard as a means of projecting a computer monitor onto a larger screen
Multiple screens	Screens used to present and interact with multimedia (either large sizes or smaller desktop displays)
Interactive whiteboards	Large computer screens that can be interacted with (also called SMART Boards)
Touchscreens	Screens developed for TVs, computer monitors, and handheld devices that can be used with fingers and hands, rather than a mouse and keyboard, for interactivity and input
E-readers	Electronic book readers for printed material, such as books, newspapers, magazines (such as the Barnes & Noble Nook, Amazon Kindle, and Sony Reader)
Video game platforms	Game systems: PCs (Windows, Mac, and Linux) and consoles (Xbox, PlayStation, Wii); handheld devices (smart phones, Nintendo DS, PlayStation PSP, Apple iPad, and iPod)
Simulations	Dedicated hardware systems, often with controls configured to replicate actual environments such as airplane cockpits

Portable multimedia is advantageous for the following reasons:

- It is convenient and easy to set up.
- It is always available.
- Updates can be made on the fly.
- It offers control over the presentation.
- It is fast and immediate.

However, there are also downsides to portable multimedia presentations. Small displays can accommodate only limited sized groups, so you cannot reach as wide an audience. Also, they are not easily presented to large groups because

FIGURE 12-1 · Portable laptops and mobile devices

you need an additional screen and projector, requiring a fair amount of equipment to set up.

Permanent multimedia systems are those that are intended to stay in one place for the duration of a contract or agreement. Some examples include a kiosk in a shopping mall to order products and a computer terminal in a museum that accompanies an exhibit.

Permanent displays are not applicable to web multimedia, as these are inherently independent of particular hardware at a single location, unless a web site is accessed from only one location and is restricted from being used by the general public. In that case, a multimedia project that has a web component would need to be password-protected and used directly by individuals. It would also need to be permanently displayed as a self-contained computer station—a kiosk, as discussed next.

Kiosks

A *kiosk* is a stand-alone computer terminal used for public information or services. Kiosks are widely used today for convenience purposes. Also, automated

FIGURE 12-2 · Presenting to an audience using a large screen

services save on costs when it comes to hiring employees. They encourage independence and self-reliance on the user's part. The self-service quality is part of the appeal (see Figure 12-3). For instance, it is typically faster and more efficient to use a computer to make a purchase than it is to go through a checkout line at a store.

Kiosks are used for interactive games and entertainment at video arcades, amusement parks, movie theaters, casinos, cyber cafes, hotels, and resorts. They are commonly available for shopping purposes, such as price checking, product searching and purchasing, and food vending. They are also increasingly used in cities for automated bike and car rentals, as well as making payments for parking spaces. And, of course, kiosks for educational purposes can be found in many museums and institutions.

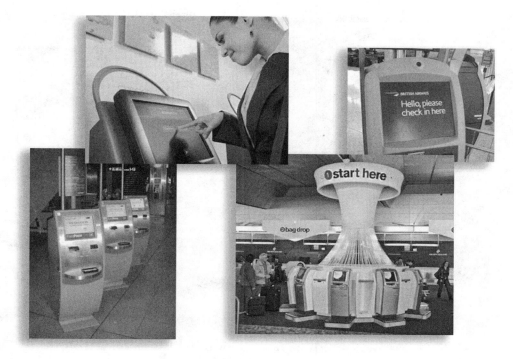

FIGURE 12-3 • Airport and hotel check-in kiosks

Projects destined for kiosk installation are particularly prone to problems and vulnerable to vandalism. They are often located in public places (see Figure 12-4), which can lead to damages requiring repairs that cannot always be addressed in a timely manner. The project needs to be housed in a well-built, tamperproof unit and secured to a semipermanent platform.

Additionally, publicly placed kiosks, such as ticket dispensers and information booths, get a significant amount of use on a daily basis. As a result, they need to be tested thoroughly using a general audience sampling, as you do not know for certain what age, gender, or educational level users will have.

Touchscreens, which will be discussed later in this chapter, are commonly used for kiosks, as they are user-friendly and easy to use.

Projection

There are a few different ways to project multimedia onto a large screen. This is done primarily for a presentation at a meeting, in an auditorium, with a museum exhibit, in a classroom, or at an event with a group of people or large audience. The purpose of projection is to allow for ample viewing at different locations in a room.

FIGURE 12-4 • Interactive kiosks for subway tickets and museum education

As discussed in Chapter 9, LCD projectors are the most common technology for projecting computer monitors onto large screens. Using an LCD projector and a few cables, you can project from a laptop, desktop computer, phone, or tablet screen onto a large screen or clean, flat wall (see Figure 12-5).

 Still Struggling

As discussed in Chapter 9, LCD projectors work by light reflecting off two mirrors inside the projector, which divide it into the three additive colors of red, green, and blue. Each color passes through a separate LCD panel that is made up of pixels. The three colors recombine as light as they pass through a prism, which is then projected through the lens. Images are projected in the form of pixels that appear as full color on the screen. LCD panels are found in many electronics, such as cell phones, calculators, alarm clocks, and cameras, since they are light-weight and use a small amount of power to run.

FIGURE 12-5 • Uses of LCD projection

Another type of projection is one that is *backlit*. Backlit LCD projection uses LED technology to illuminate a display from behind. LED displays project a brighter, sharper image than LCD high-definition monitors and TVs due to the number of LEDs used. Purchasing one is an expensive prospect, however, so it is worth looking into rental options.

With LCD projectors, the presenter or user often blocks the projection if the unit is placed directly in front of a screen. Other alternatives include rear projection or backlit interactive whiteboards using LCD technology, and front projection with an LCD mounted on top of the screen or whiteboard. A popular type of interactive whiteboard is the SMART Board, as discussed later in the chapter.

Some portable cell phone projectors allow you to show photos, video, and web sites on any flat surface. Such portable, lightweight, easy-to-use, reasonably priced projection for handheld devices provides us with the capability of sharing multimedia at a moment's notice.

Multiple Screens

Some multimedia projects require more than one screen. How does this decision affect the way users interact with or view a multimedia presentation?

A single display is fine for a web site, but multiple displays are better for slides with accompanying video, for instance, so the text explaining the concept is alongside the movie that *shows* how it is done.

Using more than one screen requires planning, money, equipment, and time, so you need to make sure it's worth the investment. Most multimedia presentations are more than adequate with a single display. You should have a valid reason for using more than one screen. Ask this question: Will the setup support both the concept (main idea) and the experience for the viewer/user?

Desktop displays intended for a single user typically do not require an advanced setup with multiple screens. Some examples are web sites, individual training/testing programs, private viewing of videos and movies, and educational programs in schools. These can be flat-screen LCDs or older CRTs, which range in size from 13 to 24 inches.

You might use additional monitors for desktop computers at home or work (for productivity and workflow purposes) as an alternative to purchasing a larger display (see Figure 12-6), which is a more costly option. The primary

FIGURE 12-6 · Dual-monitor setup for a desktop computer

FIGURE 12-7 · Multiple computer monitors used with TV and video displays

reason is to be able to multitask and increase productivity, which is a necessity for security monitoring and TV news broadcasting (see Figure 12-7).

TIP *For the pros and cons of using multiple monitors, visit www.webdesignerdepot .com/2009/05/advantages-and-disadvantages-of-working-with-multiple-screens/.*

Laptop computers are another type of screen for personal use of multimedia. These displays tend to be smaller due to the associated technology. For certain kinds of multimedia, even small displays such as these can benefit the user if more than one is used. A laptop connected to a TV for broadcast video production is one example. A medical technician using a desktop computer with patient data or diagnostic information tethered to a screen showing x-rays is another.

Presentations including photos or other images that need to be accompanied by text and diagrams are more beneficial when placed on separate screens so side-by-side comparisons can be made. When an auditorium or arena is large, there needs to be multiple simultaneous viewing locations so all members of the audience have a vantage point. Examples of this would be a political convention, music concert, or professional sporting event at a large venue (see Figure 12-8).

FIGURE 12-8 • Multiple large screens at a convention

Another scenario that would benefit from multiple large screens is when a presenter stands near the screen and interacts with it, and other displays around the room illustrate facts with diagrams and pictures that pertain to the topic. You might find presentations like this at a medical conference or technology expo, for example. Add animation, music, lighting effects, and video, and throw in special effects—such as vibrating seats, fans blowing air or aromas, and water sprayers—for a full sensory experience. This type of show is customary at Disney World, where nothing is held back in the name of entertainment.

Interactive Whiteboards

Interactive whiteboard is a generic name for the SMART Board brand (http://smarttech.com). This is in essence a very large computer screen with interactive capabilities (see Figure 12-9). A projector displays the output of a computer screen onto the SMART Board to allow users to interact with what is on the screen. SMART Boards operate like touchscreens—you can drag, tap, and erase elements using your hands, your fingers, or a pen tool as a means of affecting what is displayed. The SMART company also offers an interactive table, or SMART Table, for younger learners.

SMART Boards have increased in size, which is advantageous, but compatibility between devices is more complicated than it was in the past, and this often leads to technical problems when you least want them. Before purchasing an interactive whiteboard, do some research and make sure the hardware that will be connected to it is compatible with the particular make and model.

FIGURE 12-9 · Interactive whiteboard

Interactive whiteboards are very successful for classroom learning because they get students enthused and excited about learning due to a direct involvement with the material. Teachers can also save the lessons prepared in class for students to review at home.

Interactive whiteboards have the following features:

- Internet connection to access dates and facts and take virtual field trips
- Ability to create, animate, and manipulate objects
- Capability for active collaboration and group projects
- Hands-on learning with touchscreen capabilities
- Ability to write, edit, erase, move, and save notes with "digital ink"
- Intuitive and responsive interface
- Movability and flexibility (wall-mounted or attached to a stand)
- Screenshot recording for saving the screen in formats such as Microsoft PowerPoint and Word, to edit, distribute, or print

Touchscreen TVs and Handheld Devices

Touchscreens are displays that respond to the user's touch as opposed to relying on a mouse or stylus for input (see Figure 12-10). They are responsive and

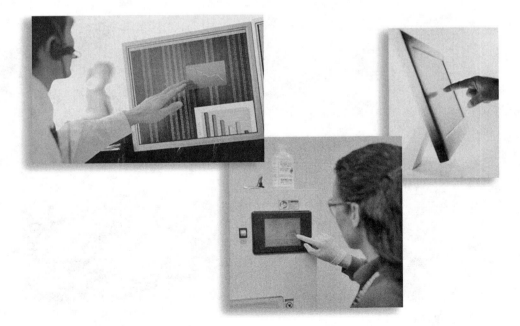

FIGURE 12-10 · Touchscreen technology

intuitive, which is the reason for their wide appeal when it comes to multimedia. The capability of pressing on exactly what you want is more natural than the disconnect that occurs when using a mouse or stylus for input and interactivity. It is easier to tap on graphics and words, type, and make edits directly on a screen than it is to set up and use separate peripherals.

Of course, using a mouse or touchpad becomes intuitive the more you use it, and your intended audience may have a lot of experience with both. However, it makes sense to offer a more instinctive user experience if it suits the purpose of the project and the technology is available and reasonably priced.

Touchscreens are less expensive to manufacture than they used to be, so they have become much more common. There are many benefits to using touchscreens, particularly due to their accessibility and usability, including the following:

- Touchscreens are faster and more efficient in the workplace for productivity and training.

- They are useful for automation processes in industry due to an immediate response to a user's actions, which could make a difference in terms of productivity and manufacturing costs.

- Touchscreens are helpful for those with limited mobility, as they are comprehensive and self-contained.

There are also some disadvantages to using touchscreens. Table 12-3 summarizes the pros and cons of using touchscreens.

TABLE 12-3 Pros and Cons of Touchscreens

Advantages	Disadvantages
They are fast and efficient.	The user interface can be too small and cause inaccuracies to occur (limited precision).
They are user–friendly (easy to use).	Screens need to be cleaned often, and scratches are more common.
They allow fluid, continuous movement.	Batteries run out more quickly due to demands on the CPU.
There is an intuitive, direct hand–to–screen correlation.	There are no keys to force a quit if a program freezes.
Portable models can be moved to different positions, for more comfortable use.	Arm and hand strain occur due to the screen angle and position.
There is less equipment to break.	Parts of the screen get covered up, making it difficult to have a complete view.

Touchscreen TVs are used for multimedia, as they allow users to directly access the media on screen. There are portable touchscreens that are essentially multimedia players with TV connection capabilities, and those designed for the car that have GPS, movies, and music features.

Touchscreen displays come in different sizes and vary in terms of quality. For desktop computers, they are useful because they have multiple functions. For example, they can be used as a touchscreen for direct demonstration to a group, as well as a regular display where input is accomplished with a physical keyboard and mouse.

The special appeal of touchscreens is that you generally find the same features as with smart phones and tablet computers, such as pinching to contract or expand the screen instead of zooming in and out, and flicking the screen instead of scrolling. A number of mobile phones and handheld devices provide touchscreens, such as the Apple iPad and iPod (see Figure 12-11), BlackBerry smart phones and PlayBook, and Motorola DROID.

Touchscreens are typically used for multimedia kiosks since they are easier and less costly to set up for a public multimedia station. They eliminate the inconvenience of needing a mouse or other input device. Usually, there is not

FIGURE 12-11 · Apple iPad touchscreen in use

enough room for a mouse. And if you do use separate input devices, they tend to disappear. A streamlined, self-contained unit is preferable; the more peripherals, the more that can go wrong.

TIP *CNET (www.cnet.com) is a very good web site for information and reviews on the latest technology. It also offers a TV site with demonstration videos, at http:// cnettv.cnet.com.*

E-Readers

E-readers, or e-book reading devices, provide avid bibliophiles and casual bookworms alike the capability of having volumes of books, stories, and articles literally at their fingertips (see Figure 12-12). Although they are not categorized in the same family as tablet computers and smart phones in terms of their multimedia capabilities, they have a considerable number of interactive features,

FIGURE 12-12 · E-readers

despite their primary function as an e-book. They are also more affordable and portable than most tablets or laptops, which adds to their appeal.

There are many e-readers to choose from, but a few of the more popular brands are the Amazon Kindle, the Barnes & Noble Nook, and the Sony Reader. Some make use of touchscreens, such as the Nook and the Reader; others do not (as a means of keeping the price lower).

Some e-reader features that appeal to consumers are a natural page appearance and screen design, as well as the overall look and feel of the device. *Electronic ink* is a display technology used to imitate the look of ink printed on paper. The result is natural-looking screen text, because it closely resembles an actual page in a book. More specifically, words appear to be typed on "digital paper" and are still readable in bright light, resulting in less eye fatigue. Some e-readers use LCD screens, which are lower in quality and have a shorter battery life.

An Internet connection is a standard feature in most e-readers, providing the ability to readily download books and look up words, dates, names, and other information relevant to what is presently being read. Some have Wi-Fi connectivity only, while others have 3G capabilities. Text-to-speech options are available for those who want to be read to or who have vision limitations.

TIP   *Take a look at these two web sites for comparisons of e-reader brands, costs, and features: http://ebook-reader-review.toptenreviews.com/ and http://ipod .about.com/od/ipadcomparisons/a/comparing-ipad-kindle-nook.htm.*

Video Game Consoles

Video games are relevant to the subject of delivery and presentation due to their inherent interactive qualities. Video games are associated with different platforms, which can be broken down into the following three categories: consoles, desktop, or handheld.

Microsoft Xbox 360, Nintendo Wii, and Sony PlayStation 3 are video game consoles that are widely used in the consumer market. Two of these companies also offer handheld portable models, such as the Sony PlayStation Vita and the Nintendo 3DS.

Video game consoles are units resembling DVD players that are attached to TV displays with cables. Players interact with them using various kinds of wired and wireless remote control devices (called *controllers*), as shown in Figure 12-13.

The first consoles were introduced in the early 1970s. In the 1980s, video arcade games were commonplace; users shelled out quarters for a chance to

FIGURE 12-13 · Interacting with a multiplayer game on the Xbox 360

beat the highest score. In the early 1980s, PCs began to replace arcades for video game use in homes. Today, numerous computer games for both individual and multiple players can be downloaded or purchased on CD for use with a desktop computer.

Handheld devices are portable and intended for individual game play. Examples are the Nintendo DSi and the iPod touch, which both have models with Internet capabilities for online game play. The DS Lite is an older model still in use that does not have a Wi-Fi feature, but players can synchronize and interact with each other in the same room with a single game card. This can be accomplished using the DS Download Play feature.

NOTE *For a video game timeline, visit www.onlineeducation.net/videogame_ timeline. For a history of video game consoles, go to www.time.com/time/ interactive/0,31813,2029221,00.html.*

Xbox Kinect and PlayStation Move are truly interactive game systems. Kinect is an add-on to the Xbox 360. With it, users' movements, facial expressions, and voice commands trigger a sensor that controls the game play, as opposed to using a remote controller that must be held. This is innovative now, but it will most likely become a standard way of interacting with multimedia games.

Wii Fit is an add-on to the Wii game system that requires a physical platform that the user stands on and it responds to their weight and movements, offering guidance with balance and fitness workouts to assist with getting in shape. You still need to use a wireless controller, but it is more of a full-body experience than just the Xbox 360 or PlayStation 3.

Still Struggling

Game consoles are manufacturer-specific, and games are purchased for the particular brand. Some game titles can be used with earlier console models, which means they are *backward-compatible*, but they are not interchangeable between products. For instance, Sony PlayStation units and games can be used only with the PlayStation; they will not work with the Nintendo Wii. This limits users somewhat, leading avid gamers to purchase or borrow other systems so they can take advantage of what each has to offer.

The supply of games for these devices and consoles appears endless. The themes range from simulation, role-playing, art and music creation, warfare, fitness, spelling and reading, car racing, dance instruction, crime-solving, puzzles, and sports.

Developing high-end 3D role-playing video games can take years to complete. Shorter, less intricate games take fewer hours and smaller teams to produce, and can be distributed more quickly.

Preparation for delivering video games requires a number of steps that will ensure the game will function properly when it hits the retail shelves or online stores. As discussed previously, each game must be tested thoroughly before final distribution, as there are many levels of interactivity to take into consideration. Any flaws or bugs that prevent smooth, uninterrupted game play will affect the profits of the game (word gets out quickly), as well as the company producing it. When a great deal of time, effort, and money are put into producing a video game title, especially those created for high-end platforms, it is crucial that user testing is factored into the development process.

Setting up and using consoles and game systems varies depending on the product, but is typically not very complicated for the average user. Providing instructions is essential. You'll also want to supply guidelines or a Help feature for using the game.

Delivering Multimedia

When a multimedia project is complete, it is time to prepare your product for *delivery* to its final destination where it will be used. At this stage in the development of the project, the media files that have been painstakingly treated and refined, and the programming that has been applied to provide interactivity, are compiled. They are then uploaded to the Web, burned to a disc, or installed on a computer that will be used to present or interact with the program. The following are some delivery scenarios:

- You deliver a multimedia project to a manufacturer of CDs or DVDs that will duplicate and distribute the product commercially through retail outlets.
- You transfer the files directly to the platform that will be used.
- You send files to the client, who will install it on the required computer(s).

Summary

This chapter covered the way in which multimedia is delivered to end users, as well as the many purposes of multimedia, including for business, education, entertainment, and finance. How you present and display multimedia should be at the crux of your project goals from the very start.

This chapter concludes our *Multimedia Demystified* journey together. The goal of this book has been to inform and guide you with the many aspects of multimedia. What lies ahead in terms of advancements to a multisensory approach to experiencing and interacting with media remains to be seen.

QUIZ

1. **What is the first phase of testing a multimedia project?**
   A. QA testing
   B. Alpha testing
   C. Beta testing
   D. Testing on the intended audience

2. **What is the kind of technology used for front projection onto a screen or wall?**
   A. LCD
   B. CRT
   C. LED
   D. RGB

3. **What is the electronic ink technology used by e-readers?**
   A. Type that appears darker than on a tablet or laptop computer
   B. Words that appear on an interactive whiteboard
   C. Ink on "digital paper"
   D. Touchscreens with editable text

4. **Multiple screens are often used for what purpose?**
   A. Viewing professional sports events
   B. Training and promoting products and services at conventions
   C. Entertaining audiences at music concerts
   D. All of the above

5. **What does LCD stand for?**
   A. Lasting computer display
   B. Liquid-crystal display
   C. Laptop computer diode
   D. Liquid computer display

6. **What are permanent multimedia displays described as?**
   A. Versatile for both stationary and movable purposes
   B. Intended to stay in one place for the duration of the contract or intended use of the program
   C. Temporary computer stations
   D. Moving around from place to place

7. **Interactive whiteboards are beneficial for education because they allow for which of the following?**
   A. Active collaboration and group projects
   B. Hands-on learning with touchscreen capabilities
   C. Internet connections to access dates and facts
   D. All of the above

8. **What are the three primary platform categories for video games?**
    A. PC, console, handheld
    B. Nintendo Wii, DS, and 3DS
    C. Microsoft, Sony, and Apple
    D. Wii, Xbox, and PlayStation

9. **In terms of presenting multimedia, what can be lit from the back or front of a display?**
    A. Touchscreen
    B. Desktop monitor
    C. LCD projection
    D. Laptop screen

10. **Kinect is a video game add-on associated with which product?**
    A. Wii Fit
    B. Nintendo DS
    C. PlayStation Move
    D. Xbox 360

Final Exam

1. Adobe produces many of the industry-standard software programs for professionals working with what kind of media?

   A. Illustration

   B. Digital imaging

   C. Web design

   D. All of the above

2. What does most screen-recording software allow you to do?

   A. Take screenshots

   B. Record screen activity

   C. Record audio while demonstrating with a computer

   D. All of the above

3. You can listen to audio, watch video and animation, and control the playback by using which of the following?

   A. Word processors

   B. Media players

   C. Image editors

   D. Illustration programs

4. What does desktop publishing software, such as Adobe InDesign, allow you to create?

   A. Digital magazines, or e-zines

   B. Web page layouts

C. Brochures

D. All of the above

5. **What are music blends created with audio-editing software called?**

    A. Mashups

    B. Prerecorded songs

    C. Sound effects

    D. Vocal recording

6. **What does the development of a multimedia project include?**

    A. Concept and planning

    B. Setting up a team

    C. Project management

    D. All of the above

7. **What is the final step in the multimedia development process?**

    A. Production

    B. Distribution and deployment

    C. Prototype

    D. Quality assurance

8. **What are authoring tools primarily used to do?**

    A. Give functionality and interactivity to a multimedia program

    B. Compress media files

    C. Edit images

    D. Create animation

9. **You should ask permission to use a photo in a multimedia project if you did not take it yourself to avoid which of the following?**

    A. A low-quality result

    B. Duplication by another company

    C. Copyright infringement

    D. Creative restrictions

10. **When trying to meet a deadline for delivering a multimedia kiosk to a client, what should you do?**

    A. Make sure that all the bugs have been fixed.

    B. Skip the testing phase, since it usually does not affect the end product.

    C. Perform the QA process with actual users after it is set up.

    D. Try to save time by bypassing potential functionality issues.

11. **What are kiosks?**

    A. Home gaming consoles

    B. Self-contained computing terminals

    C. Desktop computers

    D. Handheld devices

12. **What is Hypertext Markup Language?**

    A. Hyperlinks on a web site

    B. A programming language for developing games

    C. A markup language for preparing web pages

    D. An authoring programs like Adobe Flash

13. **Which of the following is a positive feature when using interactive multimedia?**

    A. Self-paced

    B. Simulates environments

    C. Hands-on

    D. All of the above

14. **Which of the following are the responsibilities of the project manager on a multimedia development team?**

    A. To plan, organize, and oversee the project

    B. To develop the prototype

    C. To edit the video and audio

    D. To provide content on the primary topic

15. What is *not* a potential drawback of interactive multimedia?

    A. Lack of accessibility for users with disabilities

    B. Limited memory to run programs

    C. Time-consuming to produce

    D. Allows users to explore and learn by trial and error

16. GraphicConverter is a free converter program for which kind of media files?

    A. Animation

    B. Video

    C. Graphics

    D. Audio

17. Which of the following software is better for creating vector graphics?

    A. Adobe Photoshop

    B. Adobe Illustrator

    C. Microsoft PowerPoint

    D. Apple iMovie

18. A byte of computer data is how many bits?

    A. 2

    B. 8

    C. 16

    D. 32

19. What kinds of multimedia presentations are considered linear?

    A. Sequential

    B. Hyperlinked

    C. Hierarchical

    D. Multidirectional

20. True or False: Microsoft's Bill Gates originally came up with the concept of multimedia.

    A. True

    B. False

21. True or False: Left-justified is the best type arrangement for screen-based body text when using the English language.

    A. True

    B. False

22. Which information technology pioneer developed the hypertext system in the 1960s?

    A. Douglas Engelbart

    B. Steve Jobs

    C. Ted Nelson

    D. Vannevar Bush

23. How many bytes make up an average typed word?

    A. 8 bits, or 1 byte

    B. 2KB, or 2,000 bytes

    C. 10 bytes, or 80 bits

    D. 100,000 bytes, or 10 kilobytes (KB)

24. Which of the following media elements is considered analog?

    A. Audiocassette tape

    B. Digital video

    C. Computer animation

    D. Scanned images

25. Which of the following is the primary factor in the file size of a scanned photograph?

    A. How the photo is cropped

    B. The orientation of the image (horizontal or vertical)

    C. The number of pixels

    D. How much black or white the image contains

26. What is a software program for viewing and interacting with web pages?

    A. Browser

    B. Image editor

    C. Audio-recording tool

    D. Media player

27. What is a multimedia project with multiple levels and submenus providing the user with a number of choices called?

   A. Nonlinear

   B. Spoke and hub

   C. Linear

   D. Nonhierarchical

28. True or False: CD-ROM stands for compact disc–read-only memory.

   A. True

   B. False

29. What does Short Message Service (SMS) pertain to?

   A. Text messages

   B. Email messages

   C. Blog postings

   D. Facebook postings

30. The JPEG file format is better for which kind of visual image?

   A. Vector

   B. Object-oriented

   C. Pixel-based

   D. Resolution-independent

31. What is the type of Internet server that allows users to upload and download files called?

   A. Executable

   B. External storage

   C. FTP site

   D. USB drive

32. What is a bitmap image also referred to as?

   A. A raster image

   B. A vector graphic

   C. An object-oriented shape

   D. A resolution-independent image

33. What is screen resolution?

    A. 24 PPI

    B. 30 PPI

    C. 60 PPI

    D. 72 PPI

34. Which term refers to the process of transferring video from a VCR tape to the computer?

    A. Digital recording

    B. Video editing

    C. Postproduction

    D. Analog-to-digital conversion

35. What is *narrative* another word used to describe?

    A. Multilevel web site

    B. Sequential story

    C. Animated advertisement

    D. Collage of still images

36. What are raster graphics mostly made up of?

    A. Pixels

    B. Curves with anchor points

    C. Lines

    D. Smooth-edged objects

37. True or False: The first Apple computer that revealed a graphical user interface (GUI) was in 1970.

    A. True

    B. False

38. True or False: With image resolution, the more pixels that make up an image, the higher the quality and the larger the file size.

    A. True

    B. False

39. Which color model is associated with screen-based color as opposed to paints or pigments?

    A. RGB

    B. CMYK

    C. HSB

    D. Subtractive

40. True or False: Vector and raster are the two primary kinds of digital images.

    A. True

    B. False

41. Which type of graphic is considered resolution-dependent?

    A. 3D wireframe

    B. Vector

    C. Object-based

    D. Raster

42. Color is light energy in the form of waves, which are referred to by which of the following?

    A. Signals

    B. Lightwaves

    C. Pixels

    D. Resolution

43. True or False: Times is an example of a font rather than a typeface.

    A. True

    B. False

44. What does a sans serif style of type have?

    A. Short lines or marks at the beginning and end of letter strokes

    B. Clean lines without marks on the ends of letter strokes

    C. Elongated ascenders and descenders

    D. Connected letterforms

45. **Of the following, which is the preferred option for storing large sound and video files?**

    A. Cloud storage

    B. CD

    C. Internal hard disk

    D. External drive

46. **What should headlines or titles on the screen be?**

    A. A different font and a larger size than the body text

    B. The same size and style of font as menus

    C. Slightly smaller, since body text is more important

    D. Small, so they do not draw too much attention

47. **Who is quoted as saying "The medium is the message"?**

    A. Bill Gates

    B. Steve Jobs

    C. Marshall McLuhan

    D. Ted Nelson

48. **CSS is a technique used in web design to do which of the following?**

    A. Minimize the amount of text on a web site

    B. Control the appearance of text on a web site

    C. Format images

    D. Add interactivity to buttons

49. **Which of the following has the lowest bit depth compared to that of CDs and DVDs?**

    A. Radio

    B. Telephone

    C. Both radio and telephone

    D. Neither

50. **When writing copy for multimedia, what is suggested for greater effectiveness?**

    A. Get to the point and address the main idea early

    B. Use active words

    C. Simplify by limiting excessive words or phrases

    D. All of the above

51. Which text attribute is described as the higher portion of a lowercase letter that extends above the meanline?

    A. Ascender

    B. Descender

    C. Stroke weight

    D. Cap height

52. Analog video combines brightness and synchronization into one signal, which is referred to as which of the following?

    A. Composite

    B. Consolidated

    C. Component

    D. Condensed

53. True or False: A *typeface* differs from a *font* because a font is a single size and style of type, and a typeface is a set of characters with a similar structure.

    A. True

    B. False

54. Which of the following file formats is *not* recommended for vector graphics if you want to go back and edit the lines and curves?

    A. GIF

    B. JPEG

    C. EPS

    D. PNG

55. What type size is *not* recommended if serif type will be displayed on screen?

    A. 8

    B. 10

    C. 12

    D. 14

56. Animation used in multimedia helps to do which of the following?

    A. Draw attention to buttons and navigational devices

    B. Provide feedback to users when accessing active areas

    C. Visually demonstrate a complex concept or process

    D. All of the above

57. Video games used in arcades were popular in which decade?

    A. 1960s

    B. 1970s

    C. 1980s

    D. 1990s

58. Which of the following is a characterization of 3D animation?

    A. Minimal depth

    B. Virtual reflections, transparencies, and shadows

    C. Cartoonlike characters

    D. Flat colors

59. True or False: Traditional cel animation requires 30 individual drawings for each second of animated film.

    A. True

    B. False

60. Digital animation uses a process where frames are inserted in between key frames or end frames. What is this process called?

    A. Tweening

    B. Looping

    C. Ease-in/ease-out

    D. Rendering

61. Which of the following formats is *not* recommended for saving animation files?

    A. SWF

    B. JPEG

    C. QuickTime

    D. GIF

62. **What is the primary purpose of using a storyboard?**

A. Sketching the navigational routes in a multimedia project

B. Prototyping animation frames on the computer

C. Developing the story and planning the action in the animation

D. Writing an outline of how the animation will unfold

63. **Which British photographer demonstrated the capabilities of capturing fluid motion?**

A. Eadweard Muybridge

B. Pierre Bezier

C. Tim Berners-Lee

D. Marshall McLuhan

64. **True of False: The kineograph was an early animation invention that is essentially a flip book.**

A. True

B. False

65. **What is Java?**

A. A markup language

B. A scripting language that is similar to JavaScript but more limited

C. A programming language

D. Code that uses tags similar to HTML

66. **Which kind of microphone picks up subtleties and discrete nuances, and minimizes distortion and ambient noise?**

A. Large, external microphone

B. Microphone built into a digital camera or camcorder

C. Laptop microphone

D. Podium-style microphone

67. **What does *amplitude* refer to?**

A. Power of a sound

B. Loudness

C. Volume

D. All of the above

68. True or False: *Lossy* compression means there is no loss of quality between the original and a compressed image or video file.
    A. True
    B. False

69. What is MIDI?
    A. Audio that is downloaded from the Web
    B. A compression format for sound files
    C. Music that is generated and manipulated on a computer
    D. Live-music recordings

70. Which of the following audio devices has the highest sampling rate?
    A. CD
    B. DVD
    C. Radio
    D. Telephone

71. True or False: Music recorded at 16-bit stereo has a higher sampling rate than voice recorded at 8-bit mono.
    A. True
    B. False

72. True or False: The frequency of a sound is measured by the number of wave cycles in one minute of sound.
    A. True
    B. False

73. What is a container?
    A. File type that is capable of storing many different formats for media files
    B. Music synthesizer for creating and manipulating sound
    C. Hardware used for sound recordings
    D. Editing tool for combining audio and video files

74. **When working with video, what is the aspect ratio?**
    A. The size of the uncompressed file compared with the compressed file
    B. A mathematical formula used to calculate reductions in data
    C. The width and height of a video frame within the viewing area
    D. Dimensions of the screen, such as a TV display

75. **True or False: The compression ratio of a video is the size of the uncompressed file compared with the compressed file.**
    A. True
    B. False

76. **What did DVD originally stand for?**
    A. Digital video device
    B. Digital versatile disc
    C. Digital video disc
    D. Digital virtual disc

77. **Which method is used for compressing and saving audio and video files?**
    A. File storage
    B. Codec
    C. MIDI
    D. JPEG

78. **What kind of typeface has variable line thicknesses that do not reproduce well at small sizes on the screen?**
    A. Traditional
    B. Modern
    C. Serif
    D. Sans serif

79. **True or False: Cloud computing is an online service that provides data storage.**
    A. True
    B. False

80. Which video standard for broadcast media is used by the United States and Japan?

    A. NTSC

    B. PAL

    C. HDTV

    D. SECAM

81. What is the aspect ratio for standard HDTV?

    A. 2:1

    B. 3:2

    C. 4:3

    D. 16:9

82. What is the process of writing the code to make a multimedia project interactive and functional?

    A. Authoring

    B. Compiling

    C. Goal setting

    D. Storyboarding

83. True or False: Round-trip HTML is when changes are made to a web page design and the underlying code is simultaneously updated.

    A. True

    B. False

84. What is the primary function of the W3C organization?

    A. It sets the standards and provides guidelines for web content accessibility.

    B. It makes regular HTML updates.

    C. It establishes web security protocols.

    D. It regulates what is on the Internet.

85. What is ActionScript?

    A. Scripting language used to enhance user interfaces and create more dynamic interactivity

    B. Brackets that tell the web browser how to present the document

      C. Programming language similar to C++

      D. Web design used to format pages and lay out text

86. True or False: HTML is a programming language used to create dynamic, interactive web sites.

      A. True

      B. False

87. True or False: Using color contrast is one of the most important concerns for screen-based design.

      A. True

      B. False

88. What is a CSS style?

      A. Template that allows for changes to web page layouts

      B. Diagram for structuring a web site

      C. Text editor document with HTML code

      D. Formatting guideline for web page sizes

89. What should be avoided when designing navigation for multimedia?

      A. Alphabetical categorization

      B. Numerous buttons and menus

      C. Consistent placement of elements

      D. Similar size and treatment

90. Which device has the slowest connection speed when accessing the Internet?

      A. 56K modem

      B. Wireless

      C. Satellite

      D. Cable

91. True or False: Optical resolution in a scanner is the highest number of pixels a scanner can produce with built-in optics.

      A. True

      B. False

92. When listening to audio on the Web, it occasionally stops or gets interrupted. What is this called?

    A. Buffering

    B. Streaming

    C. Bandwidth

    D. Computer speed

93. What is archiving media files the same as?

    A. Storing

    B. Backing up

    C. Saving in more than one place

    D. All of the above

94. When a computer mouse and keyboard are designed to facilitate natural handling and to help minimize discomfort with extended use, which term is used to describe them?

    A. Intuitive

    B. Organic

    C. Ergonomic

    D. Wireless

95. What does CSS stand for?

    A. Cascading style sheets

    B. Controlling similar styles

    C. Content style standards

    D. Creative style settings

96. Many computer displays and TVs use LCD technology. What does LCD stand for?

    A. Large component display

    B. Liquid-cathode display

    C. Liquid-crystal display

    D. Low cinematic distortion

97. True or False: The most important requirement when choosing a digital voice recorder is portability.

    A. True

    B. False

98. Which company produced the first game console for home use in the 1970s?

    A. Magnavox

    B. Sony

    C. Nintendo

    D. Microsoft

99. What are the primary colors in the additive color model used by computer displays?

    A. Cyan, magenta, yellow

    B. Red, blue, yellow

    C. Red, green, blue

    D. Orange, green, purple

100. True or False: Interactive whiteboards are beneficial for education because they encourage active collaboration, promote hands-on learning, and connect to the Internet for information while learning.

    A. True

    B. False

Answers to Quizzes and Final Exam

Chapter 1	Chapter 3	Chapter 5	Chapter 7
1. B	1. B	1. A	1. A
2. A	2. A	2. C	2. C
3. D	3. C	3. B	3. D
4. C	4. A	4. C	4. A
5. B	5. C	5. B	5. D
6. D	6. D	6. C	6. C
7. A	7. C	7. A	7. D
8. A	8. D	8. B	8. A
9. D	9. C	9. B	9. B
10. A	10. B	10. D	10. C

Chapter 2	Chapter 4	Chapter 6	Chapter 8
1. D	1. B	1. A	1. A
2. C	2. B	2. B	2. B
3. D	3. A	3. D	3. D
4. B	4. D	4. D	4. D
5. B	5. C	5. B	5. B
6. C	6. C	6. C	6. C
7. B	7. A	7. A	7. D
8. C	8. B	8. B	8. B
9. A	9. C	9. A	9. A
10. D	10. A	10. C	10. D

Chapter 9	Chapter 10	Chapter 11	Chapter 12
1. B	1. B	1. D	1. B
2. A	2. A	2. A	2. A
3. D	3. B	3. B	3. C
4. B	4. D	4. C	4. D
5. A	5. A	5. C	5. B
6. C	6. D	6. D	6. B
7. B	7. B	7. A	7. D
8. A	8. A	8. B	8. A
9. B	9. C	9. D	9. C
10. D	10. C	10. C	10. D

Final Exam

1. D	21. A	41. D	61. B	81. C
2. D	22. C	42. B	62. C	82. A
3. B	23. C	43. B	63. A	83. A
4. D	24. A	44. B	64. A	84. A
5. A	25. C	45. D	65. C	85. A
6. D	26. A	46. A	66. A	86. B
7. B	27. A	47. C	67. D	87. A
8. A	28. A	48. B	68. B	88. A
9. C	29. A	49. C	69. C	89. B
10. A	30. C	50. D	70. B	90. A
11. B	31. C	51. A	71. A	91. A
12. C	32. A	52. A	72. B	92. A
13. D	33. D	53. A	73. A	93. D
14. A	34. D	54. B	74. C	94. C
15. D	35. B	55. A	75. A	95. A
16. C	36. A	56. D	76. B	96. C
17. B	37. B	57. C	77. B	97. B
18. B	38. A	58. B	78. C	98. A
19. A	39. A	59. B	79. A	99. C
20. B	40. A	60. A	80. A	100. A

Image Credits

Chapter 1
Figures 1-6 and 1-7:
Source: Wikimedia Commons. The works have been released into the public domain.

Chapter 2
Figure 2-3:
Source: Wikimedia Commons. Author: Eurofruit. Released under the terms of the Creative Commons Attribution 2.0 Generic license.

Chapter 5
Figure 5-1, clockwise from top left:
Source: Wikimedia Commons. Author: Malvineous. The work has been released into the public domain.
Source: Wikimedia Commons. Author: Patsw. Released under the terms of the Creative Commons Attribution-Share Alike 3.0 Unported license.
Source: Wikimedia Commons. Author: Microsoft Games Global Marketing employees, from gamerscoreblog.com. Released under the terms of the Creative Commons Attribution-Share Alike 2.0 Generic license.
Source: Wikimedia Commons. Author: UpstateNYer. Released under the terms of the Creative Commons Attribution-Share Alike 3.0 Unported license.
Figure 5-2, clockwise from top left:
Source: Wikimedia Commons. Released under the terms of the GNU Free Documentation License.
Source: Wikimedia Commons. The work has been released into the public domain.
Source: Wikimedia Commons. Author: Andrew Dunn. Released under the terms of the Creative Commons Attribution-Share Alike 2.0 Generic license.
Source: Wikimedia Commons. Author: Simon Speed. The work has been released into the public domain.
Figure 5-3:
Source: Wikimedia Commons. Author: Lampman. Released under the terms of the GNU Free Documentation License.
Figure 5-4, left, right:
Source: Frame from Adobe Flash demo file.
Source: Wikimedia Commons. Released under the terms of the GNU Free Documentation License.
Source: Wikimedia Commons. Author: Pelotica. Released under the terms of the GNU Free Documentation License.
Figure 5-5, right:
Source: Wikimedia Commons. Author: J-E Nyström. Released under the terms of the Creative Commons Attribution-Share Alike 2.5 Generic license.
Figure 5-6: top, bottom:
Source: Frame from Adobe Flash demo file.
Source: Frames from Alyssa Smith animation.
Figure 5-7, top, bottom:
Source: Wikimedia Commons. Author: Tommato. The work has been released into the public domain.
Figure 5-8, top and bottom:
Source: Wikimedia Commons. Released under the terms of the GNU Free Documentation License.

Chapter 6
Figure 6-3:
Source: Wikimedia Commons. Released under the terms of the GNU Free Documentation License.

Figure 6-4:
Source: Wikimedia Commons. Author: Joe Mabel. Released under the terms of the GNU Free Documentation License.
Figure 6-5, bottom
Source: Wikimedia Commons. Released under the terms of the GNU Free Documentation License.
Figure 6-6:
Source: Wikimedia Commons. Author: Julien Lozelli. Released under the terms of the Creative Commons Attribution 2.0 Generic license.

Chapter 7
Figure 7-2, top left, bottom right:
Source: Wikimedia Commons. Author: Ryan J. Restvedt. The work has been released into the public domain.
Source: Wikimedia Commons. Author: Activideo. Released under the terms of the GNU Free Documentation License.
Figure 7-3, left, right:
Source: Wikimedia Commons. Author: Andrzej Barabasz (Chepry).
Source: Wikimedia Commons. Author: Norbert Schnitzler. Both released under the terms of the GNU Free Documentation License.
Figure 7-4, top, left to right:
Source: Wikimedia Commons. Author: KMJ.
Source: Wikimedia Commons. Author: JoaoMirandaBot.
Source: Wikimedia Commons. Author: Priwo.
All released under the terms of the GNU Free Documentation License.
bottom, left to right:
Source: Wikimedia Commons. Author: Wassily. Released under the terms of the GNU Free Documentation License.
Source: Wikimedia Commons. Author: Myke2020. The work has been released into the public domain.
Source: Wikimedia Commons. Author: IqRS. Released under the terms of the Creative Commons Attribution 3.0 Unported License.
Figure 7-6, clockwise from top left:
Source: Wikimedia Commons. Author: Ruiguerra. Released under the terms of the Creative Commons Attribution 3.0 Unported License.
Source: Wikimedia Commons. Author: Channel R. The work has been released into the public domain.
Source: Wikimedia Commons. Author: Halonen. Released under the terms of the GNU Free Documentation License.
Figure 7-7:
Source: Wikimedia Commons. Author: Nullcron. Released under the terms of the GNU Free Documentation License.

Chapter 8
Figure 8-2:
Source: Wikimedia Commons. Author: Jspark77. Released under the terms of the Creative Commons Attribution 3.0 Unported License.
Figure 8-5, left to right:
Source: Wikimedia Commons. Author: Szakalabombas.
Source: Wikimedia Commons. Author: Amit kdin.
Both have been released into the public domain.
Source: Wikimedia Commons. Author: Joshualam. Released under the terms of the GNU Free Documentation License.

Chapter 9

Figure 9-1, clockwise from top right:
Source: Wikimedia Commons. Author: Joe Ravi. Released under the terms of the Creative Commons Attribution 3.0 Unported License.
Source: Wikimedia Commons. Author: w:User:Acdx. Released under the terms of the GNU Free Documentation License.
Source: Wikimedia Commons. Author: Evan-Amos. The work has been released into the public domain.
Figure 9-2, middle:
Source: Wikimedia Commons. Author: Inisheer. Released under the terms of the GNU Free Documentation License.
Figure 9-3, clockwise from top:
Source: Wikimedia Commons. Author: Pierre Bauduin. Released under the terms of the Creative Commons Attribution 3.0 Unported License.
Source: Wikimedia Commons. Author: Ernie. The work has been released into the public domain.
Source: Wikimedia Commons. Author: Motoki-jj. Released under the terms of the GNU Free Documentation License.
Figure 9-4, left to right:
Source: Wikimedia Commons. Author: Equationaudio. Released under the terms of the GNU Free Documentation License.
Source: Wikimedia Commons. Author: Evan-Amos.
Source: Wikimedia Commons. Author: Eric_Chassaing.
Both have been released into the public domain.
Figure 9-5, left to right:
Source: Wikimedia Commons. Author: KennethMPennington. Released under the terms of the Creative Commons Attribution 3.0 Unported License.
Source: Wikimedia Commons. Author: Christian Sprenger.
Source: Wikimedia Commons. Author: Mariko GODA.
Both released under the terms of the GNU Free Documentation License.
Figure 9-6:
Source: Wikimedia Commons. Author: Master Sgt. Quinton T. Burris. The work has been released into the public domain.
Figure 9-8, left to right:
Source: Wikimedia Commons. Author: Dflock.
Source: Wikimedia Commons. Author: RadioActive.
Source: Wikimedia Commons. Author: Evan-Amos.
All have been released into the public domain.
Figure 9-9, clockwise from top left:
Source: Wikimedia Commons. Author: CHG.
Source: Wikimedia Commons. Author: Mmckinley.
Both have been released into the public domain.
Source: Wikimedia Commons. Author: David R. Tribble.
Source: Wikimedia Commons. Author: Kristoferb.
Both released under the terms of the GNU Free Documentation License.
Figure 9-10:
Source: Sizzling Bit Author: Brandon LeBlanc.
Figure 9-11, clockwise from top left:
Source: Wikimedia Commons. Author: BF Newpunk. The work has been released into the public domain.
Source: Wikimedia Commons. Author: Unamed102.
Source: Wikimedia Commons. Author: DanielZanetti.
Both released under the terms of the GNU Free Documentation License.
Source: Wikimedia Commons. Author: Thox. Released under the terms of the Creative Commons Attribution 3.0 Unported License.

Chapter 10

Figure 10-5:
Source: Wikimedia Commons. Author: Akrisht Pandey. Released under the terms of the Creative Commons Attribution 3.0 Unported License.

Chapter 11

Figure 11-1:
Photo courtesy of Luis Rodriguez.
Figure 11-4, top left, right:
Source: Wikimedia Commons. Author: Manuel Martin.
Source: Wikimedia Commons. Author: Tucia.
Both released under the terms of the Creative Commons Attribution 2.0 Generic license.
Figure 11-5, top right:
Source: Wikimedia Commons. Author: Seth Rossman. The work has been released into the public domain.
Figure 11-6:
Source: Wikimedia Commons. Author: Nevit Dilmen. Released under the terms of the GNU Free Documentation License.
Figure 11-9:
Source: Wikimedia Commons. Author: Yves Tennevin. Released under the terms of the GNU Free Documentation License.
Figure 11-10:
Source: Wikimedia Commons. Author: Cian Ginty. The work has been released into the public domain.
Figure 11-11:
Source: Wikimedia Commons. Author: LGEPR. Released under the terms of the Creative Commons Attribution 2.0 Generic license.
Figure 11-12, left, right:
Source: Wikimedia Commons. Author: MesserWoland. Released under the terms of the GNU Free Documentation License.
Source: Wikimedia Commons. Author: Roger. Released under the terms of the Creative Commons Attribution-Share Alike 2.0 Generic license.

Chapter 12

Figure 12-3, clockwise from top right:
Source: Wikimedia Commons. Author: Terminal 5 Insider.
Source: Wikimedia Commons. Author: Phillip Capper.
Source: Wikimedia Commons. Author: uggboy.
All released under the terms of the Creative Commons Attribution 2.0 Generic license.
Figure 12-4, left to right:
Source: Wikimedia Commons. Author: Kyoungbe2.
Source: Wikimedia Commons. Author: Phyzome.
Source: Wikimedia Commons. Author: Solomon203.
All released under the terms of the GNU Free Documentation License.
Figure 12-6:
Source: Wikimedia Commons. Author: MrChrome. Released under the terms of the GNU Free Documentation License.
Figure 12-7, left:
Source: Wikimedia Commons. Author: UMD-Eskin. The work has been released into the public domain.
Figure 12-9:
Source: Wikimedia Commons. Author: Activeducator. The work has been released into the public domain.

Index

C